BERNADOTTE

Napoleon's Marshal,
Sweden's King

BERNADOTTE

*Napoleon's Marshal,
Sweden's King*

by

ALAN PALMER

JOHN MURRAY

© Alan Palmer, 1990

First published in 1990
by John Murray (Publishers) Ltd
50 Albemarle Street, London W1X 4BD

British Library Cataloguing in Publication Data

Palmer, Alan, *1926–*
Bernadotte: Napoleon's Marshal, Sweden's King.
1. Sweden. Carl XIV Johan, King of Sweden
I. Title
948.5040924

ISBN 0-7195-4703-2

Photoset by Rowland Phototypesetting Ltd
Bury St Edmunds, Suffolk
Printed in Great Britain by
Butler and Tanner Ltd, Frome and London

Contents

Illustrations

Preface

I T IS a curious irony of dynastic history that, while only two of today's kings can claim descent from the House of Bourbon, more than half the reigning monarchs in Europe number among their ancestors a Gascon sergeant in Louis XVI's regiment of marines. He is best remembered as Marshal Bernadotte, although in Sweden his remains are interred in a sarcophagus inscribed 'Carl XIV Johan'.

Jean Bernadotte – a soldier as dashing in appearance as Murat, as brave as Ney, as eagle-eyed as Masséna – remains the most puzzling of the fourteen generals who were created Marshals of the Empire by Napoleon in the spring of 1804. Others conform to a recognised pattern: a romantic idol and a tragic hero, two austere disciplinarians, some covetous graspers, several also-rans and a virtual non-starter. But Bernadotte is not for labelling. His political opinions defy easy analysis: he was a staunch Jacobin in early years, a persistent legend maintaining that his arm was tattooed with republican imprecations, and yet by 1813 he was able to convince himself that his homeland needed a constitutional monarchy and that he was himself called to become King of the French. His contemporaries never doubted his courage in the field, their memoirs sometimes recalling an intrepidity which verged on the foolhardy; but there can be no other corps commander who, in the course of his campaigns, narrowly missed quite so many famous battles. Although he acquired a reputation for political intrigue, it is hard to think of any other aspirant to high office so reluctant to progress from rhetoric to executive action or so willing to accept a walking-on part in the major dramas of a restless decade. Nor is it only in his public career that paradoxes abound. His private life, too, is full of anomalies, not least that strange mutual loyalty which preserved a marriage to Napoleon's first love, Désirée Clary, through a dozen years of separation. The closer the personal history of Bernadotte is scrutinised, the stronger seem the contradictions within it.

Sixty years have passed since Sir Dunbar Plunket Barton completed his studies on King Charles XIV John with *The Amazing Career of Bernadotte*. Since 1930 no comprehensive biography of the Marshal-King has appeared in English. This is surprising on four counts: the publication of fresh material on his career by both Swedish and French scholars; the posing anew during World War II of questions of loyalty and obedience similar to those which had perplexed Napoleon's Marshals; the proud re-emergence of the name Bernadotte in the tragic endeavours of the first UN mediator in Palestine; and the popularity of *Désirée*, a best-selling novel by Annemarie Selinko subsequently made into a less well-known American film. In France, on the other hand, new assessments of both Bernadotte and Désirée have been made by Gabriel Girod de l'Ain and the 1700-page Swedish biography by Torvald Höjer has appeared in translation, while since 1956 the Friends of the Musée Bernadotte in Pau have published an annual bulletin containing articles which are, for the most part, devoted to the life and times of their hero-king.

The enigma of Bernadotte's character began to fascinate me some twenty years ago when, after delving into Russo-Swedish diplomacy for a biography of Tsar Alexander I, I visited Scandinavia for the first time and was surprised to see a fine equestrian statue of Charles XIV John looking out across central Oslo. I considered at that time writing a book about the soldier who was Napoleon's rival, companion in arms and eventual enemy, but put the idea aside to concentrate on other topics. Now that we are approaching the bicentennial years of the Revolution at war, it seems to me appropriate to take a fresh look at the only ranker who rose from Carnot's improvised army to found a dynasty on a foreign throne.

Although this biography is written as a chronologically continuous narrative it seems to me that Bernadotte's life falls naturally into four parts. In the first section I emphasise three points: the lesson of his early military career, especially in Corsica and Marseilles; the difference between his battle experience along the rivers Sambre, Meuse and Rhine and the schooling of Napoleon's Army of Italy; and the notoriety Bernadotte acquired from his brief embassy in Vienna. The second section deals with the vicissitudes of his relationship with Napoleon as Consul, Emperor and generalissimo of the Grande Armée. The third section covers his strange election as Prince Royal of Sweden, the reasons why he joined the final coalition against Napoleon, and the way in which the clash between his Grand Design for Scandinavian Union and his personal ambitions in France lost him the always tenuous political support of his allies. The final section narrates his activities as ruler of Sweden, both before and after his accession, and his desire to create a favourable image of himself outside Scandinavia, and particularly in France. A section of Notes and Sources affords me the opportunity to acknowledge my debt to the many books and articles which I have used and, at the same time, to indicate to readers where they may find in greater detail some of the matter included in the main body of the book.

I am grateful to Mrs Alice Petersen for translating some passages of Swedish for me and to M. Dominique Bernadaux for his kind assistance when I visited the Musée Bernadotte at Pau. Once again I would like to record my gratitude for the help I have received from the staff of the London Library, the British Library, the Public Record Office at Kew, the Bodleian Library at Oxford and also the Bibliothèque Municipale at Pau. My publishers have been most helpful and encouraging; I especially appreciate the sound guidance and advice I have received from Mr Roger Hudson. It is hard to find adequate words to express my thanks to Veronica, my wife, for the help she gave me during many journeys we have made together in the steps of Bernadotte as well as in discussing the book chapter by chapter and, most of all, in preparing a difficult Index with patience and persistence.

Alan Palmer
Woodstock, April 1990

BERNADOTTE'S EUROPE

—— Boundaries at end of 1810

▧ Added to French Empire in 1809-1810

N

SCOTLAND

Edinburgh

Bergen

DENMARK

NORTH SEA

Belfast

IRELAND

Dublin

Cork

York

ENGLAND

WALES

London

HOLLAND

Hambu
Bremen
Osnabrück

Amsterdam

Plymouth Portsmouth Dover *Walcheren*

CONFE

ATLANTIC OCEAN

Cherbourg

Channel Is.

Brest

Lorient
Quiberon

Belle Isle

Nantes

Antwerp
Boulogne
Jemappes
Amiens
Seine
Reims
Versailles Paris Valmy
Châlons
Fontainebleau
Orléans
Chaumont
Châtillon

Brussels Cologne BERG
Namur
Coblenz
Mainz
Verdun
Metz
Nancy
Strasbourg

Cassel

OF

Fran

RH

Stuttgart
Ulm

Loire

VENDÉE

Rochefort

FRENCH EMPIRE

BADEN

Basle

HELVETIA

Lyons

Chambery LOMBAR

Bordeaux

Garonne

Corunna

GALICIA

Oporto

Duero

Almeida Salamanca
Ciudad Rodrigo
Madrid

Lisbon

Tagus

PORTUGAL

SPAIN

Vitoria
Burgos Pamplona
Bayonne
Pau
Pyrenees

Toulouse

Ebro

Saragossa

Barcelona

PIEDMONT
Grenoble Turin

Marengo
Genoa

Avignon

Fréjus

Marseilles

Toulon

Ri
Milan Ve
Man

Parma

Nice
Spezia
Lucca

Bastia
Corsica
Ajaccio

El

Balearic Is.

MEDITERRANEAN SEA

Seville

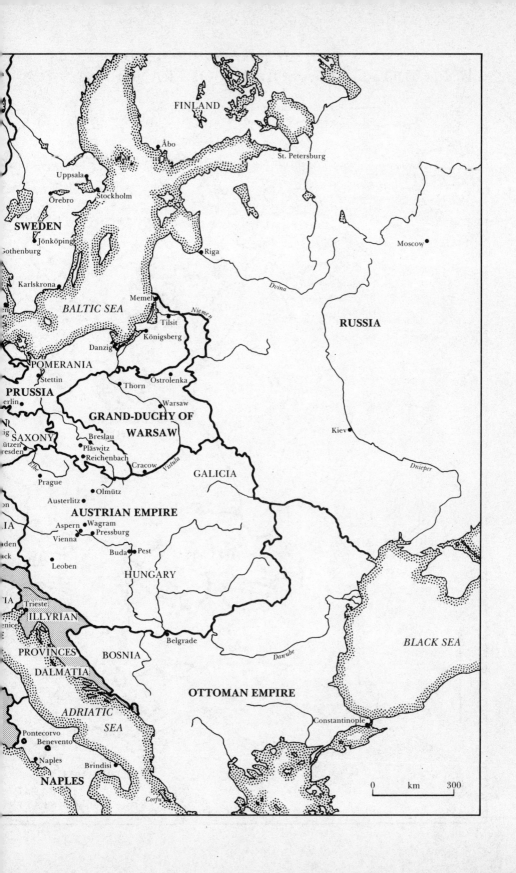

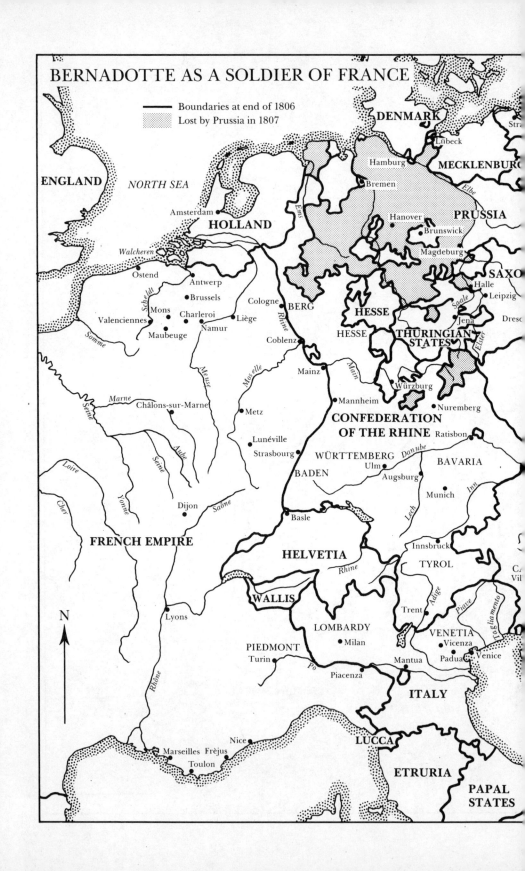

BERNADOTTE AS A SOLDIER OF FRANCE

—— Boundaries at end of 1806
Lost by Prussia in 1807

ENGLAND

NORTH SEA

DENMARK

Stra

Lübeck

MECKLENBURG

Hamburg

Bremen

Elbe

Ems

Amsterdam

HOLLAND

Hanover

PRUSSIA

Brunswick

Walcheren

Magdeburg

SAXO

Scheldt

Ostend

Antwerp

Brussels

Cologne

BERG

Halle

Leipzig

Mons

Charleroi

Liège

Rhine

HESSE

Saale

Jena

Dres

Valenciennes

Namur

HESSE

THURINGIAN

STATES

Maubeuge

Coblenz

Elster

Somme

Meuse

Moselle

Mainz

Main

Würzburg

Meuse

Marne

Châlons-sur-Marne

Metz

Mannheim

Nuremberg

Seine

Aube

CONFEDERATION

OF THE RHINE

Ratisbon

Lunéville

Danube

Loire

Seine

Strasbourg

WÜRTTEMBERG

Ulm

BAVARIA

BADEN

Augsburg

Cher

Yonne

Dijon

Saône

Munich

Lech

Inn

Basle

FRENCH EMPIRE

HELVETIA

Innsbruck

Rhine

TYROL

C

Vil

N

Lyons

WALLIS

Trent

Adige

Piave

Tagliamento

Rhône

LOMBARDY

Milan

VENETIA

Vicenza

PIEDMONT

Turin

Mantua

Padua

Venice

Piacenza

Po

ITALY

Nice

Marseilles

Fréjus

LUCCA

Toulon

ETRURIA

PAPAL

STATES

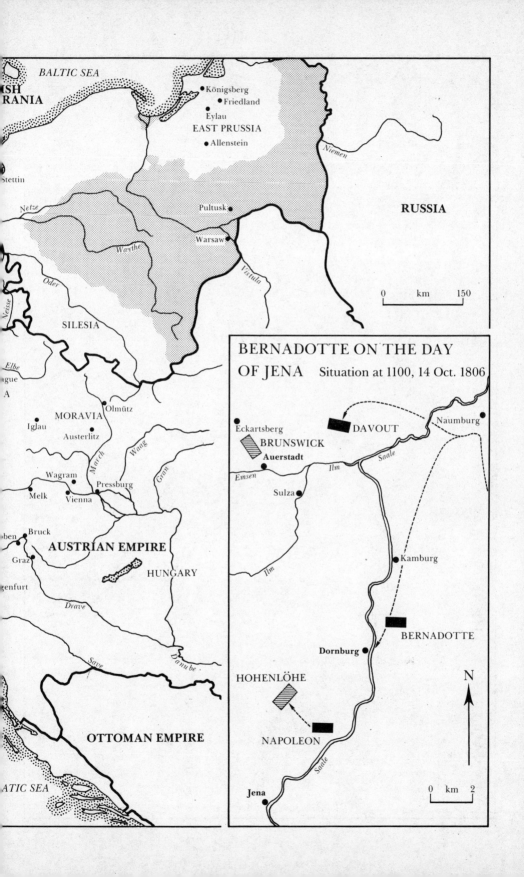

BALTIC SEA

ISH
RANIA

Königsberg
Friedland
Eylau
EAST PRUSSIA
Allenstein

Stettin

Niemen

RUSSIA

Netze

Warthe

Pultusk

Warsaw

Oder

Vistula

0   km   150

Neisse

SILESIA

Elbe

ague

A

MORAVIA

Olmütz

Iglau

Austerlitz

Waag

March

Gran

Wagram

Pressburg

Melk

Vienna

ben

Bruck

AUSTRIAN EMPIRE

HUNGARY

Graz

genfurt

Drave

Save

Danube

OTTOMAN EMPIRE

ATIC SEA

BERNADOTTE ON THE DAY
OF JENA   Situation at 1100, 14 Oct. 1806

Eckartsberg

DAVOUT

Naumburg

BRUNSWICK

Auerstadt

Saale

Ilm

Emsen

Sulza

Ilm

Kamburg

BERNADOTTE

Dornburg

HOHENLÖHE

N

NAPOLEON

Jena

Saale

0   km   2

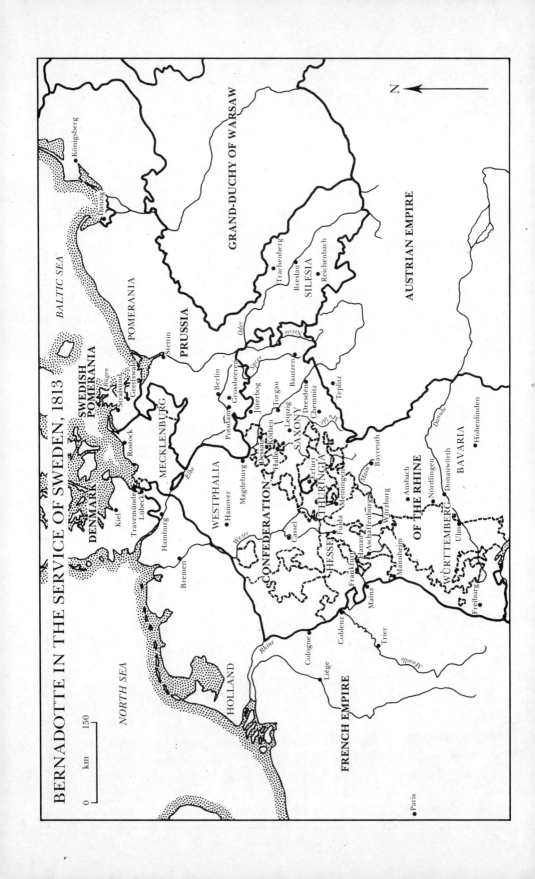

BERNADOTTE IN THE SERVICE OF SWEDEN, 1813

N

NORTH SEA

BALTIC SEA

Königsberg

Danzig

SWEDISH POMERANIA

Rügen
Stralsund
Greifswald
Stettin

POMERANIA

PRUSSIA

GRAND-DUCHY OF WARSAW

Trachenberg

Breslau
Reichenbach

SILESIA

AUSTRIAN EMPIRE

DENMARK

Kiel
Travemünde
Lübeck

Rostock

MECKLENBURG

Hamburg

Bremen

HOLLAND

Berlin
Potsdam
Grossbeeren
Jüterbog
Dessau
Köthen
Halle
Magdeburg

WESTPHALIA

Hanover

Weser

Elbe

Oder

Spree

Neisse

Torgau
Leipzig
Bautzen
Dresden
Chemnitz
Teplitz

SAXONY

Erfurt

THURINGIA

Meiningen

Cassel

Fulda

HESSE

Frankfurt

CONFEDERATION

Hanau
Aschaffenburg
Würzburg

Main

Bayreuth
Ansbach

OF THE RHINE

Nördlingen
Donauwörth

Hohenlinden

BAVARIA

WÜRTTEMBERG

Ulm

Freiburg

Mainz
Mannheim

Coblenz

Cologne

Liège

Trier

Rhine

Moselle

Danube

FRENCH EMPIRE

Paris

0   km   150

Part I
Soldier of France

Chapter 1
Royal Marine

THE south-western corner of France, inland from the Basque coast at Hendaye to the Pic Long of Bigorre, is the forgotten marcher border of Christendom. From the early eighth century until the middle of the eleventh, it was a natural flood-plain for Islam. A hundred years after the death of the Prophet Mohammed an Arab army had sped northwards from Pamplona to raid as deeply into France as Bordeaux and Poitiers. This incursion, and later raids too, made the pastoral people of the Pyrenees foothills cluster protectively in small towns beneath hilltop castles. Anxiously they waited for a new wave of bandits or pillagers to come through the passes. Yet some intruders forayed no further. They were content to winter along the banks of the *gaves*, the mountain torrents which fed the River Adour. Eventually these newcomers settled with indigenous Celts and Goths from older migrations to form a distinctive community, with a language of its own which has survived in the outlying villages of the foothills. Gradually the towns attained a loose unity, first in the principality of Béarn and later in the Kingdom of Navarre. And, after the Saracen tide had finally receded, one town – thirty-five miles north of the Spanish border and sixty miles inland from the Atlantic – achieved local primacy. By 1450 Pau, on a plateau above the confluence of its own *gave* and an even smaller stream called the Hédas, was marked out as the administrative capital of Béarn.

Jean Baptiste Bernadotte was born in Pau on 26 January 1763. His birth and early life are steeped in the narrowly local patriotic customs of which the Palois – as the people of Pau are called – were possessively proud. Traditionally the gloom of winter was lightened by three weeks of carnival before Lent closed in upon Pau. In 1763 the masqueraders were accordingly out in the streets soon after dark fell on that last Thursday in January. They were not fancifully dressed, with the mocking grandeur of patrician Venice, but wrapped in improvised costumes, faces hidden and distorted behind masks. They weaved their way from the open square outside the castle up the Rue des Cordeliers towards the town's northern limits. Along the route, at the corner of a narrow street known as the Rue Tran, they had to pass a three-storeyed house with two rickety balconies looking down on a small courtyard and with dormer windows set in a pointed attic. This was the Maison Balagué; and on the second floor was the home of Henri Bernadotte, an attorney (*procureur au sénéchal*) at the king's magistrature down the hill and across the Hédas. There had been Bernadottes in Pau for at least a century and a half, the name apparently coming from a farmhouse in which a Germaine de Bernadotte was living in the early years of Louise XIII's reign. And Henri's wife Jeanne, a farmer's daughter from neighbouring Boëil, also came from a family held in high respect. As some of her kinsmen were among the revellers that evening, it was reasonable for them to pause at the Maison Balagué and serenade the Bernadottes with carnival banter.

Reasonable – but, on this particular evening, ill-timed. For Jeanne Bernadotte was awaiting the birth of her fifth child in nine years; the sudden appearance in the courtyard of grotesque torchlit masks brought forward a confinement not expected until early March. A boy was born a few hours later. Already Jeanne had lost two of her four children and so frail was the new baby that Father Poeydavant hurriedly baptised him next morning. Little care was taken over the choice of a name, presumably because it seemed certain he would not survive. The Bernadottes had a nine-year old son, whose patron saint was John the Evangelist. If he won the fight for life, the new baby would also be known as 'Jean', with 'Baptiste' as a second name to distinguish him from his brother.

Against all expectation, Jean Baptiste survived. In later years he sat for more portraits than any other son of Pau; canvases in the galleries of France, Sweden and Norway show a soldierly sovereign of character, consequence and pride. Looking at these paintings, it seems almost as if Bernadotte's face was shaped by the image of distorted masks which startled his mother on that carnival evening in January 1763: a long nose is set between piercing eyes, as steely as in a bird of prey, and offset by jet black hair, coarse and curly. But this is fantasy. Bernadotte's nose and dark hair are characteristic of the menfolk of central Béarn. It is as if, by some freak of heredity, a physiognomic strain has preserved for over a thousand years the imprint of those Semitic incursions, when Saracen horsemen swept through the passes of the Pyrenees.

Young Bernadotte, like any other Palois, would have been more aware of a prouder moment in Béarn's past than its pillaging by the Caliph's warriors. For, during the religious struggles of the sixteenth century, the intermarriage of Pau's seigneurial family of d'Albret with the Bourbons left an enduring mark on French history. In 1553, in the royal castle above the *gave* and the Hédas, was born France's one truly popular monarch, Henri IV, Henry of Navarre.

'A considerable town', the pioneer agricultural theorist and traveller Arthur Young noted in his journal when he came to Pau on the eve of the French Revolution, 'but I question whether anything would ever carry a stranger to it but its possessing the cradle of a favourite character.' Young was right, and visitors today may still see the enormous tortoise shell in which 'our Henry' was cradled. Through two centuries of Bourbon rule Pau basked in the afterglow of Henrician Legend: the child born with a full set of teeth, whose father rubbed garlic on his lips and silenced natal bawling with a sip of Jurançon wine; the boy sent ten miles up the valley to till the fields of Coarraze beside peasant sons; the Gascon gallant who, at eleven, was singled out by the prophetic astrologer Nostradamus, in Catherine de Medici's presence, as the progenitor of France's kings; the astute general who escaped murder during the Wars of Religion because he was relieving himself in a pigsty when the assassins came for him; the lover of Gabrielle d'Estrées, the mistress he would have married in defiance of the Pope, had she not died mysteriously as the Court made ready for her wedding; and the tactful diplomat who, when he swallowed up his native principality in a national kingdom, assured his earliest compatriots that he was merely 'giving France to Béarn'. In May 1610 a religious fanatic mortally stabbed Henri IV when his coach was snarled up by draymen's carts in a narrow Parisian street. Nearly five hundred miles away, at Pau, they long refused to believe their king was dead.

To seven generations of Palois boys Henry of Navarre remained a hero. Many may have boasted of matching the least estimable qualities of his private life, but how could they hope to emulate his public exploits? They were not of princely birth, and there was no place for a hierarchy based on merit in pre-revolutionary France.

One youngster from Pau – a member of the lesser nobility – did indeed use the army to climb the ladder of fame: Jeanne de Gassion, born a year before Henry was murdered, fought in Saxony as an auxiliary commander beside King Gustavus Adolphus of Sweden during the Thirty Years' War and added such lustre to Condé's victory at Rocroi that he was created a Marshal of France. Poor Gassion fell mortally wounded outside Lens within a few weeks of his thirty-eighth birthday and, except in Pau, his name was scarcely remembered a century after his death. But Bernadotte would have heard of the first Béarnais to win a Marshal's baton; and almost certainly he will have known that Gassion made his military reputation in the service of Protestant Sweden.

Bernadotte probably received his formal education from the Benedictines, who maintained a good school in Pau. Only two boyhood friends are known by name: Jean Gré was two years his senior and Louis Camps three years his junior; both were later to serve him in Sweden. So long as Henri Bernadotte practised law in Pau no one doubted the profession his sons would follow. At fourteen Jean Baptiste became the French equivalent of an articled clerk, with every prospect of a long apprenticeship ahead of him in the office of Maître de Batsalle, a family friend who was attorney to the Navarre Parlement. But at Easter 1780 Henri Bernadotte – who had been fifty-two when Jean Baptiste was born – suddenly died, leaving debts which forced his widow to move into a smaller house in the Rue Tran. Her elder son was now qualified as an attorney, a dutiful bachelor who could contribute to the well-being of his mother and sister. Her youngest child, on the other hand, would be a financial burden for several years to come.

When his father died Bernadotte was just seventeen. He seemed outshone by a brother who thought himself socially gifted and was their mother's favourite. Had Jean Baptiste stayed in Pau, poring over the law books, he might well have remained 'the other Bernadotte', denied any chance to assert an identity of his own. But what choice was there for him? He could not seek apprenticeship in Bayonne, or any other city in south-western France, so long as he was bound to Maître de Batsalle. In Brittany or Poitou he might well have gone to sea. Along France's northern or eastern frontier he could have joined an élite regiment, for King Louis's proudest troops were recruits from Alsace, Franche-Comté, Picardy and Champagne. In south-western France, however, there was no regional link with any branch of the king's army. Nor, despite a string of fortresses planned by Vauban in the previous century, was there an old tradition of military service in Béarn and Gascony. But one regiment, only founded a few months before Bernadotte was born, had its depot at Collioure, the ancient fortified port where the northern slopes of the Pyrenees tumble down to the Mediterranean. During the 1770s the Régiment Royal-la-Marine had attracted recruits from the Pyrenean provinces in increasing numbers. Conditions of service were said to be good; officers and NCOs were Frenchmen, not foreigners; and a regiment raised for service overseas had a more romantic appeal than the line army units garrisoning the north and the east.

Late in August 1780 Captain de Lassus, a recruiting officer for the Royal-la-Marine, arrived in Pau. He was a Béarnais himself; and the regiment's colonel, the Marquis de Lons, was also born near Pau. The recruiting drive opened up for young Bernadotte a means to escape from the tedium of a notary's office. For, provided that the local civil authority stamped approval on his form of enlistment, there was no reason why he should not serve his king as a marine infantryman over the next eight years, or even longer. Moreover in 1780 the army regulations still held out to any intelligent ranker the prospect of a commission, and eventually the command of a company. It is probable that, as Jean Baptiste knew of Colonel the Marquis de Lons through his work in the courts, he assumed like any other proud Gascon lad that the Marquis had heard of him; and, indeed, Lons does seem to have known Henri Bernadotte and looked with some favour on a son of that family who was prepared to join his regiment. Jean Baptiste realised, of course, that he had little chance of getting his papers stamped in Pau itself, where Batsalle and his own brother had influence. But to the west of the town, in the small municipality of Billère, the Maire was readily obliging. At the first weekend in September, just five months after his father's death, Bernadotte set out by coach for Tarbes. Ahead lay Perpignan, the road southwards to Collioure, and six weeks' stern discipline at the regimental depot.

Today Collioure is a small tourist resort, not yet spoilt. Earlier in this century the light and colour of its bay and harbour attracted Matisse, Derain and Dufy; now sun-bathers and surfboarders follow the artists to what travel brochures have dubbed the 'Vermilion Coast'. But, in the 1980s as in the 1780s, a French army is in training at Collioure, far more amphibious than the Royal-la-Marine but still making use of the old fortress and Vauban's barracks, where Bernadotte and other recruits in Captain de Brassac's company slept three or four in a bed and first learnt their musketry and drill. Not that the recruits stayed long at Collioure. As soon as they had completed their basic training they were sent to Toulon and then on to Bastia, the administrative capital of Corsica. The regiment had been in the island since August 1778. For in a terrain historically and geographically Italian, Louis XVI's Governor needed a strong garrison to make a truculent people appreciative of French rule.

Throughout the eighteen months Bernadotte spent in Corsica, the island was more peaceful than at any time during the previous half-century. The Corsicans had struggled against Spain, against the Genoese Republic, against France and against each other until, by 1780, their all-consuming fire of passionate hatred was at last burning low. A change of attitude in Paris allowed the Governor, the Comte de Marbeuf, to spend French money generously; he improved communications and encouraged new enterprises, such as the growing of flax and tobacco, or the mulberry plantations which Marbeuf's friend, Carlo Buonaparte, wished to set up near Ajaccio, over ninety miles from Bastia. The principal task of the Marines was to protect the military engineers from bandit raids, especially the men building the road through Corte – where Marbeuf had built a fine villa – up into the wooded mountains around Vizzavono and down the Gravone valley to Ajaccio. But the Royal-la-Marine was no regiment of saints; Corsican farmers complained of poaching, of the theft of food, and of worse. When disciplinary action was taken against offenders it was often arbitrary and frequently brutal, as in most armies of the eighteenth century. Nor were living conditions so good as in the mainland towns, where the authorities had long recognised the need to construct barracks or provide other military housing for a garrison. Poor sanitation and inadequate food continued to undermine the health of many recruits. Service in Corsica might not provide training for battle, but it ensured a harsh schooling of character.

On one occasion Bernadotte, who was befriended by the Governor's Béarnais chef, encountered an impatient Marbeuf, visiting the kitchens to hasten preparations for a civic banquet. But he never met the Buonapartes, as the future imperial family still called itself. Almost certainly he spent some weeks on duty in Ajaccio, where he may well have noticed the lawyer Carlo Buonaparte's house in the Via Malerba, which was bigger than any lawyer's home back in Pau. Only four of Carlo Buonaparte's children – known later as Lucien, Louis, Eliza and Pauline – were living in Ajaccio at the time, and neither Jerome nor Caroline was born. Joseph, the eldest son, was five years younger than Bernadotte but was away in France, at school in Autun; and, thanks to Marbeuf's patronage, the second son, Napoleon, was a cadet at the military academy in Brienne. Yet if Bernadotte did not know the Buonapartes personally in Ajaccio, his turn of duty in Corsica gave him in later years an advantage over other Marshals of the Empire: some may have fought there, but Bernadotte alone had seen for himself the ambiguities of loyalty which faced socially ambitious families on an island only half assimilated in Bourbon France.

In May 1782 Bernadotte was transferred from a fusilier company to the crack detachment in the regiment, the grenadiers. Over the following month, however, the temperature shot up rapidly, the scourge of malaria returned to the marshes along the eastern coastal plains, and Grenadier Bernadotte went down with a fever. As soon as he was well enough to travel, he was given the six months' leave to which he was now entitled. By the autumn he was home in Pau, with his mother, sister and brother; and there, rather surprisingly, he remained for eighteen months, his furlough extended by sick leave with the authority of the Marquis de Lons and support from the regimental depot doctor. Presumably the fever was chronic; perhaps the physicians of Pau were more sympathetic than skilled; and possibly his family sought to tempt him back to the notary's office. Once during this long leave Bernadotte and a gendarme officer named Castaing picked a quarrel – probably over a woman – and a duel was fought with swords in the woods to the west of Pau: Castaing was wounded, and Bernadotte won new respect from his contemporaries in the town.

The Royal-la-Marine left Corsica in April 1784 and was stationed at Besançon when Bernadotte returned to active service. By November the regiment had joined the garrison at Grenoble. There, early in 1785, he suffered so grave a recurrence of his illness that one doctor, finding him motionless on a bed, was prepared to certify him dead, a verdict successfully disputed by a medical colleague. He went back to Pau for a further spell of leave. But his family ties were weak. He seems still to have resented the preference shown by his mother for her elder son. Never again did he set foot in Pau. Although he remained sentimentally attached to the Gascon loyalties of the Béarnais for the remainder of his days, not once in later years did he even come within sight of the Pyrenees.

Bernadotte's 'family' was now, as he often remarked, the army. He became a Corporal on 16 June 1785 and a Sergeant less than eleven weeks later. Yet, despite this rapid promotion, his prospects for climbing out of the ranks seemed poorer than when he had enlisted: the threat of national bankruptcy made Louis XVI's ministers impose drastic cuts on military spending from 1783 onwards; at the same time, the French officer corps became more exclusive, with commoners forced to accept a subordinate role in the military hierarchy. There was a change, too, in the command of the Royal-la-Marine: the Marquis de Lons, regimental Colonel for more than sixteen years, had received a largely honorific post at Court, and on New Year's Day 1784 was replaced as Colonel by the young, haughty and irascible Louis de Merle, Marquis d'Ambert. Some junior officers and NCOs found d'Ambert impossibly tyrannical, but the new Colonel was impressed by Bernadotte's obsessive concern for the small details of garrison duty and his smart appearance on parade. In Corsica Bernadotte had been derisively addressed as 'Monsieur' by NCOs who thought the young Gascon recruit gave himself airs. Now, at Grenoble, he was known as 'Sergeant Belle-Jambe' – a nickname implying, not so much that the Sergeant was a foppish dandy, as that he aspired to a level of elegance which others in the regiment grudgingly admired.

There was, it is clear, a special relationship between Colonel d'Ambert and his ambitious Sergeant. For many years d'Ambert was a high dignitary within French Freemasonry. Significantly, in March 1786 a surviving letter sent by Bernadotte to his brother in Pau is signed, for the first time, with a symbolic flourish used by French freemasons; almost certainly Bernadotte had recently been received into a Masonic Lodge, established under d'Ambert's auspices within his regiment. During this winter of 1785–86 the Colonel gave Bernadotte increased responsibilities. He trained recruits, supervised the issue of uniforms, became an instructor in swordplay. The letter which he sent to his brother on 9 March 1786 describes how during that winter he had been sent out on three occasions to bring back fugitive deserters: twice they were within half an hour of Chambéry, where they could have slipped across the frontier and so shaken off their pursuers; and at the end of February he had followed 'a young man of rank' for more than 170 miles before arresting him in Avignon, where he was seeking sanctuary in a papal enclave. 'I was praised by my regimental Major, and all the officers', Bernadotte wrote contentedly. Some patrols sent in pursuit of deserters would come back to their barracks empty-handed, the officers suspecting that the sergeant in command lacked zeal or welcomed bribes, or both. No such accusations could be levelled at Sergeant Belle-Jambe. His worst offence at Grenoble seems to have been the fathering of a daughter on Catherine Lamour, spinster. Even then Bernadotte retained from those months of apprenticeship in Pau a legalistic sense of honour; for, before she was born, he formally acknowledged paternity at the notary's office. The child lived no more than a few days.

Grenoble, the old Burgundian city and capital of Dauphiné, was proud of its fifteenth-century Palace of Justice. It was the seat of a parlement, one of thirteen regional courts in the Kingdom of France, and its lawyers were jealously possessive of what they respected as their ancient rights, particularly over the raising of loans by the government in Paris. Eleven other provincial towns had parlements, among them Pau. What happened in the Béarn Parlement mattered little to the King's ministers, for Pau was an isolated backwater, away from the main stream of French political life. Grenoble, however, was different; it lay close to the most enlightened cantons in Switzerland. Accordingly when, in 1788, Louis XVI's government sought to centralise administration by curbing the powers of the parlements there were noisy demonstrations down in Pau – but in Grenoble the mood of the people was so defiant that it seemed to threaten revolution. The hereditary military governor of Dauphiné – himself Grand Master of a Freemasons' Lodge – was ordered to arrest and disperse the members of the Grenoble Parlement for having denounced their sovereign's edicts. And on Saturday, 7 June, the Governor duly sent two companies of infantry into the centre of the town to escort some of Grenoble's most respected citizens into exile. The soldiers were not issued with ammunition, for the Governor wished them to carry out their task quietly and discreetly.

Unfortunately for the troops it was market day. The women selling fish and vegetables in the Place aux Herbes shouted insults. Some twenty young Grenoblois started throwing stones. The soldiers sought to clear a path with their bayonets; and a hatter's apprentice was mortally wounded. Hurriedly the Governor called out the rest of the garrison to police his streets. But as the troops marched towards the Palace of Justice they were pelted with tiles torn from the roofs by the angry townsfolk.

The Royal-la-Marine was not the only regiment stationed in the city; it shared garrison duties with the Austrasie Light Infantry, who had recently served in India. Colonel Boissieux of the Austrasie was struck in the face by a tile but, remembering the Governor's orders to avoid provoking violence, insisted that his men should fall back to barracks rather than avenge the attack on their commander. Colonel d'Ambert, however, was more hot-tempered than his brother officers; a detachment of marines fired on the demonstrators, two of whom fell dead. After two hours of rioting the Governor gave up the attempt to arrest the Grenoble Parlement and withdrew his troops. The townsfolk celebrated their victory by breaking into the Governor's cellar and looting his best wine.

Legend maintains that Bernadotte commanded the patrol which opened fire that Saturday. His insolent manner is said to have angered the women in the market-place; he was allegedly arrested on the Governor's orders and only released through the intervention of the War Minister, at the insistence of the King. Yet this tale is without foundation. Bernadotte, promoted Sergeant-Major four weeks previously, was certainly in the streets of Grenoble that Saturday, the first time in his life that he came under attack. But the reminiscences of eye-witnesses of the Day of Tiles, published after Bernadotte became a famous and controversial figure, make no reference to his activities; the Governor reprimanded, not one of d'Ambert's senior NCOs, but a junior officer. Nevertheless Bernadotte had been present at a decisive moment in French history. News of Grenoble's act of defiance spread across France, increasing demands for summoning the States-General, that cumbersome and half-forgotten assembly of deputies no King had convened for over 170 years. Eight weeks after the Day of Tiles, Louis XVI gave way; a royal decree summoned the States-General for the following spring.

By May 1789, when the States-General met at Versailles, Bernadotte's battalion had left Grenoble and moved down the Rhône, to the outskirts of papal Avignon. Nobody could remember such a bad harvest as in the previous autumn, and food stocks ran low during the winter. Violent protests over the price of bread in several towns at the end of March were followed by sporadic disturbances across a wide area of Provence. With the coming of summer, however, it was clear that the greatest threat to the social order lay in Marseilles, France's third-largest city. Arthur Young, who spent the first week-end of September 1789 in the sprawling port, found the cafés strewn with newspapers and noted that the current state of revolutionary politics was the chief topic of conversation. By then the provincial Governor had responded to a frightened plea from Marseilles's manufacturers and shopkeepers and called on the Royal-la-Marine to join five other regiments already keeping watch on the turbulent city; and Bernadotte was in Marseilles during the tense weekend which so excited Arthur Young's interest.

Among the traders who petitioned the Governor to reinforce the garrison was François Clary, a wealthy silk manufacturer with a house off the Place Saint Michel. Clary was, at sixty-three, the father of thirteen children, three of whom still lived at home. Many years later the youngest child, Désirée, described to her court chamberlain an incident that summer, when she was eleven:

> One day a soldier presented himself with a requisition billeting him in our house at Marseilles. My father, who had no wish to be disturbed by the noise which soldiers usually make, politely sent him back with a letter to his colonel requesting that an officer might be billeted on us instead of a soldier. The soldier who was sent back in this way was Bernadotte, who was afterwards to marry me and become a King.

For many historians this episode is too coincidental to ring true. They point out that Bernadotte habitually gave full play to that Gascon raconteur's licence which enjoys fabricating what ought to have happened out of what might have done. But the tale originated with Désirée rather than with her Gascon husband, and she was recalling a scene from an impressionable age not, as some scoffers claim, from her infancy. Moreover is the coincidence really all that implausible? By 1789 Bernadotte was a senior NCO, high in the favour of Colonel the Marquis d'Ambert and, if tittle-tattle may be believed, of Madame la Marquise, too. He was smart on parade, ambitious, familiar with a higher level of society than most rankers, and sufficiently astute to manipulate for his own ends the billeting arrangements of his regiment. He was, too, like his Colonel and

Clary, a Freemason. Under normal conditions no soldiers, whether officers or men, would have been found lodging with the Clarys. But François Clary, thinking presumably as much of his silks as of his daughters, had already emphasised his need for protection from mob violence. It made more sense to quarter a ranker of Bernadotte's experience and self-discipline on the family than some greenhorn lieutenant. Désirée never indicated in her flow of reminiscence if d'Ambert did indeed send an officer to be billeted on the Clarys; probably not. Another nine years passed before Désirée was formally introduced to General Bernadotte. By then she was well acquainted with the ways and wiles of soldiers seeking a quick path to pinnacles of glory.

By the end of the year 1789 the revolutionary temper in Marseilles was more volatile than in Paris. In the capital the insurrectionary energies of the people seemed satisfied in October, when the royal family returned from Versailles escorted by the National Guard, the militia hurriedly raised in July and August. By the late autumn this Parisian National Guard, with Lafayette at its head, could claim a responsible status. In Provence, on the other hand, the militia was still play-acting, striking revolutionary attitudes because there seemed no prospect of power. Time and time again through the winter of 1789–90 the political clubs in Marseilles asked the military commandant to remove all line regiments and entrust the safety of port and city to the National Guard. But officers and NCOs who had made the army their career despised a people's militia. The commandant, ignoring the menacing tone of the clubs, kept the line regiments within the city gates.

In several garrison towns there were mutinies. At Marseilles, too, many disaffected soldiers responded sympathetically to club propaganda and among these rebels against authority were some marines. Not, however, Sergeant-Major Bernadotte. In 1788 he had completed his eight-year term of enlistment and could have left the army for good. He preferred to remain in the Royal-la-Marine, giving his loyalty not so much to his sovereign as to the regiment itself. The political abstractions which so perplexed Lieutenant Buonaparte, converting an officer who hated civil disorder into the spokesman of Corsica's revolutionaries, meant little to Bernadotte at this time. Nor indeed did his harassed King's token pledge to uphold 'constitutional monarchy and freedom with justice'. What still mattered to Bernadotte in that winter was the advancement of his military career. For, only a few days after his twenty-sixth birthday, 'Sergeant Belle-Jambe' acquired an even smarter uniform. As Adjutant-Major he became a warrant officer on the Marquis d'Ambert's regimental staff. 'My Colonel, right or wrong', might well have been Bernadotte's toast that February.

Under the haughty Marquis d'Ambert's colonelcy, however, 'wrong' was always more likely than 'right'. On a Saturday evening, six weeks after Bernadotte's promotion, the Colonel's coach arrived back at the Aix Gate after a tour of inspection in the surrounding countryside. A sentry of the Marseilles National Guard demanded to see the Marquis's pass before allowing him through the gate. D'Ambert told the wretched man what he thought of sentries who wished to inspect the passes of regimental colonels, adding some derogatory remarks about the National Guard in general. When the duty officer, Captain Gautier, backed up the sentry, Colonel d'Ambert – who sounds as if he had been drinking heavily – issued a challenge to the revolutionary leaders in the municipality: a single company of his regiment would take on the National Guard of Marseilles and sweep the vile scum into the sea. Surprisingly, the Marquis was allowed through the gate unharmed.

That night exaggerated tales of this exchange of insults fanned the embers of revolt in the city. On Sunday morning – 21 March – a mob was in the streets. So too was Bernadotte; he accompanied several members of d'Ambert's staff to the Hôtel de Ville to give an explanation of what had happened. Unfortunately, shortly afterwards, the Marquis joined them, whereupon some of the mob broke into the council chamber threatening to lynch him. Bernadotte and his companions drew their swords, refusing to leave their commanding officer. As a compromise it was agreed that the incident should be reported to the Constituent Assembly in Paris, where the Colonel's folly could be debated and his fate determined. A letter, drafted by Bernadotte and with his name at the top of a list of twelve NCOs in the regiment, accompanied the official complaint from the municipality and urged the assembly to note that their Colonel had gone to the Hôtel de Ville to make reparation for the previous evening's misunderstanding. It would be at least a week before the incident could be debated in Paris. Meanwhile d'Ambert and his bodyguards remained in the Hôtel de Ville, virtually under self-imposed house arrest.

The Colonel could count on Bernadotte's loyalty, not least because of his respect for Masonic solidarity. But he lacked support from the regiment as a whole; his irascibility made him far from popular with his men. Couriers carried other messages from Marseilles to Paris: an address from the rankers to the King claimed that their Colonel had regularly defrauded them of some 25,000 livres a year since taking command; and, less sensationally, a majority of his junior officers wrote to the Minister of War asking for his removal, for the sake of the regiment. The Colonel's alleged insults at the Aix Gate were detailed in the *Moniteur Universel*, the semi-official gazette, on 28 March, while the following day's issue reported a short debate on the incident in the Constitutent Assembly. The deputies deplored the episode but characteristically shrank from giving Marseilles a firm lead. It was, they argued, by no means clear what offence had been committed. Here, they felt, was a question to be decided locally. But the deputy from Marseilles was more adept at buck-passing; France was a constitutional monarchy; the marines were a royal regiment; the Colonel's conduct, so the deputy argued, was thus a matter for the King to judge.

After seventeen days at the Hôtel de Ville the Marquis d'Ambert, still protected by Bernadotte's improvised bodyguard, was therefore handed over to the custody of Maître Chomel, the King's seneschal at Marseilles. Next day – Thursday, 8 April – Chomel examined the evidence and ordered d'Ambert's release. Discretion, however, kept the Marquis at the seneschal's court until three o'clock on the Friday morning when Bernadotte, a junior officer and an escort of the National Guard accompanied him to the Rome Gate. They saw him set out along the road to Piedmont, and – as they assumed – into exile. He never rejoined his regiment.

Yet, though d'Ambert was off stage, another act of the drama had still to be played out in Marseilles. In fury over the news of the 'aristo' Colonel's release, some hotheads burst into the seneschal's home, forcing him to flee the city. The Jacobin Club renewed the demand for all line regiments to be replaced by the National Guard. So explosive was the mood of the mob that, within a fortnight, the Royal-la-Marine received orders to pull out of Marseilles and establish a camp at Lambesc, beween Arles and Aix. They were fortunate to be away from the port. A Major of the Vexin Regiment who remained in Marseilles was lynched by the mob on 2 May as he was on his way to the Hôtel de Ville. By the autumn the only unit of the King's army still garrisoning the forts which protected the great Mediterranean port was a regiment of Swiss mercenaries.

Discipline within the Royal-la-Marine wavered at Lambesc, as the Jacobin virus spread through its ranks. Not until 25 June was Morard d'Arces appointed to succeed d'Ambert as colonel of the regiment. During the intervening two months attempts were made to create a military democracy, with the soldiery electing officers at meetings convened in Lambesc church. In later years Bernadotte claimed that the marines chose him as colonel of the regiment, that he thanked them from the pulpit for this vote of confidence but insisted they should consider themselves bound by the familiar obligations of command and obedience. It is probable that recollection may well have tidied up these events in Lambesc church, bringing a moralising orderliness to a meeting which, in reality, never ran so smoothly for Bernadotte. For why should the marines have backed the former protector of an unpopular Colonel? But, although the events at Lambesc remain muddled and confused, it is at least clear that someone at the camp had sufficient personality to hold the regiment together. There were many desertions and several officers resigned their commissions, but the Royal-la-Marine escaped the mutinies which brought bloody repression to the garrison at Nancy that summer. Soon after Morard d'Arces's arrival, the regiment left Provence, shaking off the revolutionary infection as it moved further westwards. By late July Bernadotte's battalion was on the Atlantic coast, near Rochefort. Throughout the 'third year of liberty' the marines kept watch on the islands off the Charente estuary – a dull duty, relieved only by rumours of embarkation for a colonial adventure in Haiti.

In the spring of 1791 all units of the old army lost their names: the Royal-la-Marine became the 60th Regiment of Infantry. Bernadotte deplored the loss of identity, but he welcomed another reform which gave officers the right to fill some vacancies in the lower commissioned ranks with nominees, chosen by direct election. An energetic Colonel, Henri de Boulard, took command of the 60th in January 1792 and found to his dismay there were only 768 men in the regiment. Since Boulard wished speedily to double the strength, he needed loyal backing from so experienced an instructor as 'Sergeant Belle-Jambe'. There seemed little doubt that Bernadotte would at once be elected to commissioned rank. To his consternation, however, the officers passed him over. They chose a sergeant-major whose career he had himself advanced, a man who seems to have had political connections injudicious to ignore. With some embarrassment, Colonel Boulard assured Bernadotte it would not be long before his brother officers unanimously gave him their support.

But, after nearly twelve years with the marines, the decisive break had come in Bernadotte's career. For at the end of March 1792 – a day when, a thousand miles away, all Stockholm was mourning Gustav III, a gifted king shot at a masquerade ball – an order reached Boulard's headquarters from the War Ministry in Paris: Adjutant J. B. Bernadotte was commissioned as a Lieutenant in the 36th Regiment (late Anjou Infantry); he must travel at once to Brittany and join the 36th Infantry at St Servan, near St Malo. 'I suffer a serious loss in having to leave the 60th Regiment in which I . . . had hoped to spend an agreeable career', Bernadotte wrote to his brother that Easter; and for the rest of his life his talk would revert, with sentimental nostalgia, to his days as a Sergeant with the marines. But he left the 60th as soon as he could hand over his duties, taking the coach from Rochefort to St Servan in the fourth week of April, 1792.

That month war came to Europe, with revolutionary France challenging Habsburg Austria. At the age of twenty-nine Lieutenant Bernadotte was about to set out on his first campaign. Curiously enough, Captain Bonaparte – six years his junior, but with the prestige of a military academy behind him – was also at that moment travelling by coach along the dusty roads of France, though on a longer journey and with less confidence for the immediate future. For Napoleon, having dabbled so long in Corsica's feuds that he neglected a summons back to his regiment, was hurrying to Paris in fear of court martial. He need not have worried: more urgent concerns troubled the capital in that first summer of war. Before lasting peace returned to Europe, the wheel of fortune was to lift Lieutenant Bernadotte to royal Stockholm and Captain Bonaparte down to Rochefort and the roadstead in the Charente, where HMS *Bellerophon* awaited a fallen Emperor.

Chapter 2

The Revolution at War

FOREIGN observers believed that in challenging Austria and Prussia the politicians of Paris were courting disaster. The French, Edmund Burke declared, had become 'architects of their own ruin'. It was assumed that internal chaos was weakening France month by month and that the army lacked executive direction; more and more experienced officers would defect and the Revolution would have become an episode in history before the end of the year.

Bernadotte's first two months of active campaigning seemed to confirm the prejudiced confidence of France's enemies. His battalion left St Servan for the war zone on Sunday, 15 July 1792, under orders to join the Army of the North. He assumed that his men were marching to Cambrai; 'several regiments are to muster there', Bernadotte explained in a letter to his brother. But the war was going badly for the French. The first assaults on Austrian positions at Tournai and Mons ended in a panic rout; by mid-July the Duke of Brunswick was assembling a predominantly Prussian army at Coblenz, ready to invade Lorraine, while the Austrians would march southwards from Flanders into Picardy. Four days before Bernadotte left St Servan the Legislative Assembly in Paris declared 'the Fatherland in Danger' and called urgently for thousands of volunteers. Small wonder if, as the 36th Infantry headed towards Normandy, the War Ministry was hastily revising plans for armies which, as yet, existed in name only.

In five days Bernadotte's battalion covered eighty miles. Friday night was spent at Mayenne, well on schedule to reach Cambrai by 6 August. But so grave was the threat in the east that fresh orders went out from Paris: the regiment was no longer needed at Cambrai; it should join General Custine's Army of the Rhine, in Alsace. The line of march was changed, to skirt the capital and make for St

Dizier on the upper Marne, and the men managed more than twenty miles a day across the plain of Champagne. The going was slower after St Dizier, through thickly wooded hills around Lunéville, but on 10th August the regiment marched into Strasbourg. It was a date history remembers well. For, while an uneasy calm prevailed in Alsace, on that blazing hot Friday in Paris the sovereign people unleashed the Second Revolution; a mob, supported by the National Guard, burst into the Tuileries Palace and slaughtered King Louis's loyal Swiss Guards. By nightfall the Assembly had suspended the King's authority; the fate of the royal family was in its hands, to be decided ultimately by the revolutionary Commune of Paris.

While Napoleon had a grandstand view of the assault on the Tuileries from a shop-window in the Place de Carrousel, Bernadotte was far removed from the making of history; he was seeking billets in what was for him merely another garrison city. To Eugène de Beauharnais, an eleven-year-old schoolboy in Strasbourg that summer, it seemed as if 'Everything breathed a Love of Glory and of Fatherland'. At Dietrich's tavern, four months before, Captain Rouget de Lisle had first sung his patriotic 'War Song of the Army of the Rhine', which, upon its publication in June, the volunteers from Marseilles appropriated as their anthem of revolution. If Bernadotte, like the people of Strasbourg, was elated by a sense of expectancy, it remained unsatisfied. For the long march to Alsace was followed by anticlimax. Seven weeks went by before the 36th Infantry saw action. Throughout August and September all military operations were dependent on the political drama in the capital. On Saturday 11 August the provisional executive council of revolutionary ministers sent commissioners to every army, to require a new oath of loyalty to the French Nation rather than to the King: any officer reluctant to take the oath or suspected of disloyalty might be arrested. Many veterans of the old army chose to emigrate rather than await the arrival of the commissioners. Three regiments in the direct path of Brunswick's invading army lost their commanding officers at this crucial moment in France's history.

No such crisis of loyalty shook the 36th Infantry. As Bernadotte had already told his brother, 'the purest patriotism' sustained a regiment in which 'discipline is regularly observed'. But it was different northwards along the frontier. The commander of the Army of the Centre – the Marquis de Lafayette, hero of the American War and idol of the National Guard three years before –

sought refuge beyond the Rhine, taking some twenty staff officers with him into emigration. Two days later the fortress of Longwy was surrendered to the Duke of Brunswick. Within a fortnight the vital citadel of Verdun capitulated. In Paris rumours of treachery and betrayal led to the killing of over a thousand innocent men and women held in the prisons. Revolutionary patriotism sank to the lowest level of bestiality. It seemed impossible that anything could stop an invading army less than ten marching days from the capital.

Yet, improbably, on 20 September Generals Dumouriez and Kellermann defeated the Prussians at Valmy and threw back Brunswick's troops. Although cannon fire from what had been the King's artillery regiments checked the Prussian assault, the victory was decided by non-professionals in the infantry battalions, volunteer fanatics uplifted by revolutionary songs and slogans which many had learnt when storming the Tuileries six weeks before. The victory at Valmy was a signal encouraging other French commanders to go forward. Two days after Valmy Bernadotte's battalion was on the march, moving forty miles up to the advanced lines at Weissenburg. Within a week he was in the vanguard of General Custine's army invading the Rhineland.

Bernadotte was present at the capture of two cities on the left bank of the Rhine, Speyer and Mainz, but he gained no battle experience. For three months he served as garrison adjutant at Bingen, superintending the movement of traffic along the great river. There he celebrated his thirtieth birthday, just five days after King Louis was guillotined in Paris. At that moment there were no enemy troops anywhere within France's natural boundaries, but the immediate military prospects for the new Republic looked bleak. The volunteers who made possible the defeat of the Prussians at Valmy in September and the Austrians at Jemappes in November, had enlisted for only one campaign. By the end of the year some 170,000 of them were back home again, leaving the army so wretchedly depleted that General Custine could muster scarcely more than half the numbers he possessed when he marched to the Rhine. Desertion, administrative corruption, and political confusion among the factions in the National Convention all weakened the army's effectiveness in the field. When in March 1793 the Prussians recrossed the Rhine, Custine's army was swept back to the lines of Weissenburg. A subsequent attempt to relieve the beleaguered fortress of Mainz ended in disaster: in July the unfortunate Custine was summoned to Paris; a month later, he perished under the guillotine. Such should have been the fate of General Dumouriez, too, after defeats at Neerwinden and Louvain, had he not saved his life by defecting to the Austrians.

These early campaigns in the Rhineland made a deep and disagreeable impression on Bernadotte, for the buffetings of war knocked the noblest ideals awry. He had seen the revolutionary exultation of the previous autumn give way to cowardice and mutiny: two of yesterday's popular heroes had deserted to the enemy while his own army commander, disgracefully neglected by the politicians in Paris, was executed on trumped-up charges of treason. By now Bernadotte himself wished to get away from the German frontier and return to his native city, for Spain had joined the growing list of France's enemies and, as he wrote to his brother, Pau was 'close to the theatre of war'. He urged his brother to use family influence to secure for him a colonelcy in the new Army of the Pyrenees. He sent home both a record of his military service and descriptions of hand-to-hand fighting to impress the authorities in Béarn with his zeal. One letter decribes how he rallied panic-stricken volunteers facing an Austrian counter attack at Rulzheim, south of Speyer, in May 1793:

> I shouted at them, cursed them, begged them, ordered them . . . There is the sound of a thousand musket shots, some of which miss me only because I push aside musket barrels with my sword. My horse stumbled but I kept in the saddle . . . 'Soldiers, rally here. Retreat no further . . . With your bayonets and courage, what more defence do you need? If death comes for us, let us perish shouting "Long Live the Republic, Long Live the Nation". If we march forward together against these hirelings, it will be no easy task for them to defeat us' . . . I formed them in battle order; I checked the panic, which would have enveloped six other battalions . . . All the officers congratulated me on my energy and my triumph. The soldiers speak of me with enthusiasm.

Perhaps the skirmish at Rulzheim did, indeed, follow such a pattern, with Bernadotte showing both courage and initiative. Perhaps he did possess the physical agility and gift of spontaneous oratory to make this battle scene a reality. He may well have responded to the cowardly confusion around him in this way, for there is ample testimony to his bravery in later campaigns. But on this occasion there is no record of his heroism except his own letter, written nine days after the incident: 'Nobody informed the General of my conduct', he explained to his brother. 'The actions of junior officers often pass unnoticed'. If Bernadotte's account was forwarded to the headquarters of the Army of the Pyrenees, it went unnoticed there, too. For although he continued to urge his brother 'to leave nothing undone to get me a battalion' in the Pyrenees, he was never to fight in Spain or along the Spanish frontier.

The General to whom Bernadotte referred in his letter was the unfortunate Custine. He was succeeded in command of the Army of the Rhine by Alexandre de Beauharnais, father of the schoolboy who had found life at Strasbourg so exhilarating. It was unfortunately exhilarating too for the General, to whom the charms of an officer's daughter in the city were irresistible. Alexandre de Beauharnais, still only in his early thirties but long separated from his wife Josephine, looked handsome on parade, but he was no leader of men. The war along the Rhine, simmering when he took command of the army in early summer, never came to the boil; and Mainz, so far from being relieved by Beauharnais, surrendered to the Prussians. At that point the General thought it expedient to return to the Loire on sick leave. He made little impression on Bernadotte or any other junior officer; it was by vote of his men that Bernadotte was promoted Captain that summer, not through any commendation of his commanding general. When, in the following July, the name of the *ci-devant* Vicomte de Beauharnais joined the long list of officers to perish under the guillotine, his death aroused scant interest outside Paris. But, in a topsyturvy world, the Beauharnais stock was to show resilience and durability. Exactly half a century later – in the summer of 1844 – Captain Bernadotte's son and General de Beauharnais's granddaughter were preparing for their coronation as King and Queen of Sweden.

Bernadotte held the rank of Captain for only three weeks. For early in August 1793 the votes of 660 out of 1203 electors in his regiment raised him to Lieutenant-Colonel, although his promotion was not confirmed by the War Ministry until the following February. The election came as the 36th Infantry was on the move again, away from the Rhine and across to the marshy villages along the Belgian frontier. For in this battle-pitted corner of the continent, a French army under General Jourdan was seeking to thwart the Duke of York and the Prince of Coburg, who were conducting a leisurely campaign in the hope of capturing Dunkirk. Bernadotte's troops fought their way along the line of the Yser, south-east of Ypres;

they took Wervik and Menin and threatened to cut off the British from their base at Ostend. They did, it would seem, nothing wrong. But when Jourdan won the decisive battle of Wattignies in mid-October, Bernadotte was in reserve. After the near-panic at Rulzheim there was a certain reluctance that autumn to test the mettle of the 36th Infantry.

As yet Bernadotte's war service had been creditable, but not outstanding. Jourdan was only a few months his senior in age and like him had served in the ranks before the Revolution, but he became a Major-General (*Général de division*) as early as July 1793, with command of the Army of the North soon afterwards. Jourdan, however, had three advantages over Bernadotte: battle experience in America, rather than the policing of Corsica and Grenoble; an interlude of civilian life in his native town (Limoges), so that he was free to enlist in the National Guard as soon as the Revolution began and become a Captain immediately; and the opportunity to win distinction at Jemappes and keep good order at Neerwinden while Bernadotte was still skirmishing, unobserved, in the wings of Custine's sideshow. But in the following year Bernadotte's fortunes were to change swiftly. For, in Lazare Carnot, France at last found an effective war minister who levied troops to serve for more than one campaign and drew up a grand strategic plan for the Republic's fourteen armies. Apart from some months in 1795, when he was under a political cloud, Carnot 'organized victory' between August 1793 and September 1797. Without his perceptive genius there would have been no triumph in Italy for Bonaparte and no lasting fame for the lawyer's son from Pau.

Carnot was himself a soldier. He passed out of the Military Engineering School at Mezières as a star pupil. In October 1793 he insisted on coming to the Front and serving as an officer at Wattignies to assess the strength and weakness of the republic's soldiery in battle. Subsequently Jourdan resented the War Minister's constant presence at headquarters and, after a clash of wills, Carnot sent the victorious General back home to Limoges in disgrace. But Carnot knew how to bring cohesion to the army as a whole. He implemented the long-discussed 'Amalgam' reforms by which regiments of the line and the relatively untrained volunteers were integrated in new units, to be known as 'demi-brigades'. For Bernadotte the Amalgam meant both the end of the 36th Infantry Regiment and further promotion. On 4 April 1794 he became Colonel of the 71st Demi-

Brigade, which comprised his old battalion, two battalions of volunteers and a company of artillery. In General Pichegru's spring offensive of 1794, Bernadotte led these troops forward along the upper waters of the Sambre into Belgium.

Their first experience of battle was disastrous, almost a repeat performance of Rulzheim. The demi-brigade was fighting together after less than a fortnight's training and ran into hardened Austrian troops. 'If you disgrace yourselves by fleeing from the enemy, I shall not remain your Colonel', Bernadotte shouted as his men wavered. He tore the epaulettes from his shoulders and threw them dramatically to the ground. The gesture was effective; his men rallied around their Colonel and repulsed the Austrian assault. Bernadotte won renown as a queller of mutinies in the army as a whole, not merely in the 71st Demi-Brigade. On several occasions his fury erupted in a Gascon theatricality which was awe-inspiring. He rescued his immediate superior, General Marceau, from an angry mob of mutineers who seemed about to lynch him. His ability to impose discipline by rhetoric and example impressed the divisional commander, General Kléber. It was natural that so formidable a personality should catch the attention of Antoine de Saint Just, the austere Jacobin who arrived at headquarters in the castle at Guise on 2 May to keep watch on the army as a Representative of the People.

The *Représentants en Mission*, itinerant representatives of the sovereign people, were a familiar and dreaded phenomenon of the Republic's early campaigns. They came, generally two at a time, to root out what they saw as treachery, incompetence and indolence. Both Saint Just and his companion, Philippe Le Bas, were feared as active revolutionaries, close allies of Robespierre on the Committee of Public Safety: Saint Just, a contemporary declared, 'has the stiff, intolerable pride of a reformed reprobate, who atones for youthful aberrations by a life of virtue'. He knew nothing of warfare, seeing military science as an extension of active politics, a matter of resolutely attacking prominent objectives. Although some former volunteers resented the strict discipline which Bernadotte imposed on his demi-brigade, their colonel's energy in sustaining an assault on Austrian positions won Saint Just's warm approval. He proposed that Bernadotte be immediately promoted General. Other officers scaling the ladder of success were glad of a helping hand from Representatives who had the Committee of Public Safety apparently in their power; at Toulon, for example, Brigadier Bonaparte owed much to the backing of Robespierre's brother, Augustin. Bernadotte, however, was too proud, or too canny, to accept promotion at the whim of a Jacobin emissary. He 'had not the talents necessary for so high a rank', he explained with rare modesty. But next day a confidential message to his divisional commander set the record right: General Kléber was to understand that should promotion in the field 'again be offered me, I shall accept'.

Saint Just and Le Bas were at headquarters for four weeks. The Generals in the field knew that Jourdan, reinstated to favour, was on his way northwards with substantial reinforcements from the Moselle; until he arrived they wished to stand on the defensive. But Saint Just was moved by other considerations. For several weeks there had been murmurs of discontent among members of the Convention who resented the arbitrary character of Robespierre's dictatorship. If Robespierre went, there was little chance of the two Representatives surviving him. A courier sent post-haste early on Saturday, 24 May, warned Saint Just of the 'alarming revival of factions' and pressed for his immediate return to Paris. But Saint Just did not want to face his critics empty-handed. On Sunday evening he summoned a Council of War at Cousolre: 'The Republic requires a victory tomorrow', he peremptorily told the senior commanders. Dutifully the infantry was sent across the Sambre on Monday morning, even though hopelessly outnumbered; and by nightfall the men were back in their lines, with the Austrian defences undented. Desperately Saint Just ordered another assault. On 29 May – the Thursday on which Saint Just belatedly left for Paris – Bernadotte's troops again forded the river. This time the demi-brigade remained on the far bank until an Austrian counter-attack drove it back on the following Tuesday. By then Jourdan had reached the Sambre.

The grand strategic plan, carefully scrutinised by Carnot at the Ministry of War, envisaged the total defeat of the Austrians and their allies in the Low Countries: General Pichegru would advance through Flanders to the lower Scheldt to deal with the Dutch and the Duke of York's puny expeditionary force; General Jourdan would assume overall command of three armies and, having cleared eastern Belgium, wheel about and make for the Rhineland. A third attack was launched on the Austrian positions on 12 June; for four days Bernadotte and the advanced brigades of the army were engaged in heavy fighting. On the battle's second day the two Representatives of the People returned from Paris, Saint Just still demanding a battle honour won speedily: those who denied the Republic a triumph would, he threatened, face 'the People's justice'.

The full force of Jourdan's armies – beween 75,000 and 80,000 men – was turned against the Austrians on 18 June. Saint Just constantly interfered, insisting on the bombardment of Charleroi, even though its garrison was so short of provisions that it could not long sustain a siege. After a week's frontal assault on one of Vauban's most formidable citadels, Charleroi surrendered on 25 June, and for the first time the cumbersome baggage waggons of the Republic's Army clattered over the cobblestones of Hainaut. Thirty-five miles due north lay Brussels, a tempting objective. But Jourdan and Kléber were more concerned with the approach of the main allied army under Coburg on their right flank. Next morning the French vanguard – commanded by the future Marshal Lefebvre, who had been like Bernadotte a Sergeant on the eve of the Revolution – found Coburg holding the plain of Fleurus, eight miles north-east of Charleroi. It was an old battlefield: German Protestants were victorious in 1622; and the French inflicted a crushing defeat on Louis XIV's enemies sixty-eight years later.

The third, and most famous, Battle of Fleurus was a strange clash of arms. Coburg always observed the precepts of the textbooks and it began with all the calculated precision of a setpiece eighteenth-century engagement. On Kléber's orders, Bernadotte led the 71st Demi-Brigade against the Austrian flank in the woods around Baymont at a time when it seemed as if Coburg might break through to Charleroi and split the French army in two. In his despatches Kléber subsequently praised Bernadotte's bravery at the head of his troops, the example he set to young volunteers plunged into bitter hand-to-hand combat for the first time. More significant for the future, however, was Bernadotte's quick response to the warning of enemy reinforcements. When four squadrons of Dutch cavalry came to aid their Austrian allies, he amended his original plan, detaching four companies to protect his own flank from the new danger. No other Colonel took so many prisoners that day. Tactically the battle was drawn, with the French losing far more men than their enemies. But Jourdan and Kléber were left masters of the field and strategically Fleurus became a decisive victory for the Republic. As the fighting died away, Kléber galloped over to the 71st Demi-Brigade and greeted Bernadotte: 'Colonel, I appoint you Brigadier-General on the field of battle'. From his divisional commander Bernadotte welcomed the promotion he had declined so recently from Saint Just.

Victory at Fleurus opened the way to a rapid French conquest of the Austrian Netherlands. In Paris the deputies in the Convention were swift to recognise the battle's significance: the chief threat to the Republic, invasion from the North, receded; a formal decree, published in the *Moniteur* four days later, announced that Jourdan's united forces 'shall be known in future as the Army of Sambre-et-Meuse' and 'deserve the gratitude of their country'. Earlier in the month Saint Just had sought a Jacobin triumph, a victory for Robespierre to celebrate on 8 June at his Festival of the Supreme Being. But the good news from the Sambre reached Paris too late to be appropriated by this curious cult. To republicans cynically indifferent to the *Révolution Doctrinaire* of the Jacobins, Fleurus restored faith in a *Révolution Militant*. Carnot, already infuriated by Saint Just's interference with his war plans, began publishing a special army weekly, *La Journée de Camp*, which became a daily paper on 20 July. A week later the temper of the Convention turned against Robespierre, Saint Just and the whole surviving Jacobin faction. On 28 July, 1794 – 10 Thermidor, Year II, by the Revolutionary Calendar – they perished under the guillotine.

Thermidor is remembered as the end of the Revolutionary Terror. It was also, in a sense, an army coup that failed to happen – not least because there was no General on horseback to seize executive power in Paris that July. Within a few days the dismantling of the Jacobin tribunals promised greater freedom for all citizens. Yet the soldiery benefited most from the first administrative reforms, for in August the army was placed under the control of a specially constituted Military Committee. The *Représentants en Mission* were still sent out to the battle fronts, but never again did they seek to impose their will at Councils of War, as the fanatical Saint Just had done.

After Fleurus, Jourdan could thus conduct operations at his own pace. The Sambre-et-Meuse became the earliest élite army of the Revolution, its prestige antedating the fame of the Army of Italy by some twenty months. No fewer than six future Marshals were serving in its ranks during the winter of 1794–95: Jourdan himself, Bernadotte, Lefébvre, Ney, Soult and Gérard. By the first week of

October the Sambre-et-Meuse had carried the war to German soil, north of Aachen; Brigadier Bernadotte, with Colonel Michel Ney in support, showed such enterprise in fording the Ruhr between Aldenhoven and Jülich that the whole Austrian position was turned: 'I cannot speak too highly of General Bernadotte and of Ney who every day afford me new instances of their skills and courage on the Rhine; I am delighted that I gave them the posts they hold', Kléber wrote to Jourdan.

Soon Bernadotte could look out across the Rhine at the towers and spires of Düsseldorf. But, as Jourdan thought it impossible to cross so broad a river in winter, he was content for the army to dig in along the left bank until the spring. His forward troops were sent back to the Meuse (Maas) in Limburg where the 71st Demi-Brigade again distinguished itself, at the siege of Maastricht. There, for the fifth time in fifteen months, Bernadotte was promoted: he became a *Général de division* (Major-General) on 2 October 1794. No higher permanent rank could be attained in the revolutionary armies. Brigadier Bonaparte – having committed himself more positively to the Robespierrists and, in consequence, spent eleven days purging his Jacobinism in Antibes prison after Thermidor – was to wait another twelve months before reaching such a pinnacle of distinction.

By the early months of 1795 Bernadotte was back in a countryside he knew already. His division was spread along the left bank of the middle Rhine as far as Bingen, although Mainz was still in enemy hands. A general peace seemed close at hand: Prussia and much of northern Germany went out of the war by the Treaties of Basle (April and May 1795); Hesse Cassel followed Prussia's example in August; and Bernadotte's fears for his kinsfolk in Pau were removed when Spain made peace that summer. Along the Rhine an unofficial truce prevailed: the Austrians remained at war; for three months Bernadotte kept anxious watch on the Rhine from the bastions of Andernach, alert against a surprise assault.

From mid-July he was helped by aerial reconnaissance. He received regular observers' reports from a Montgolfier balloon of the *Corps Aérostatier*, a novelty assigned to the Sambre-et-Meuse by Carnot on the eve of Fleurus. When Kléber seized the initiative and crossed the Rhine in force near Düsseldorf on 4 September 1795, it was assumed that this thrust would draw the Austrian reserves northwards. Bernadotte, however, was unsure of the position on the far bank. His artillery bombarded Neuwied. Was it effective? Were there cavalry reserves in the hills beyond the river, waiting to sweep down on any landing parties he might put across? At six in the evening of 11 September he decided to see for himself and risked a balloon ascent from Andernach, staying aloft for over twenty minutes. By then the evening sun should have been behind his own positions and lighting up the right bank of the Rhine and the high ground beyond Neuwied. But he could see little; a storm threatened and the balloon cable nearly broke. Although Bernadotte has the distinction of being the first General to make an aerial reconnaissance, the experience convinced him that, militarily, Montgolfier balloons were unreliable toys. Never again did he resort to aerial reconnaissance. Despite the stormy weather he sent his men forward across the Rhine next day. By the end of the week they had joined Jourdan and Kléber along the River Lahn, poised to come down on the Main from the north, with Mainz or Frankfurt as potential prizes.

Yet the campaign as a whole was bungled. The Austrians threatened to turn the French flank, and on 14 October Jourdan ordered a swift withdrawal, back to their old positions beyond the Rhine. Even so the French were fortunate to escape total disaster. General Marceau, already for several years a warm companion-in-arms of Kléber, had by now also become a close friend of Bernadotte. Their surviving letters show an easy *tu-et-toi* familiarity; they understood each other's moods and intentions well. But at the end of that autumn their mutual telepathy failed to function. As Marceau's troops were crossing the river near Coblenz he ordered them to set fire to some Rhine barges: they would, he thought, provide a smoke screen to cover the French withdrawal. The burning barges were carried northwards by the strong current; nine miles downstream they fired the bridge of boats at Neuwied on which Kléber and Bernadotte were retreating. Such an emergency showed Bernadotte at his best: he goaded his men to extremes of courage by his Gascon rhetoric. The rearguard held off the Austrians while pontoons were repaired and the army crossed to safety. Marceau, whose temperament was as theatrical as Bernadotte's, declared he would shoot himself in mortification. Fortunately his aide-de-camp had the good sense to remove his pistols, whether before or after the threat of suicide remains unclear.

For the next eleven months Bernadotte and Marceau worked

in tandem. The Austrians, wheeling north-westwards from their bridgehead at Mainz, sought to reach the line of the Moselle and make Jourdan abandon Coblenz. Marceau was forced back behind the River Nahe into the Soonwald and the wooded hills and vineyards of the Hünsruck. Both armies, short of food and supplies, were bogged down in the mud of an early winter until, in mid-December, Bernadotte's division occupied Kreuznach, on the Nahe. At once the Austrians counter-attacked; there was grim street-by-street fighting for several hours. Moreover when the troops found themselves in a town after weeks of wintry bivouacs, they began looting freely from its terrified inhabitants. Many generals left fallen cities at the 'disposal' of their captors; but not Bernadotte. At Kreuznach he threatened with severe punishment any culprits apprehended and he insisted on recompense for householders who had suffered. 'An army without discipline can win a victory, but cannot make use of it', he declared uncompromisingly. For the moment, however, there was no question of winning a victory. Throughout the first five months of 1796 the French and Austrian commanders observed an armistice, keeping the lines they held at the end of the year.

From the Hünsruck, Bernadotte moved in January 1796 to new headquarters at Boppard, eight miles upstream from Coblenz, where he was to serve as Governor later in the year. In both winter seasons there was a fine choice of social entertainment in Rhineland towns and villages. Rhenish patriotism was, as yet, local rather than German national in sentiment. The Rhinelanders felt more at ease with Alsatian officers like General Kléber than they had with the many Magyar and Bohemian nobles in Emperor Francis's army; the officers of the Sambre-et-Meuse bore little resemblance to those blood-stained monsters against whom emigré aristocrats had warned the Rhinelanders a year or two ago. Even the Generals were young bachelors: Marceau was only twenty-six, and though Bernadotte complained to his brother that he was an old man before his time, he celebrated a thirty-second birthday at Boppard. The sometime Sergeant Belle-Jambe still dressed smartly and looked imposing, especially in the saddle. He had admirers: there was, for example, 'the canoness' – as the free-thinking Kléber nicknamed her in a note from Cologne at Easter 1796 – who 'spoke to me of you for more than an hour with expressions of the liveliest tenderness and high regard'. Later in the year his staff thought Bernadotte might marry a Fräulein Potgeisser, whose father was a banker in Coblenz. Whether he would get that doe-eyed brunette, Träntchen, or her young sister, the blonde Rhine-maiden Lischen, was a matter of amused speculation. He chose neither.

The grand strategic plan for the year 1796 had been approved by Carnot during the first week of January. Three French armies would attack the Austrian Empire: the main front would be in Germany, where General Jourdan would lead the Sambre-et-Meuse against Mainz and across Franconia to the borders of Bohemia while General Moreau's Army of the Rhine-et-Moselle would strike eastwards from Alsace into southern Bavaria and ultimately the Tyrol; but there would also be a second front in Piedmont, where General Napoleon Bonaparte's Army of Italy would tie down Austrian troops who might otherwise have engaged Jourdan or Moreau. It was felt that, as General Bonaparte was a 'young man of talent', he might with luck reach the Lombard plain and threaten Milan. There was no supreme commander and little contact even along the Rhine between Jourdan and Moreau, let alone between the armies north and south of the Alps. Napoleon, however, made certain he kept in close touch with the political leaders of the ruling Directory. He had been frequently in Paris and knew them well enough not to be inhibited by any constraints in a War Ministry directive. The Army of Italy went over to the offensive in the second week of April, and even before the Armistice expired along the Rhine Napoleon had won the battle of Lodi and entered Milan in triumph.

For the Sambre-et-Meuse 1796 was a disastrous year. Jourdan could only produce a replica of the last campaign: Kléber crossed the Rhine near Düsseldorf, Bernadotte at Neuwied; and everyone met on the Lahn, where the Austrians duly counter-attacked, forcing Jourdan to order a retreat to the Rhine. Since on this occasion the French would not oblige with fire-barges, there now followed a slight change in scenario, with the Austrians sending heavy rafts downstream to batter the bridge of boats. The effect was much the same: the bridge creaked, groaned and began to float away; and Bernadotte once more struck fine attitudes, keeping the foe at bay while his division crossed to safety. By midsummer, while Moreau's Rhine-et-Moselle was heading for the upper Danube, the Sambre-et-Meuse was back in winter quarters. South of the Alps, in what the strategists of Paris had seen as the secondary front, Napoleon had already gobbled up Bologna,

crossed into Tuscany, and come to within a few days' march of
Florence.

Jourdan tried again a fortnight later. He took Würzburg while
Kléber entered Frankfurt. Bernadotte pushed ahead to Darmstadt
and on to Nuremberg. But he was uneasy. He was troubled by the
intermittent character of the resistance offered to his advance.
Where exactly was the Austrian commander-in-chief, the Archduke
Charles? It was reported that his army lay somewhere between
Bernadotte's own right flank and Moreau's vanguard, more than
sixty miles to the south. The Archduke, not yet twenty-five and a
brother of Emperor Francis, was a gifted strategist. No French
general would lightly dismiss a threat from Charles's army: could
it be, Bernadotte wondered, that he was playing a cat and mouse
game with the Sambre-et-Meuse?

Bernadotte's doubts came to a head in the third week of August
when he reached Altdorf, a small university town fifteen miles
south-east of Nuremberg. The townsfolk, who were dominated by
the University Rector, irritated him with complaints of ill-usage
by the French soldiery: for once he treated such representations
brusquely. His principal worry was the order he had received from
Jourdan to advance to the Danube at Regensburg – then still
known as Ratisbon. There, at the approach to the Austrian border,
Bernadotte's corps would be joined by the main body of the Sambre-
et-Meuse and, so Jourdan believed, by units of Moreau's army
following the Danube eastwards. But Jourdan's strange order left
Bernadotte's corps exposed to a possible flank attack by an Austrian
army which was said to outnumber the French by three to one.
Moreover, if Archduke Charles succeeded in sweeping aside Bernadotte, he would then be in a position to cut off Jourdan and Kléber
from their bases on the middle Rhine.

With slightly more than 9000 men, Bernadotte pushed ahead
across the plain of Neumarkt to the heavily wooded high ground
around the village of Deining, almost halfway between Nuremberg
and Regensburg. The Austrian attacks became so severe that Bernadotte was forced to halt on 21 August, fall back on the Deining
heights, and give battle next day from daybreak until dusk. He
personally led an attack on the Austrian centre in the early evening
which checked the Archduke's assault and enabled the French to
begin a long retreat under cover of darkness. That night a howitzer
caisson caught fire and a series of explosions shook wagons and

frightened horses as the men stumbled back around the edge of the Neumarkt plain. The main body of the Sambre-et-Meuse was twenty-five miles to the north, at Amberg. Like Bernadotte's corps it was now pulling back fast, on Bamberg. For the Austrians the news from the Italian Front seemed so bad that Archduke Charles was looking for a decisive victory in Germany to serve as a counterweight to Napoleon's triumph should it become necessary to negotiate a general peace.

Bernadotte retreated through five days of desperate skirmishing in summer heat. Surprisingly he was able to maintain strict discipline and good order on the grim march. By 27 August, when he rejoined the main army at Forchheim, he was extremely weary and suffering from a lance wound on the top of his forehead: 'Had I not been wearing a hat, I should not have lived', he wrote to his brother. Morale was low at Forchheim: the Armies of Italy and of Rhine-et-Moselle seemed to be hammering the Austrians on the anvil, as Carnot intended; Napoleon, on the shores of Lake Garda, was threatening an advance into the Tyrol; and, on the day that Jourdan's general retreat began, Moreau's army gained a victory at Friedberg, five miles east of Augsburg. Only the Sambre-et-Meuse failed to consolidate its early successes. The good companionship which had bound together Jourdan's officers for more than two years was broken. Both Kléber and Bernadotte were angry with Jourdan for a lacklustre strategy they could not understand.

The crisis in command came to a head on 1 September. On that Thursday morning Jourdan summoned a Council of War at Schweinfurt and announced that he would give battle to the Archduke Charles on the high ground above the Main at Würzburg. Every senior officer opposed him: the troops, and the cavalry horses, were exhausted; the French were outnumbered, their supplies were low and they needed to get back to the Rhine without more losses. But, for political purposes, Jourdan remained adamant. Next morning neither Kléber nor Bernadotte was on duty. Both Generals had reported sick and both missed Saturday's battle outside Würzburg, at which Jourdan was, predictably, defeated by the Archduke. Presumably the two generals were genuinely ill, for no action was taken against them as malingerers: Kléber had already been out of action with a fever for several days in August (as, indeed, had Jourdan, who suffered from malaria) while Bernadotte's lance wound needed treatment. Not until the following Sunday was

Bernadotte back on duty: 'The soldiers', wrote one of his staff officers later, 'received him joyfully, as if welcoming back a father, but the officers more coldly for having left them at a critical moment'. It was not the last occasion in his career when, for good and sound reasons, Bernadotte missed the hour of battle.

On that Sunday he found his old division behind the Taunus hills, helping General Marceau hold some sixty miles of the River Lahn, so as to give Jourdan a chance to get his main body of troops back to Cologne. Even now, poor Jourdan made an error of judgment, summoning Bernadotte's troops to support the left of his line on the eve of an Austrian attack which lost Marceau's depleted force the town of Limburg. But next day (18 September) Bernadotte and Marceau brought their troops together to fight a rearguard action as they retired northwards through Freilengen to the village of Altenkirchen. Next night a Tyrolean marksman hidden in a neighbouring wood fired at Marceau and mortally wounded him. Bernadotte had to leave his friend to be taken prisoner by the Austrians. Despite the best medical attention, Marceau died two days later.

By now the campaign was virtually over. While Bernadotte was seeking to keep a bridgehead at Neuwied, an Austrian cavalry escort brought back Marceau's body, under a flag of truce; the Archduke asked that he might be informed of the day of Marceau's funeral so that the Emperor Francis's army could pay homage to a heroic adversary. As Governor of Coblenz, Bernadotte arranged for his friend's ashes to be interred beneath a pyramid of stone; an eloquently simple inscription recalled 'A soldier at 16, a General at 22' who met his death at twenty-seven. Twenty years later when Byron visited the Rhineland he was so impressed by the dignity of the monument that Marceau's name is honoured in the third canto of *Childe Harold's Pilgrimage*.

Soon afterwards Jourdan, an amiable and astonishingly unambitious military leader, resigned his command having, as he informed the War Department in Paris, 'lost the confidence of my generals'. Kléber seemed to be Jourdan's natural successor, but the command went, instead, to the competent and thoroughly unimaginative Pierre de Beurnonville. The Sambre-et-Meuse, saluted 'as deserving the gratitude of their country' two years before, had fallen from grace. During the closing months of 1796 it became fashionable in Paris to disparage Jourdan's campaign, his army's

achievements and the military reputation of his subordinate commanders. Many of the sixty newspapers in the capital were no more
than gossip-sheets, serving a limited reading public. But some were
by now seeking a wider circulation. Prominent among these journals
was the new and ambitiously named *Gazette Générale de l'Europe*.
In issue no. 26 the *Gazette* attacked Bernadotte's conduct early in
the year, accusing him of having 'for twenty-four hours given over
the city of Nuremberg to plunder'.

Copies of the *Gazette* reached Coblenz in the last week of October.
Bernadotte was especially proud of the iron restraints he imposed
on his troops on the march; and when he read the paper's allegations,
his brother officers found it hard to calm his anger. Not even
Kléber's cynical indifference to journalism and to Parisian politics
could douse the fire and flame of his friend's Gascon temper. He
wished to set out at once for Paris (which he had never visited)
and fight a duel with Duperon, the journalist who concocted so
groundless a libel. Since October 1795 the executive power in the
French Republic had been shared by five Directors, among them
Lazare Carnot. In high indignation Bernadotte now formally wrote
to the Directory, asking to be put on half-pay so as to come to Paris
and 'attend to his private affairs'. At the same time he complained
– as he had to his brother after the Rulzheim incident – that
individual feats of arms went unnoticed. This obsessive grievance
lacked foundation: Bernadotte's achievements were often mentioned
by Jourdan in his despatches and given publicity in the *Moniteur*.
The Directors, in refusing his request to be put on half-pay,
urged him to treat the calumnies with silent contempt; they wrote
appreciatively of his military talents and service. But fair words
were not enough for Bernadotte. On 10 November, the *Moniteur*
printed an open letter from Bernadotte to the Directory claiming
'just reparation' for Duperon's 'mendacious assertions'. Slowly the
Directors prepared to take action over an episode they would far
sooner have ignored. They were anxious to keep a hot-headed
General with a grievance away from the capital.

Side by side with Bernadotte's aggrieved assertions in the *Moniteur* of 10 November was printed a letter from General Bonaparte
praising the purity of Genoese republican sentiment. Theoretically
the Italian campaign, like the German, should have been over by
now: 'All Italy is French', Napoleon had written to the Directors
as early as 21 June. But the Austrians showed unexpected resilience.

By mid-November, Napoleon was admitting that he was 'on the eve of losing Italy' unless he could bring separately to battle the two armies which the Austrians had thrust into the field against him. 'Reinforcements! Send me Reinforcements . . . Not on paper, but here now and under arms', he wrote to Paris on 14 November. Although over the next three days he won the battle of Arcole, and so prevented any union of the Austrian armies, he continued to badger Carnot for troops: 'Send me 10,000 men from the Rhine . . . and you may expect millions, victories, and a good peace', he wrote temptingly at the beginning of December.

France needed peace. The strain of four years' intermittent campaigning was throwing the Republic into near-bankruptcy, with only the loot from pillaged Italy keeping treasure in the coffers. Yet although peace talks between French and Austrian representatives continued throughout the last two months of 1796, the Emperor Francis would make no concessions. The fear that the Emperor had the strength and confidence to order another winter offensive in Italy finally decided Carnot on a change in strategic priorities. Since there was no prospect of a favourable outcome to any campaign in the German lands, Napoleon must crush the Austrians south of the Alps, and perhaps even wheel northwards into Austria. He should be given the reinforcements he demanded from the Rhine. And what better way to calm Bernadotte's ruffled temper than by giving him command of the troops who were to cross the Alps and strengthen the French hold on the Italian plain? Over the Duperon calumnies he had, after all, taken pride in emphasising the skill with which he could keep good discipline on the march. To bring reinforcements from Metz to Milan would put his claims to the test – and also keep him away from Paris.

On 7 January 1797, Bernadotte received orders which placed him under the command of General Napoleon Bonaparte in Italy. He would lead a division of the Sambre-et-Meuse from Coblenz to Metz where he would be joined by a second division, from the Army of Rhine-et-Moselle. His staff were to prepare an itinerary which would enable his corps to cross the Mont Cenis Pass and arrive in Lombardy ready to give battle to old adversaries in a strange terrain. The order to prepare a long mid-winter march was unexpected but Bernadotte was hardly surprised by the decision to strengthen the Army of Italy. Despite the recent rebuffs to the Sambre-et-Meuse it was still fashionable in Coblenz to admire Napoleon's victories with studied condescension and a certainty that when his offensive lost its momentum he would turn for aid to the hard-plodding veterans from Germany. In Paris, where Lazare Carnot was well aware of the patronising attitude of the Rhineland officer corps, there may well have been second thoughts over the new appointment. 'Major-General Bernadotte, who is leading the troops sent to you from the Army of Sambre-et-Meuse . . . has already won our approbation', ran the formal letter from the Directory to Napoleon, 'We hope you will be able to report favourably on his services to you.' As a testimonial for a General who believed he had deserved well of the Republic the message might, perhaps, have been more warmly worded.

Chapter 3
Beyond the Alps and in Paris

N O LOGISTIC enterprise so repeatedly feeds history with legend as the crossing of the Alps by an army on the march. The deeds of Hannibal, Charlemagne and Napoleon are so well remembered that they evoke a series of melodramatic images in the mind: African elephants in an icy snowscape; Frankish horsemen seeking speedy routes to the Lombard plain; or that wild-eyed charger which never, in reality, carried the First Consul over the Great St Bernard. By contrast, Bernadotte's passage of the Alps – undertaken three years before Napoleon's – has provided no familiar episode to set beside these pageant scenes from romanticised history; his men were at odds with Nature rather than with an active enemy manning a line of fortified positions. Nevertheless the long winter march of 1797 was an astonishing achievement; for Bernadotte a triumph of organisation, endurance and discipline.

Yet there was a moment, less than a fortnight after Bernadotte left Coblenz, when it seemed as if he might not, after all, be crossing the Alps. A hurried letter to Kléber shows how enthusiastically he had thrown himself into the preparatory paperwork, with staff officers of his own selection working beside him in Metz. Having served for so long in the ranks, he knew the need of soldiers on the march for food, good quarters and welfare. On 18 January he wrote for the first time to Napoleon (who had defeated the Austrians at Rivoli four days before); it was a flattering letter to which was attached a long, but admirably precise, itinerary and a request that supplies should be ready at Lyons, Grenoble and Chambéry to sustain his men as they headed for the Alps. When he reached Dijon on 28 January, with nearly a third of the journey to Milan completed, he could claim that his men's behaviour in the countryside had been exemplary. It was therefore a disagreeable surprise to find awaiting him in Dijon fresh orders despatched from Paris six days earlier by the Minister of War, Charles Petiet: at the request of General Moreau, Bernadotte was to return to Coblenz, ready for service once more along France's eastern frontiers, this time as Moreau's close partner. Nothing was said of a replacement commander for the army on the march.

'The first duty of a soldier must be obedience', Bernadotte piously wrote to Napoleon next day, reporting his receipt of the new orders from Petiet. In reality neither General believed in so simple an article of soldierly faith any longer: Napoleon had convinced himself long ago that, for a commander of genius, obedience was always dependent on the promptings of common sense; and Bernadotte's experience in the field was encouraging a similar independence of judgment. Nevertheless it was as well to affirm the importance of orders when writing to a commander-in-chief whom you had never met, especially if you had every intention of ignoring them. It was reasonable for Bernadotte to argue that if these 20,000 men whom he had bullied and cajoled across Lorraine and into Burgundy saw their General turn back and head for the Rhine they would desert by the hundred, if not by the thousand. Bernadotte sent Napoleon a copy of the wretched Petiet's directive together with a covering letter in which he emphasised his desire to serve under a commander whose triumphs he had so admired from afar. He would, he told Napoleon, press ahead to Chambéry and take no notice of Moreau's alleged appeal for his services until 'I can be informed what will best suit your intentions'. Next day he notified Petiet that he was resuming his march to the Alps.

By 2 February Bernadotte's three columns had left Dijon for Lyons, where they turned along the Guiers valley and up a rocky defile to the Col-de-Couz before dropping down to the Army of the Alps's depot at Chambéry, where General Kellermann, the hero of Valmy, was in command. There on 17 February Bernadotte received from Petiet confirmation of his original appointment to Italy; and no further attempt was made to lure him back to the Rhine. At Chambéry, too, the first orders from his general-in-chief awaited him. He was now Napoleon's man, eager (as he wrote soon afterwards to Kellermann) 'to champion the glory of the Army of Italy'. Significantly, with an echo of the patronising mood of his brother officers in the Sambre-et-Meuse, the impact of Bernadotte's proud phrase was then diminished by a confident hope that the 'young general' will 'not prove ungrateful'.

Kellermann, whose knowledge of raising and training armies went back to the Seven Years' War, was impressed by the bearing of these reinforcements, marching in such good order from Rhine to Po. So confident was Bernadotte of the discipline within his own division that he allowed 6000 men a few days' leave before leaving France, and none deserted, even though they knew that ahead of them lay the 140 mile journey through the Mont Cenis Pass to Turin. By 20 February they had left Modane and were more than 4000 feet up in the mountains. Captain François, one of the few officers whose journal has survived, remembered the six-hour climb up the Mont Cenis road that Monday, with heavy snow falling and regimental drums beating to keep the column pressing forward across the crest of the pass; and then, in icy darkness, those four endless hours as the long line of weary infantrymen slipped and slithered down the highest peaks into the cheerless foothills of Piedmont. It was Wednesday night before they reached the comparative comfort of Turin. Next day a French royalist agent observed, 'Fine young men . . . from Coblenz . . . marching forwards gaily (*gaiement*) and tirelessly . . . crossing Piedmont without causing any trouble or the slightest havoc (*le moindre dégât*)'; he took care to let King Louis XVIII, in exile in western Germany, know what he had seen. For this was not the behaviour which the people of Piedmont had come to expect from an army of the French Republic passing through their land.

Bernadotte reached Milan at last on 22 February. But Napoleon was not there. The general-in-chief, having sent a message that 'he greatly desired to make General Bernadotte's acquaintance' was some 260 miles away in Ancona, and most of his commanders were along the rivers Adige and Mincio, where Mantua had surrendered after a long siege at the start of the month. Bernadotte's staff therefore found themselves dealing in the first instance with Colonel Dominique Dupuy, military commandant of Milan, an officer who was jealously proud of Bonaparte's triumphs and resented intruders. The Army of Italy had evolved military conventions of its own: it expected to be paid in cash by the general-in-chief, from seized booty and indemnities; and having gained its earliest victories in threadbare uniforms and short of tents and baggage, it took pride in an improvised self-sufficiency which depended on successful

ravaging in the towns and villages through which it passed. Bonaparte personally may have tried to check the looting: when his
troops entered Verona in June 1796 he promised them a bonus of 24
livres each not to pillage the city; and he rebuked the Government's
representative, his fellow-Corsican Antoine Saliceti, for removing
chalices from churches and selling them in the streets. But the Army
of Italy remained essentially a Jacobin host, setting up satellite
republics in Milan and Bologna. It exported the Revolution in a
style unfamiliar to the Sambre-et-Meuse. 'Our methods of warfare
here are so different from all others', Bonaparte had warned the
War Ministry, while Bernadotte was on his way southwards to
Chambéry.

To Dupuy, and many other battle-hardened veterans in Milan,
the parade ground newcomers from the Rhine were pampered
'gentlemen', as distinct from the citizen army which had stormed
the bridges of Lodi and Arcole and sent the Austrian whitecoats
reeling back from Rivoli. Straw spread across the floors of emptied
convents was quite good enough to welcome Bernadotte's men to
Lombardy, argued Dupuy. When their officers remonstrated with
him on finding the convents had housed Austrian prisoners who left
the straw filthy, Dupuy lost his temper. He even sneered at the fine
bearing and manners of 'these *messieurs*' to their commanding
general in person, and he declined to act on Bernadotte's order to
quarter the 88th Demi-Brigade, the main sufferers among his troops,
on the people of Milan. Dupuy's conduct was too much for
the one-time Sergeant Belle-Jambe. He at once placed the military
commandant of the city under arrest for insolence and insubordination.

This show-stopping entry by Bernadotte on to the Italian stage
was, however, spoilt a few days later. General Friant's brigade,
having discovered that the rank and file of the Army of Italy were
paid regularly in cash, demanded a prompt settlement of arrears
before resuming their march to the Front; and only after Bernadotte
thundered at them with the full force of his customary histrionics
were they cowed into dutiful obedience. There were, too, unfortunate repercussions of the Dupuy affair, for the colonel was a friend
and protégé of General Alexandre Berthier, Napoleon's indefat-
igable chief of staff. A written rebuke to Bernadotte, signed by
Berthier on the authority of the general-in-chief, pointed out that
any dispute with the commandant of Milan should have been

referred to his immediate superior, the commanding general in Lombardy. The letter ended with a brief recital of Dupuy's virtues, as shown in so many encounters with the enemy, and a suggestion that the newcomers from Sambre-et-Meuse might learn from their brave comrades already in Italy 'how to suffer silently a certain deprivation of life's necessities'. According to the (slightly suspect) memoirs of Bernadotte's own chief-of-staff, the tone of the letter stung his General into threats of challenging Berthier to a duel. Fortunately it required only a few more days of marching along the mud-spattered causeways between the Mincio marshes for Bernadotte to bring the general-in-chief's reinforcements at last to field headquarters at La Favorita, outside Mantua. There, on 3 March 1797, he met Napoleon for the first time.

'He received me very well', Bernadotte said afterwards, 'but I saw in him a young man of about twenty-six or twenty-seven who wants to appear fifty – and that's a poor lookout for the Republic'; and Napoleon allegedly commented, cryptically, 'There goes a French head above a Roman heart'. But since neither judgment appeared in writing until many years later, it is probable that the two men never leapt to such shrewd assessments at first sight. The meeting was certainly friendly, despite the tension Bernadotte had aroused in Milan. With Austria about to seek recovery of her lost mastery, this was no time for dark murmurings of duels between senior commanders, and Napoleon took pains to defuse that heavy concentration of Gascon anger. As general-in-chief he still remembered what as emperor he often forgot – that unity of command depended on maintaining an Olympian detachment, well above the jealous squabbling of lesser gods.

In late February Bernadotte's old adversary the Archduke Charles came south to take command of an Austrian army which was, on paper, considerably larger than the French but in reality consisted of about 50,000 men scattered haphazardly over a wide area of north-western Italy. But Napoleon did not intend to allow the Archduke to take the initiative. With Bernadotte's reinforcements from beyond the Alps, he believed the Army of Italy strong enough to penetrate the heart of the Habsburg lands, and perhaps even to threaten Vienna. When Napoleon inspected his new brigades after their long and weary march he was impressed with their bearing and panache: 'Fine troops, in splendid condition and well disciplined', he was to recall in exile twenty years later. Despite the strictures of Berthier, he had such confidence in Bernadotte that he immediately gave him command of the 4th Division, which was to concentrate at Padua on the right wing of the whole army. It comprised, for the most part, veterans drawn from the Sambre-et-Meuse; there were even members of what Bernadotte called his 'military family', men whom he had commanded as long ago as Fleurus. Wisely, however, Napoleon encouraged gradual integration; and he attached to the 4th Division Joachim Murat, a young cavalry brigadier whose horsemanship at Dego in the previous April had already won praise from the general-in-chief.

Spring came late that year. In the first days of March the 4th Division advanced as far as the River Piave without encountering much resistance, but the snow then began to fall heavily and all activity ceased for a whole week. By Thursday, 16 March, the division had reached the banks of the Tagliamento, an unpredictable river, always ice-cold at the end of winter, normally twisting in a succession of streams across a broad and stony channel between high banks, but often so flooded by melting snow that fords ceased to exist. Shortly before noon Bernadotte, travelling along the old Via Postumia, arrived at Valvasone, a crossing known to the Roman legions; he found the Austrians in prepared defences on the far bank. Colonel Lahure, who commanded the 13th Regiment, describes how the French pitched camp, even lighting fires for a midday meal so that the enemy assumed there would be no attempt at a crossing that day. Once the Austrians relaxed, Bonaparte ordered the guns to open up on the Austrian positions, while Bernadotte hurriedly brought his division to arms. 'Soldiers, never forget that you come from the army of Sambre-et-Meuse and that the eyes of the Army of Italy are upon you', Lahure claims he said, with an over-quoted flourish of battle-eve rhetoric. More convincing is the simpler encouragement noted by Captain François in his journal: 'Let's go, lads, show yourselves worthy of the Army of Italy. Forward!' (*Allons, mes enfants, montrez-vous dignes de l'armée d'Italie. En avant!*) Yet, whatever the form of his pep-talk, Bernadotte at once suited action to words. He galloped down to the river, found the ford, dismounted, and led the crossing on foot. Antoine Lavalette, Napoleon's aide-de-camp, watching from the right bank, saw Bernadotte wade through 'numerous branches of the river under the most murderous fire'. Once Bernadotte's division had secured a foothold on the left bank, Austrian resistance crumbled. Napoleon, says

Captain François, 'congratulated us and our Gascon Major-General on our valour'.

The French captured six guns and took over five hundred prisoners in that Thursday's surprise assault. The 4th Division rested on Friday and resumed the pursuit of the Archduke early next morning towards the River Isonzo, which cuts a channel from the Julian Alps southwards to the Gulf of Trieste. On the left bank is a formidable and barren limestone plateau; and on the right a line of fortified towns, a short distance west of the river. One of these bridgeheads, Gradisca, a walled overgrown village grouped around an old castle, lay directly in the path of the French right wing; and Archduke Charles thought it worth leaving a garrison of 3000 men in the town to check the French advance. Napoleon first saw Gradisca about ten on the Sunday morning after crossing Tagliamento. From the high ground to the west, it looked a minor obstacle: Bernadotte must either take Gradisca or blockade it; he would himself remain with General Sérurier's division, higher up river, and expect Bernadotte to join him before nightfall; and he galloped off northwards, with Berthier and his staff. Bernadotte was disconcerted: verbal orders, imprecisely defined, were an unwelcome novelty. He tried to bluff the Austrian commandant into surrender. At the same time he ordered Colonel Lahure, who went forward under a white flag for parleys with the garrison, to note the state of Gradisca's defences. Like Bonaparte, Lahure minimised what he saw: dry ditches and walls in such poor repair that it would be easy to scale them, he reported confidently. Bernadotte decided on a frontal assault, another feat of valour and enterprise to catch the eye of the Army of Italy. This was a tragic error. The 4th Division was equipped for rapid movement: it had no ladders for scaling the defences of a town. Bernadotte ordered his artillery to pound the Novapalma gate and then sent his infantry forward to complete the work of the cannon. In three hours of grim fighting the division lost five hundred men before Gradisca was taken.

Bonaparte's despatch to Paris paid tribute to the personal bravery of Bernadotte, Murat and Lahure and to the ardour of the division as a whole; but that night, at his bivouac on the hills above the Isonzo, the general-in-chief received his Major-General frigidly: what impulsive folly led Bernadotte to throw away five hundred lives in storming a small town whose garrison would soon have run out of food and water? It was a question still puzzling Napoleon in exile on St Helena; the answer lay, he suspected, in that envy and jealousy which kept apart old and new units within his army. But Bernadotte's champions then and later blamed Bonaparte for having postulated a strategic objective without defining how tactically he wished it attained.

Over the remaining two and a half weeks of the campaign Bernadotte saw little action. While Napoleon pressed northwards into Carinthia with three divisions, he was left to organise advance depots in Novapalma and Gradisca. Eventually he took the field in pursuit of a Croatian division, which withdrew into Carniola (Slovenia). Father Joseph Weiniger, parish priest in what is now the Yugoslav cave resort of Postojna, was startled by the arrival of the French vanguard on 27 March, with General Murat 'riding majestically' at the head of his cavalry; but not for another six days did the core of the 4th Division reach the village, 'led by Bernadotte, with bands playing and pennants flying'. Although Napoleon's staff officers complained that Bernadotte's men had raided churches at Codroiopo after crossing the Tagliamento, Father Weiniger was full of praise for the troops billeted on Postojna: they 'exacted nothing in money or goods'; it was Passiontide on the Sunday they marched into the village and when present at Mass, 'their behaviour was Christian and respectful'. But, for the commanding general, there were welcome fruits of victory in Carniola. On Napoleon's orders Bernadotte sent a detachment from Postojna to Idria (now Idrija), where his men seized the quicksilver mines and foundries. This raid netted over three million francs for the fast emptying coffers in Paris. Almost a quarter of the sum was later reimbursed to Napoleon, while a 50,000 franc share was appropriated by Bernadotte himself, with the sanction of the general-in-chief.

From Laibach (Ljubljana) Bernadotte hurried to Klagenfurt and followed Napoleon into Styria, joining him at Schloss Eggenberg, outside Graz. Over the following fortnight Bernadotte was initiated into power politics. For by now Napoleon exercised the authority of an independent pro-consul, impatient with the ruling Directory in Paris, most of whose members he despised. The Directory sought a good, lasting and rewarding peace and, to stave off bankruptcy, needed it quickly. So, too, did Napoleon, but for different reasons: his line of communications was over-stretched; he was threatened by uprisings in the Tyrol and in Venice; and, although his forward troops were within a hundred miles of Vienna, he had no wish to

risk a decisive battle in the Hollental, for the limestone barriers of
the Schneeberg and Raxalpe were more formidable than the heights
above the Rivoli plateau, where he had consolidated his hold on
northern Italy three months before. When, therefore, the Austrians
proposed a truce, to be followed by a provisional peace settlement,
negotiated at Leoben between the commanders in the field, they
found Napoleon readily responsive. But he was determined that, in
any final settlement, the map of Europe would be re-drawn as he
saw fit, not to accommodate the wishes of that Gang of Five in
Paris.

While the peace talks continued at Leoben, Bernadotte's headquarters were seven miles away, up the Murtal, in the village of St
Michael. In the first instance Napoleon looked for advice to Berthier
and to General Masséna, old companions in arms who knew their
Italy well. But a settlement with Austria also required decisions
about the Rhine frontier and Belgium; and here the general-in-chief
could turn to Bernadotte, who would ride down to Leoben for
consultation. Not that Napoleon gave much weight to German
affairs. He secured a renunciation of Austrian claims on Belgium,
but he was more concerned with fostering republicanism in Italy
and acceptance of French primacy throughout the peninsula. The
future of the left bank of the Rhine, so recently a prime objective
of government policy, might remain in limbo.

The detailed settlement was, however, deferred for later discussion, not least because Napoleon cynically realised he could
obtain better terms if he overthrew the Venetian Republic and gave
Austria some pickings as compensation for land lost elsewhere. An
armistice, the 'Preliminaries of Leoben', was concluded on 18 April
and the French at once began their withdrawal from Styria and
Carinthia. Bernadotte became Governor of the occupied province
of Friuli, with his headquarters at Udine, and including Gradisca
and the Tagliamento fords as well as the growing port of Trieste.
These responsibilities stretched his resources and made it difficult
for him to impose the iron discipline which he thought essential for
good order. While he was on his first visit to Trieste there was
serious trouble a hundred miles away in the Laibach garrison: for
the latent hostility between his 'gentlemen's army' and Masséna's
'citizens' exploded in duels among officers and affrays in the street.
Fifty Frenchmen died before the troops were pulled out of Laibach.
Soon afterwards, in May, Bernadotte turned his attention south-

wards, providing troops for the occupation of Venice and the overthrow of the city's oligarchy. He was, it seemed, indispensable. A request for three months' leave, long overdue, was brushed aside by the general-in-chief: 'I cannot begin to think what you would wish to do with yourself when, day after day, you are rendering such brilliant services to the Republic', Napoleon wrote smoothly. A visit to Paris was all Bernadotte sought; he was unique among France's finest soldiers in never having set foot there.

There were sound political reasons why Napoleon did not want Bernadotte hurrying off to the capital, with time on his hands, at that moment. For throughout the summer of 1797 the shadow of a military coup hung over Paris, and Napoleon had no intention of allowing power to pass to any general whom he could not control. Late in March there had been elections for one-third of the seats in the two chambers of the French legislature: the Council of the Ancients (men over forty) and the Council of the Five Hundred. Widespread apathy allowed royalist agents, heavily subsidised from London, to secure a landslide victory in both Councils for moderates who looked favourably on the idea of a restored constitutional monarchy. Within the Directory itself there remained a triumvirate of committed Republicans (Barras, Reubell, La Revellière), but the other two Directors (Carnot and Barthélemy) were more responsive to shifts of allegiance in the Legislature, although mistrusting each other. The news of the elections made Napoleon profoundly uneasy for, although he always treated the Directory with casual contempt, he had remained on close political terms with the regicide Barras for three and a half years, and he had no wish to see the creation, by others, of some new constitutional device. Most alarming to both Barras and Napoleon was the unanimous election on 19 May of General Pichegru as presiding chairman of the Council of the Five Hundred. For, although Pichegru enjoyed a high reputation as conqueror of the Netherlands, he had been suspected of treasonable links with exiled royalists for over a year. Barras sent a personal emissary to Napoleon's headquarters asking for military assistance if the Directors decided on action against the elected Councils.

Two days after Pichegru's success, Bernadotte detained at Trieste a prominent Royalist agent, the Comte d'Antraigues – who unsuccessfully claimed diplomatic immunity as a counsellor in the Russian Legation at Venice. He sent d'Antraigues under escort to Milan, forwarding confiscated documents found in his portfolio to the

general-in-chief. These papers may well have compromised some
eminent figures in the Army of Italy, for it is known that in the
previous October Louis XVIII had urged d'Antraigues to seek
the 'conversion' of Napoleon and his chief officers. At all events,
d'Antraigues was mysteriously allowed to escape from custody.
Not, however, before he had provided Bonaparte with clear proof of
Pichegru's contacts with leading émigrés and with William Wickham
who, as British minister in Switzerland, was Pitt's chief spymaster on
the continent. Bonaparte entrusted a memorandum on the Pichegru
affair to Barras's emissary; he also sent to the Directory what he
selected as the most damning material seized by Bernadotte.

When, in the fourth week of June, Barras studied these revelations
he was in a quandary. He seems to have suspected that Bonaparte
had tampered with the evidence. Even if it were genuine, he dared
not move against the President of the Council of the Five Hundred
without an army to back him, but the Constitution denied the
Executive Directory any right to concentrate troops in the capital.
As Bonaparte offered no ingenious solution to this dilemma, Barras
turned from the Army of Italy to the Sambre-et-Meuse, since
February under the command of General Louis Hoche, who in
1796 had tried unsuccessfully to lead an invasion of Ireland. Now,
to his surprise, Hoche was ordered to bring 15,000 men across
France from Coblenz to Brest, apparently for another expedition to
Bantry Bay. But Barras had every intention of ensuring that Hoche's
division should linger in, or near, Paris. On 16 July, with the
Sambre-et-Meuse approaching the capital, the Executive Directory
sought to strengthen the government by a ministerial reshuffle.
Among other changes Talleyrand, a shadowy figure in Philadelphia
twelve months before, became Foreign Minister. General Hoche
was appointed War Minister but, at 29, he was ruled constitutionally
too young for ministerial office; the post went, instead, to General
Schérer. But there was still no concerted move to unseat Pichegru.

In Milan, where by now he was living in almost royal state,
Bonaparte sought to sift fact from rumour in the news from Paris.
A succession of his most trustworthy officers were despatched to
the capital: General Sérurier in June, soon to be followed by
General Desaix – who in his private journal described Bernadotte
as 'full of fire, vigour, fine enthusiasms . . . not popular, because
he is said to be mad'; and in the second week of July Antoine
Lavalette, Bonaparte's highly intelligent aide-de-camp. At the end

of the month he sent General Augereau, a swaggering and terrifying bully, too politically inept to emerge on top himself in any power struggle.

On 9 July Bonaparte mounted a fine show for the proclamation of the Cisalpine Republic, and for the *Quatorze Juillet* celebrations he presided over a magnificent fête and military parade outside the Castello, at which Bernadotte was present. Next day the general-in-chief dictated a fiery letter to the Executive Directory: 'Are there no Republicans left in France? . . . One stroke and you can save the Republic. Arrest the émigrés. Root out foreign influence. If this needs force, call upon the armies.' Soon afterwards a clumsily phrased denunciation of royalism and an affirmation of loyalty to the Constitution was drafted by Augereau and despatched to Paris above the names of his divisional commanders. But one signature was missing: J. B. Bernadotte. The commanding general of the 4th Division preferred to send his own, impeccably republican, letter to a city in which he remained personally unknown. It stood out in *Le Moniteur*, well calculated to catch the eye. When *Le Grondeur*, an allegedly royalist newspaper, sought to make mischief from this show of independence, its editor received so blistering a response from Bernadotte that, across the Channel, the *Morning Chronicle* on Wednesday, 6 September, printed a translation and gave its readers a flavour of Jacobin invective. 'I desire, sir, that you will honour me with perpetual oblivion', ran one passage in translation. 'My opinion and yours do not accord. A republican, both by principle and conviction, I will, to the moment of my death, oppose all Royalists and enemies to the Directory.' Thus did the political creed of the future King Charles XIV John first intrude into the London Press.

By that Wednesday one, at least, of Bernadotte's immediate ambitions had been realised: he was established in Parisian society. For in the second week of August Bonaparte had unexpectedly ordered him to take five captured Austrian flags to the capital and ceremonially present them to the Directory; he even 'paid me the expenses of my journey', as Bernadotte triumphantly wrote to his chief of staff a couple of hours before setting out from Milan. More remarkable still was Bonaparte's commendatory letter, introducing to the Directory 'this excellent general, who made his reputation on the banks of the Rhine, and is today one of the officers who contributes most to the fame of the Army of Italy . . . You see in

General Bernadotte one of the foremost champions of the Republic, one whose principles and character make it impossible that he should sacrifice the cause of liberty or the ties of honour.' At the same time he praised the troops from 'the Rhine and Sambre-et-Meuse' who, 'in crossing the Tagliamento and in taking Gradisca showed that courage and that zeal for military glory for which the armies of the Republic are renowned'. Bernadotte left Milan on Thursday, 10 August. By Sunday week he was in Paris.

His coming surprised and puzzled Augereau. He was well aware of the general-in-chief's irritation with his Gascon companion in arms and believed he had himself received clear instructions on how to handle any crisis threatening the Republic. Napoleon never revealed, then or in later reminiscence, what made him change his mind and send Bernadotte to the capital: to let the Directory have five Austrian regimental colours, captured at Rivoli but left by mistake at Peschiera when the first consignment was despatched in June, he said at the time. But, as they were not trophies seized by the 4th Division, why Bernadotte? He seems to have assumed that the purpose of his mission was to breathe Republican fire into the Directors and make certain they sent reinforcements should the war with Austria flare up again. Yet these were, in effect, the instructions already given to the earlier emissaries from Milan. There is little doubt that, after his show of independence over the collective affirmation of loyalty, Bonaparte wanted Bernadotte out of the way. If, during the peace talks, the Austrians continued to deny France gains in the Rhineland, it would be easier to reach final terms without the presence at Udine of so partisan a hero of the German campaigns. With their commander playing the Parisian power game, deft administrative juggling could integrate 'gentlemen' and 'citizens' by painlessly breaking up the 4th Division in his absence. Bonaparte thought he had the measure of Bernadotte by now: flatter him with fulsome praise, press him into sending analytic reports of what he observed, convince him that he alone was the trusted envoy of an all-powerful warlord, and he would serve as the voice of the Army of Italy in the capital, loyal and authentic.

Not simply a voice but, it would seem, a megaphone too. For Bernadotte was fêted by the Directors, hailed in the Assembly as bearing a name 'equally famous on the banks of the Rhine and the Tagliamento', lionised in the salons, welcomed back to the fraternity by Kléber and other friends who had come to Paris with Hoche;

and wherever he was entertained, he would speak in generous terms of the army in Italy and its extraordinary commander. Almost every day he penned a bulletin back to Milan for the general-in-chief: Napoleon (not inexperienced in such matters) heard, more than once, how Paris was repugnant to soldiers of honour, as a 'home of intrigue'; he was told of Pichegru's weaknesses ('a man swollen with pride, who thinks his very name worth an army . . . we showed the utmost reserve towards each other'). More significantly he heard that 'we are in danger of being forced to invest those to whom the Law is entrusted with consular power.'

That warning was sent on 1 September. It is from the diaries of the time, rather than his own correspondence, that we catch a glimpse of him next day, among thirty guests at Talleyrand's dinner table in the Rue Taitbout. On that Saturday evening he entertained the assembled company with an account of exactly how Bonaparte celebrated *Quatorze Juillet* in Milan; he then proposed they lift their glasses in a toast to the Constitution. His companions included a choleric military threesome – the Generals Augereau, Junot, and Lannes – and the most dazzling plants in the hot-house society which the Directory cultivated: Thérèse Tallien, a half-Spanish courtesan whom the wits dubbed 'government property'; Catherine Grand, the good-natured dumb blonde who was to become (eventually) Princesse de Talleyrand; and, in formidable contrast, the intellectually elevated Germaine de Staël, together with her lover and protégé, Benjamin Constant. Clearly Bernadotte left an impression on the dinner party: no one seems to have jotted down anybody else's table-talk that evening. Yet one guest, General Augereau, had himself been in Milan on 14 July and could well have amplified Bernadotte's dramatic account of these festivities. But more pressing matters were uppermost in that slow-moving mind. For on Sunday the triumvirate within the Directory – Barras, Reubell, La Revellière – appointed Augereau military commander in the capital. Soon some 12,000 troops were on the move across the city and narrow streets resounded with the ominous clatter of horse-artillery over the cobbles. At four o'clock next morning – Monday, 4 September, 1797: 18 Fructidor, Year V – the firing of cannon alerted Parisians to France's first military coup in more than a century and a half.

The Fructidor coup surprised no one – except apparently General Pichegru, who was rudely awakened by Augereau and made his prisoner. Orders of arrest and deportation were issued by the triumvirate against their two fellow Directors (Barthélemy and Carnot) and fifty-three alleged royalist deputies in the legislative councils. No one was executed; Carnot was allowed to escape to Switzerland; only seventeen prisoners were deported to Cayenne, eight of whom – including Pichegru and Barthélemy – escaped. By noon Augereau was military master of the capital. All was peaceful. It was his turn to report to Napoleon: 'General, my mission is accomplished. Paris is calm and astonished. The crisis which threatened to be terrible has passed off like a fête.'

But where, meanwhile, was Bernadotte? Barras says he kept away from the Luxembourg (the executive mansion of the Directory) on Sunday, Monday and Tuesday. No one was surprised to hear that Talleyrand, a lame ex-bishop and diplomat, should have spent 18 Fructidor indoors, playing whist, watching from behind his curtains, and waiting; but it seemed odd that a hero so recently praised for glories won on the Rhine and the Tagliamento should shun the chance to win new renown beside the Seine. Yet Bernadotte missed the Fructidor Coup, as he had missed the battle of Würzburg, exactly twelve months before. Next day he justified his inaction in a carefully phrased letter to Napoleon: 'Had the Republican cause been in peril I should certainly have taken action. But as there was not the slightest ground for fearing such a disaster, I did not think it my duty to thrust yet another sword into a rash business (*échauffourée*), already far too military in character.' This argument made good sense, at least in retrospect: Augereau's troops had no difficulty in carrying out the tasks assigned to them. It is, however, puzzling that Bernadotte should have kept his head down on Sunday, the eve of the coup, when there was so much military activity around the city. Was he, one wonders, sleeping off a dinner-party at which he had spoken too eloquently? Augereau, a fellow guest, is reported to have been well fortified with good champagne before the coup began.

Yet Bernadotte's cautious abstention, whatever its cause, cost him nothing. For although Barras's memoirs may have scoffed at his inaction, the triumvirate encouraged him, at the time, to linger in Paris: having lifted 'that proud bandit' Augereau into the saddle on one Sunday, they were wondering by the next whose hand was firm enough to help him down again. Augereau, wrote Lavalette, was impossible, 'a man beside himself'. The triumvirs were unpleasantly aware that, with Carnot and Barthélemy gone, there remained two vacancies in the Executive Directory: if Talleyrand had thoughts of filling one of them himself, Augereau certainly wanted the other. Better, therefore, to keep the voluble Gascon republican on hand in Paris as long as possible. It was a pleasant surprise for Bernadotte to receive, shortly after the coup, four excellent horses, two ornate pistols, and a sword of honour – gifts for past services suddenly remembered by an appreciative, if depleted, Directory; and on the next Monday, when (as his letters show) he was preparing to leave Paris, a deputation of veteran volunteers waited on him to express pleasure that he should be in residence in the capital. That evening, recognising that Barras was still the dominant Director, he called on him at the Luxembourg; over the following weeks he came there again and again. The few days originally set aside for this visit to Paris lengthened into seven weeks.

Bernadotte had, of course, ambitions of his own. Not, it would seem, to join the Directory: he recognised that he lacked political experience; and Barras succeeded in persuading the Council of the Ancients to outmanoeuvre Augereau by electing two nonentities, the ex-Jacobin deputies Merlin and François, to replace Barthélemy and Carnot. But Bernadotte would almost certainly have accepted an appointment as Minister of War or as general-in-chief on the Rhine, provided that he was given the independence already accorded Bonaparte in Italy. A further turn on the Rhine and Moselle seemed probable in mid-September when General Hoche, who had returned to Hesse in the previous month, died suddenly in Wetzlar. Kléber and Bernadotte each believed that the other had been offered the succession to Hoche but turned it down. In reality the Directory preferred to use the German command as a way to disembarrass themselves of Augereau. Any possibility that Bernadotte might go to the War Ministry was vetoed by Napoleon, who had no wish to see the Army of Italy dependent on Gascon whims and enthusiasms. Nevertheless, Bonaparte certainly did not want him back at Udine, as commander of the 4th Division; and it was at Bonaparte's suggestion that, on 20 September, the Directory nominated Bernadotte as general-in-chief of the Midi. It was, after all, the region of France he knew best. Headquarters would be in Marseilles; and he could count on having four divisions under his command.

But the Directory – and, more surprisingly, Napoleon – misjudged their man. A provincial command for a name feared equally

on the Rhine and the Tagliamento? Back to towns where, a mere
ten years before, he imagined that the proud quintessence of soldiery
was being Sergeant Belle-Jambe on parade? A dignified refusal
reached the Luxembourg for Barras on 27 September: to command
the Midi, Bernadotte explained, required deep understanding of
human nature and a firm and conciliatory character; these were
qualities which, as a simple soldier, he did not possess. Briefly he
looked to wider horizons, a campaign in India perhaps, or even a
landing in Canada, but increasingly he felt called back to Udine.
Rumours that Bonaparte was breaking up the 4th Division prompted
a sad letter of reproach. It was followed by assurances that he would
soon return, to take up once again his old responsibilities in the
Army of Italy.

The news was far from welcome to Bonaparte; he had already
appointed General Kilmaine, a dashing Irish-born cavalry commander, to take over the 4th Division, convinced that Bernadotte
would accept the Midi. But another post was hurriedly found for
Charles Kilmaine; and when Bernadotte reached Udine on 13
October, Napoleon came in person to greet him. For the past seven
weeks the general-in-chief had been in residence fifteen miles away
at the Villa Manin in Passeriano, the finest palace built by any Doge
on the Venetian mainland; and there he was conferring regularly
with Austrian plenipotentiaries sent to neighbouring Campo Formio
to negotiate a peace treaty. Although Bernadotte warned Napoleon
that at the first reversal of fortune he would find every faction in
Paris against him, he agreed that France needed a peace settlement
in Italy, even at the cost of handing over occupied Venice to Austria
as a conciliatory gesture. His support heartened Bonaparte, who
invited him to dine next day at the Villa Manin, where there would
also be Austrian guests. Bernadotte was told to bring his chief staff
officer, General Sarrazin, with him; they were to 'arrive early', in
good time for pre-prandial talks.

Sarrazin later gave two accounts of the visit, both written after
he was out of favour with Napoleon and with Bernadotte. Yet
although there may be shafts of malice in his record, the tale rings
basically true, not least because the private conduct of General
Bonaparte at twenty-seven so closely anticipates the public behaviour of the Emperor Napoleon when confronted with ministers or
foreign envoys who dared displease him. Bernadotte and Sarrazin,
knowing that their host dined at five o'clock, obeyed his order to

come early; they reached the Villa Manin at three on a late autumn afternoon, when the snow was already covering the Friulian Mountains, away to the north and west. Géraud Duroc, Grand Marshal of the Palace in later years, was duty aide-de-camp that Saturday: he asked Bernadotte and Sarrazin to wait, as the General was finishing letters for Paris. If Sarrazin is to be believed, his divisional commander thereupon complained angrily and loudly to the unfortunate Duroc: 'Tell the general-in-chief it is inconvenient for General Bernadotte to be kept waiting in an antechamber. Even the Executive Directory in Paris never subjected him to so mortifying an experience.' The haughtiness of language may well be a later embellishment; the sense of affront seems real and convincing.

His mortification was, it seemed, to be short-lived. For those ringing Gascon tones brought Bonaparte out to greet him. 'With angelic smoothness, but tight-lipped in suppressed anger', says Sarrazin, he apologised: never, he explained, would he stand on ceremony with a general whom he regarded as the right hand of his army; and he led the two men out, deep in conversation, down one of the long colonnades, which reach towards the Passeriano parkland like crab's claws, or the Doric crescent of the Piazza San Pietro in Rome. What, Bonaparte wondered, had Bernadotte thought of Hoche as a commander? When the guest praised his qualities, his host disagreed. They went on to analyse the generalship of Augereau, Kléber, Masséna, and Sérurier, with every point made by Bernadotte flawed on appeal to the maxims of military science. Mischievously Napoleon even set out the technical excellence as a master of heavy cavalry of Charles Kilmaine. A historical survey of great commanders followed: no doubt, he asked, Bernadotte had opinions on Alexander the Great, Hannibal, and Caesar? What views did he hold on the fighting qualities of the hoplites, as drawn up in a Macedonian phalanx? None at all? Then his general-in-chief would enlighten him. And the composition of a Roman legion?

By now Bernadotte was mopping his brow as though it were midsummer. At dinner came a respite: Josephine was a gracious hostess, and Bernadotte renewed acquaintance with an Austrian cavalryman, General Marfeldt, whom he had met at Leoben. When their host's table talk drifted ominously back towards military science through the ages, Marfeldt deftly turned the conversation to the marching capabilities of infantrymen. Here was a subject in which Bernadotte was more experienced than his general-in-chief.

The verbal sparring continued. It is hard to escape the impression that this was neither the time nor place for such a discussion. Each Austrian guest at the table had fought against France; each would do so again.

In these strange conversational exchanges, Napoleon may genuinely have been testing the depths of Bernadotte's knowledge. His miscalculation over the Midi command showed that he did not understand the Gascon newcomer so well as the band of brothers with whom he had shared the battle-honours from Montenotte to Rivoli. On the other hand, he may – as Sarrazin indicates – have simply wished to squeeze the egoistic stuffing from the latest Parisian toy lion. If so, he was successful: it was a chastened Bernadotte who sat beside his chief staff officer on the drive back to Udine that evening. How, he wondered, was Bonaparte so knowledgeable at twenty-eight? That, no doubt, was the advantage of having been at college in Brienne while the Royal-la-Marine were foot-slogging across Corsica and Provence. Perhaps he should retire from active service and read all he could of distant campaigns and the theory of war. At thirty-five was he too old to brush up his military history convincingly? Sarrazin claims that he reassured him in every moment of doubt.

The humiliating stroll at Passeriano made a deep impression. Bernadotte's personal staff noticed a change of leisure habits that winter: he rode less, he sent for books; he even talked about them to his aides. He continued to admire Napoleon's generalship and he now respected his book-learning. Yet he was never in awe of him. The letters he had sent to Milan from Paris show that in the summer of 1797 he consistently underestimated Napoleon's power and influence. He guessed that Napoleon would receive reports from Augereau and Lavalette as well as from himself, but it seems unlikely he suspected that Napoleon was also in regular correspondence with Barras and Talleyrand. On his return from Paris Bernadotte exaggerated the importance of his own passing contacts with the Directors and their ministers. When peace broke out in Italy other generals acquiesced in the breaking up of their divisions; but not Bernadotte. So sharp were his exchanges with Bonaparte over the pending dispersal of the 4th Division that the more reverential Napoleonic historians condemn his attitude as insolent and insubordinate.

In this, however, they misread his character. Service under

Jourdan had accustomed him to a critical independence of judgment in contrast to the adulation which Napoleon customarily received from the superb army he created and led from Nice to Leoben. In Vienna during that winter of 1797–98 there was never any doubt that Napoleon was already the real master of the hated republic, as the letters and journal of the young Metternich clearly show. But Bernadotte saw him against a different backcloth. For despite the showmanship in Milan on *Quatorze Juillet*, Napoleon remained to Bernadotte a gifted outsider, favoured by good fortune. Old prejudices lingered alongside newer jealousies. To a soldier from Henri IV's Pau, who had stood guard along the quay at Bastia when Corsica's loyalty was still in question, it seemed impossible for the Directory in Paris to turn to a lawyer's son from Ajaccio and find in him the coming century's Frenchman of destiny.

Chapter 4
Undiplomatic Interlude

A FEW days after Bernadotte's visit to Passeriano the war against Austria came at last to an end. On 18 October 1797 a peace treaty was signed at Campo Formio. The city of Venice and the Venetian hinterland were, as Napoleon intended, handed over to Austria in return for recognition of his new order in Italy, the cession to France of Belgium, and agreement on holding a congress at Rastatt to settle the future of western Germany. Napoleon finally left Italy on 19 November, paid a hurried visit to Baden to make certain that the diplomats had begun talking in Rastatt, and hastened to Paris for a triumphal reception in the second week of December. Bernadotte was not to meet him again for nearly two years.

Once the excitement of peacemaking died down, Bernadotte began to look to the future. He said farewell to the 4th Division in mid-November, but he remained south of the Alps, with three demi-brigades under his command at Treviso. Although Berthier took control of the army when Napoleon set off for Rastatt, Bernadotte still hoped he might himself become general-in-chief in the peninsula. There was also that Indian project which he had mentioned to Barras, and he expected eventually to receive command of a division in Napoleon's forthcoming invasion of England. Yet, when no new appointment had come by the end of November, he became restless. From an angry letter to Barras it seems as if he seriously considered retiring to the countryside, to cultivate the soil and his mind. During his autumn visit to Paris he had begun to negotiate the purchase of land at Dourdan, a heavily wooded region some thirty-five miles south-west of the capital. But he was willing to accept further military duties: why should he not become commander-in-chief of the Ionian Islands, establishing at Corfu a

French republican administration for the former Venetian possessions at the mouth of the Adriatic? The suggestion received warm
support in Paris from Napoleon, who already looked upon the
Ionian Islands as stepping-stones to help France expand in the
eastern Mediterranean and the Levant. At his prompting the Corfu
command was duly offered to Bernadotte and, on the last day of
the year, accepted. With eager impatience Bernadotte at once drew
up – for the 'Commander of the Army against England' – a prelim-
inary report on how France could effectively garrison the Ionian
Sea.

Napoleon, however, was not a generalissimo; he was not even
Minister of War. The Directors had thought his duties closely
defined; his post was at Boulogne. They were alarmed by the
enthusiastic reception accorded him in Paris, where he seemed to
linger longer than the exigencies of war required: better, Barras
argued, to keep in reserve a military counterweight, an impressive
General on horseback who could be summoned to the capital should
Bonaparte's ambition threaten to overturn the Republic. But who?
Augereau, in Mainz, would demand too heavy a political price for
his support. If the alternative was Bernadotte, why isolate him on
an Ionian island? Within a week of ordering him to Corfu the
Directors changed their collective mind; Bernadotte would remain
in Milan, as general-in-chief in Italy. In a typical instance of
Directory maladministration the news reached him casually, as a
sentence in a letter which Napoleon sent from Paris at the end of
the first week in January. Nevertheless the new commander of
the Army of Italy was elated. It was the post he most desired:
confirmation, as he saw it, that he possessed finer qualities of
leadership than his personal enemy, Berthier; recognition that, as
a general, he was a natural successor to the hero of the hour,
Napoleon himself.

Yet, despite a flow of fair words, that popular idol continued to
mistrust Bernadotte. Privately he deplored his promotion. Had Italy
remained tranquil, leaving a general in Milan with no greater
responsibilities to exercise over the peninsula than did the general
in Marseilles over the Midi, then Napoleon might have accepted
the Directory's decision. But in that same week bad news from
Rome made yet another Italian campaign probable. For shortly
after Christmas there had been a riot outside the residence of
the new French ambassador, Joseph Bonaparte, Napoleon's elder

brother. During the disturbances the military attaché, Brigadier-General Jean-Pierre Duphot, was killed. When news of the murder reached Paris it was seen by Napoleon as an affront both to the Republic and to his family. Joseph and his suite left Rome next day, the ambassador holding the Papal gendarmerie responsible for Duphot's death. Napoleon urged the Directory to let the French Army occupy Rome, end the temporal power of the papacy, and proclaim a Roman Republic. He recommended that this task should be entrusted to Berthier, who had already seen service in the Papal States. As for Bernadotte, since he had made such friendly contact with the Austrians at Leoben, why not send him to Vienna as ambassador?

This possibility appealed also to the Foreign Minister, Talleyrand, himself an ambassador in London six years ago. Before the Revolution the Vienna embassy had been a prize post, where the gentlemen diplomats of the aristocracy could preen themselves to advantage, but competent envoys of distinction were now in short supply. In Madrid, however, General Bernard-Nicolas de Perignon had over the past two years enjoyed a position of authority and influence at Court, even though his military reputation was made in command of the army which marched victoriously into Catalonia. Vienna required a similar soldierly representative of the republic, an ambassador who could ride with dignity in the Prater, insist firmly on fulfilment of the peace treaty and scorn the blandishments of royalist agents. It is true that Perignon possessed the polished manners of the old officer class, but Talleyrand was impressed by the little he had seen of Bernadotte's personality and the speed with which he established himself in Parisian society. He had witnessed the Gascon panache when those captured regimental colours were handed over to the Assembly and yet he had repeatedly heard him affirm sound republican sentiments. Bernadotte, he was convinced, must be France's man in Vienna. No one observed the courtesies by enquiring among the Austrians at Rastatt if he would be acceptable to Emperor Francis; and no one, for that matter, consulted the General. On 11 January 1798 he was formally named as ambassador of the Republic at the Imperial Court.

Napoleon's message, telling him he would receive command of the Army of Italy, reached Bernadotte on the morning of 18 January at Verona, when he was already on his way to consult Berthier over fitting out his expedition to Corfu. He left immediately for Milan.

By that evening he had travelled twenty-five miles, to Desenzano Castle at the foot of Lake Garda. There he found two urgent despatches awaiting him: another letter from Napoleon, saying he was appointed ambassador in Vienna; and a request from the chief of staff of the Army of Italy that he should hasten to headquarters as speedily as possible. This latest swing of fortune was as unwelcome as the revised orders he had defied at Dijon twelve months before. Now, as then, he continued his journey. But at Milan came confirmation from the Foreign Minister, expressing his conviction that in this 'highest rank' of a new career Bernadotte would 'show talents as estimable as those which have formed the basis of your military reputation'. More practically Talleyrand added, 'You will make arrangements to go without any delay to your destination.'

Bernadotte regarded his ambassadorial appointment as extraordinary and, for a soldier, almost a disgrace. His first inclination was to reject a post for which he doubted if he had the necessary background. But Talleyrand's instructions effectively sugared so bitter a pill: the ambassador was promised a salary of 144,000 francs a year, half of which would be made immediately available to him, together with about 12,000 francs for the journey; in purchasing power this ambassadorial salary was equivalent to £280,000 (slightly under half a million dollars) a year in modern terms, with over £23,000 in travelling expenses. At one stroke the Directory was thus proposing to treble the General's personal fortune, offering far more than he might expect to earn as commander-in-chief in Milan or military governor in Corfu. With misgivings, and a request for constant advice, he let Talleyrand know he 'was accepting the important mission with which the Directory has just entrusted me'. Before setting out from Milan for the Austrian frontier he set aside almost a sixth of the salary in order that, within two months, General Ernouf could complete on his behalf the purchase of an estate outside Paris. He does not appear to have expected to remain long at the Court of the Habsburgs.

It seemed natural to take with him Generals Sarrazin and Mireur, old companions from early days in the Sambre-et-Meuse. But Talleyrand drew the line at so much army top-brass. The ambassador was, however, reluctantly allowed four military aides of lesser rank: among them was Captain Etienne Gérard, a veteran of Fleurus, who distinguished himself in Napoleon's later campaigns and became (in 1830) a Marshal of France. Since it was clear that any ambassador at Francis II's court would need good briefing on the Polish question, Bernadotte also included his adjutant Antoine Maurin, who was reputedly an illegitimate son of the last Polish king. He was to return first to Paris and join him later in Vienna, together with a refugee from Russian Poland, Maleszewski – whom the Austrian authorities regarded, not unjustifiably, as an inveterate subversive. From Paris Talleyrand sent two young career diplomats. One, Emile Gaudin, had already served as second secretary at Constantinople and brought his wife with him to Austria. Apart from Mme Gaudin this improvised French embassy was an all-male establishment.

Bernadotte's appointment startled Vienna. No one seems to have expected the conclusion of peace to be followed by the rapid resumption of diplomatic relations. It was little more than four years since the Emperor's aunt, Marie Antoinette, was guillotined in Paris: one brother and two of her sisters were still living in Vienna, while 'Madame Royale' – Princess Marie Thérèse, at 19 the only surviving child of Louis XVI and Marie Antoinette – had been in residence at Schloss Belvedere since being exchanged for a French Jacobin prisoner-of-war two Christmases before. When the treaty was signed at Campo Formio it was assumed that any contact between the Empire and the Republic would take place in the conference at Rastatt. Cobenzl, the ablest negotiator among Austria's diplomats, was there; so, too, were the former Imperial minister in Brussels, Count Franz Georg von Metternich, and his son, Clemens. Since Archduke Charles was in Prague, there remained in Vienna merely a residue of great families and four figures of imperial eminence: the amiably confused emperor, who celebrated his thirtieth birthday in the second week of February; his highly pregnant consort and cousin, Maria Theresa; his former tutor and effective chief minister, Prince Colloredo, the Court Chamberlain, to whom everything concerned with revolutionary France was satanic; and Baron Franz von Thugut, the Foreign Minister, who regarded the Campo Formio settlement as little more than an armistice.

On Thugut's intructions Cobenzl wrote to Talleyrand from Rastatt explaining that it was far too soon for Emperor Francis to receive an ambassador. The protest was sent off to Paris on Saturday, 10 February. That was far too late: Bernadotte was already in Vienna. Three mud-spattered carriages stopped at the city gates on Thursday afternoon. Their coming was 'totally unexpected', the

British ambassador (Sir Morton Eden) reported to London; and the whole party spent the night at the neighbouring White Swan tavern. Next day they sought help from the Spanish ambassador, who found them temporary accommodation. Protocol made it impossible for Thugut to receive Bernadotte until his credentials had arrived. Gaudin, who was bringing them from Paris, was delayed by frontier guards at Linz; he was detained for two days as a suspected spy and did not reach Vienna for another fortnight. Meanwhile there was a search for an embassy residence. Since the Metternichs, father and son, were at Rastatt, the Spanish ambassador suggested they might lease their town house to the French; they refused. So, too, did other aristocratic families. But, two years before, Prince Karl von Liechtenstein had been fatally wounded in a duel; and Bernadotte successfully negotiated a lease of his old apartments at the Palais Geymüller, Wallnerstrasse 8. It was – and it remains – a solid classical mansion, built in 1688 but given a touch of pedimented grandeur some thirty years later. The Court Privy Chancellery in the Ballhausplatz (the centre of government) was 400 yards away, the Imperial Palace of the Hofburg slightly further.

Bernadotte presented his credentials to Thugut on 27 February and left visiting cards at the town palaces of the great families. None would receive him, although some met him at a dinner given by the Spanish ambassador. On 2 March the future King of Sweden was introduced to the intricacies of Court protocol, when he was granted an audience with Emperor Francis in the Hofburg. He made a good impression, even on a traditionalist like Colloredo. When Thugut answered his protests at the honours shown to the French royalist exiles in Vienna by pointing out to him the difficulties of refusing to acknowledge their status and titles at court, he seemed reasonable; but he pressed, with more belligerence, complaints from Venice that the Austrian troops who occupied the city in the second week of January were ill-treating French citizens for wearing tricolour rosettes in their hats. It was ominous that the French Republic attached as much importance to symbolism as the émigrés, who would wear white cockades and the crosses and cordons of the old chivalry.

'The disposition of the public mind in the capital has been, for some time, strongly pronounced against the French, and that disposition is much increased by the conduct of those who comprise the French Embassy', reported Morton Eden to London on 17 March, with smug self-satisfaction. For Bernadotte was beginning to cause offence. As soon as his old adversary, Archduke Charles, arrived in Vienna from Prague, the ambassador had asked for an audience and the Archduke agreed to see him on Monday, 12 March. On Sunday morning, however, Charles discovered that the Emperor required his attendance on a shooting party next day: he sent an aide-de-camp to the Wallnerstrasse, asking Bernadotte to postpone his visit until Tuesday, a change of plan to which the ambassador raised no objection at the time. Yet a few hours later he sent a military attaché to the palace with a curt message that, since the Archduke would not see him on the agreed day, he had no wish for an audience. He appears to have brooded over the Archduke's change of plan and decided, after dinner, that the Republic had been slighted.

Within a month of taking up his post in Vienna the General was bored and ill-at-ease. Fear of having to fraternise with French émigrés imposed odd restraints on the social life of both the ambassador and his staff; there was little for Bernadotte to do except ride in the Prater. He began to stock a cellar and build up a good library during these weeks of relative inactivity. Legend maintains that on at least one evening he was host to the violinist and composer Rodolphe Kreutzer, who brought with him to the Wallnerstrasse his friend, Beethoven. Kreutzer was a Frenchman by birth and a radical in temperament, and a visit to his socially ostracised compatriots is not improbable. Other embassies, particularly the Russian, cultivated virtuoso performers; 'If music be the food of diplomatic life, play on', Bernadotte may well have thought. Yet if so, he was soon surfeited, and the appetite sickened and died. Never again did he respond to any sound more melodious than the rhythmic beat of drums on the march.

On Easter Day – April 8th – he could be seen once more playing the republican cavalier against a Habsburg court backcloth. For on that Sunday the Empress presented her five-week-old baby, Marie Clementine, at the altar of the Burgkapelle and emerged from the seclusion of childbirth. She at once officially received the French ambassador, who reassured her over the safety of her mother, the Queen of Naples, said by rumour to be threatened with Jacobin conspiracies. Bernadotte, who allegedly talked to the Empress with animation about music, remained in the palace for what Eden describes as 'a gala reception' to honour the baby Archduchess and her mother. Almost certainly he will have noticed, on this occasion, the baby's eldest sister, a doll-like six-year-old with blue eyes whom Berthier was to escort to Paris in 1810 as Napoleon's second bride. But he will not have seen there Tsar Paul's ambassador, Count Andrew Razumovsky; for that distinguished patron of music, fearing lest court etiquette gave precedence to a Frenchman over a Russian, avoided so disastrous an embarrassment by absenting himself that day entirely. Amid such social pitfalls it was agreed that Citizen Ambassador Bernadotte acquitted himself well; but for the last time.

Over the next week there was steady activity in the Wallnerstrasse for the Viennese secret police to observe and note down. On Monday Captain Maurin arrived from Paris, accompanied by Maleszewski – two Poles together. On Tuesday the ambassador gave orders to a tailor to cut and sew, as speedily as possible, three red, white and blue strips for a large flag. On Wednesday and Thursday he drew from his 'bankers all the money for which he had credit' (as a current report in Vienna noted) and notified 'the director of the theatres, that he could not accept a box which was offered him in consequence of a desire he had expressed some time before, because he intended soon to leave Vienna'. Finally late on Friday afternoon – 'at seven in the evening', according to the police: 'shortly before dusk', according to Sir Morton Eden – a tricolour flag was unfurled on the balcony of the Palais Geymüller. It billowed out peacefully, while most Viennese were eating their evening meals.

Embassies in Vienna did not fly national flags; and to flaunt in the heart of the capital insignia associated so recently with the public execution of Marie Antoinette was, at best, insensitive. Moreover the young men of Vienna were about to enjoy a weekend of patriotic self-congratulation; Colloredo and Thugut looked benignly at celebrations to mark the response a year ago to the Emperor's call for volunteers who would have valiantly defended Lower Austria from invasion, if only Bonaparte had not stopped short at Leoben. Predictably the unfurling of a French flag by a French general soon led to a riot. An angry mob blocked the narrow Wallnerstrasse. Stones were thrown through windows. Two coaches were smashed. One intrepid rioter – a child, says Eden – climbed to the balcony, tore down the flag and threw it to friends below who carried it in triumph to the Schottengasse. There, rather oddly, they found

Count Colloredo's berlin standing with flambeaux lit; and the hated tricolour was set alight with torches from the Court Chamberlain's carriage.

Accounts of Bernadotte's reaction to the gathering of an angry crowd vary considerably. A German eye-witness, whose version was translated into English and put on sale in London the following month, blamed him for inciting the mob with a fiery speech in Gascon French none could understand: 'All would have been well with the crowd had not General Bernadotte, with furious air, grasping with one hand the handle of his sabre and clenching the other, run to the gates and by offensive measures and vulgar abuse driven to extremity the rage of the people.' The version of events sent by Morton Eden to London was extremely hostile to the French: it maintained that, when requested by the police to hurl down the flag so as to calm the crowd, the ambassador had angrily insisted that his orders from the Directory were to display and defend at all costs the insignia of the republic; but Eden admits that the mood of the crowd threatened the lives of the embassy staff. A police report, used by the German eye-witness, claimed that 'The General was in a situation which appeared to have its origin in an indulgence little suited to the character of a man of any education and least of all to that of a man of his rank.' This haughty comment has, understandably, angered Bernadotte's champions. Nevertheless it is highly likely that Bernadotte had drunk too much wine on that Friday and, indeed, on the Sunday five weeks before, when he sent an insulting message to Archduke Charles in the evening after accepting, with good grace, the Archduke's change of plan a few hours earlier. He enjoyed his wine; and his cellar is known to have included 100 bottles of champagne and 100 bottles of a favourite white burgundy brought from Trieste, as well as local wines. If he was soon to set out from Vienna, as the director of theatres had been told, small wonder that he did not wish to leave such treasures for others to imbibe.

There remain many puzzling features over this 'riot of 13th April', as the French called it. Why did the Austrians allow several hours to pass before sending the cuirassiers to clear a straight and narrow road so close to the centre of affairs? Why did the Spanish and Dutch envoys, when invited by Bernadotte to act as mediators, both return sympathetic messages of concern but discover that their health was too delicate to allow them out in the streets of Vienna after dark? And why throughout Saturday, 14th April, did Bernadotte continue angrily to reject every conciliatory gesture by the Austrian authorities? Emperor Francis sent Colloredo in person to the Palais Geymüller to express his regrets, promise an inquiry and urge the ambassador not to let the riot endanger Austro–French relations. But Bernadotte was adamant. He demanded passports and a safe passage across the frontier for himself and his staff. By Sunday morning Vienna knew the French ambassador was leaving the city, convinced that his country had been insulted. According to Eden, he delayed his departure until midday on Sunday, leaving with an escort of cavalry at a time when he could be certain of good public attention. He had been in Vienna for just sixty-six days; his mission was to be remembered only for the manner of its ending.

Next morning Baron Thugut saw Eden and the two men met again on the following Saturday. They were united in deploring the Directory's contempt for the niceties of diplomacy, especially the contacts of Bernadotte's staff with Polish dissidents. 'The present French Government is incompatible with the old established governments of Europe', Thugut remarked. He argued that war was inevitable; Jacobin agents had provoked a riot in Rome at Christmas, enabling Berthier to march into the city and empty the Pope's treasury two months later and Bernadotte was now engineering a similar crisis so that France could resume hostilities against Austria. There seemed to him no other explanation of the ambassador's behaviour and intransigence. He was confident of Austria's prospects in a new campaign: France was corrupt, war-weary and disorganised; the Austrians were negotiating with Berlin and St Petersburg and had strengthened their hold on the Adriatic by occupying Venice and Venetian possessions in Dalmatia. Thugut was eager for a British subsidy and support from the Royal Navy in the Mediterranean. Eden believed the money would be forth-coming: he feared that, so long as England was threatened with invasion, no ships could be spared for operations east of Gibraltar; but he had sent details of Bernadotte's activity by express courier to London, and he urged Thugut to await the reactions of Mr Pitt to news of the embassy drama.

Bernadotte may well have provoked the riot, but not with any intention of renewing the Austrian war. His letters to his friend General Ernouf show the mounting impatience with which he had been awaiting a definition of his task of Vienna. But even after

Maurin arrived from Paris on 9 April with clarification of his instructions, his mission seemed peripheral to the general policies of the Directory: he was to discredit the émigrés, encourage the Poles, topple Thugut in favour of Cobenzl and insist on strict observance of respect for the Republic and all its symbols. Maurin brought Bernadotte both hard fact and rumour: that the invasion plan against England was shelved; that Bonaparte was concentrating an army at Toulon; and that he was picking generals for an expedition to Egypt, among them his close friend, Kléber. Angrily Bernadotte began to suspect that the Vienna embassy was little more than a place of banishment, well away from the grand decision-making in Paris. Accordingly, a day before unfurling the flag on the balcony, he wrote to Talleyrand asking to be allowed to resume his military duties. First, however, he would carry out the letter of his instructions and fly the tricolour to enable the Austrians to see that the Palais Geymüller was an embassy of the French Republic. But he can have been neither surprised nor displeased when the Viennese mob gave him an excuse for hastening what he regarded as his return from exile.

Over the next few weeks nothing went as any participant in this curious drama anticipated. Bernadotte expected to be summoned urgently to Paris for consultation: he was kept in idleness for a month at Rastatt, where a dreary congress waited for people who never came to settle problems no one dared raise. Talleyrand, angry with Bernadotte for leaving Vienna precipitately, expected the Directory to censure him for hot-tempered imprudence. So too did Napoleon. The Directors, however, affected to treat him as a hero, praising his zeal for the honour of the flag and the courage with which, despite the fate of Duphot, he harangued a hostile mob. Eden's reports show there was inconsequential confusion in Vienna, too. Thus Thugut, who had expected to lead Austria into war, found that Emperor Francis was transferring many of his responsibilities to the more patient and adroit Ludwig Cobenzl. Yet Cobenzl had the most topsy-turvy experiences of all. For having hurried from Rastatt to Vienna, he heard from Paris that Bonaparte was going to the congress to settle affairs face to face with him; and so, on 8 May, he set out again on a gruelling five hundred mile return journey. Napoleon's carriage was indeed on the road that Tuesday but it was crossing Provence from Aix to Toulon for, despite any message Talleyrand may have sent to Cobenzl, the new commander of the

Army of Egypt had no intention of travelling to Rastatt when Alexandria and Cairo were awaiting him. Eventually Cobenzl found himself at Seltz, locked in endless and inconclusive discussions over the flag incident with Nicolas François de Neufchâteau, himself recently one of the Directors. But Cobenzl's misfortunes were still not over. For, in his absence from Vienna, Thugut recovered a hold on the Foreign Ministry which he did not relinquish for two and a half years.

If Bernadotte hoped for high military advancement when he left Vienna, he was disappointed. While still at Rastatt he was given command of the 5th Division, at neighbouring Strasbourg. He refused the post on grounds of ill-health; he would, he said, retire from active service and enjoy a quiet life (*'vie simple et tranquille'*). Not, however, before he had raised a small storm in Paris. He travelled to the capital and insisted that the *Moniteur* publish letters exchanged between Talleyrand and himself; they paid tribute to his services in the 'two careers to which he had been called', and offered him the post of envoy to The Hague, an honour he declined. After rendering a scrupulous account of his expenses as an ambassador, and ensuring that Gaudin received generous compensation for losses he had suffered in the Vienna disturbances, Bernadotte was prepared to settle in the countryside and put the whole episode behind him.

This, however, proved impossible. The flag incident, the riot and the abrupt departure remained associated with him long afterwards. He was to meet again, under very different circumstances, many people he had known in Vienna, including the Emperor Francis and the Tsar's ambassador, Andrew Razumovsky. Clemens Metternich, whom he encountered in Rastatt, remembered the undiplomatic interlude when a princely Bernadotte was waiting on the steps of a throne. In London, during the autumn of 1798, *The Times* could refer to 'Bernadottes' collectively, as envoys who 'diffuse . . . the seeds of revolution'. But fortunately for the General this generic term did not pass into common usage. That earlier reputation – 'a name equally famous on the banks of the Rhine and the Tagliamento' – was more to his liking.

To magnify the importance of the 'riot of 13th April' was easy, and in retrospect all these events seem trivial affairs. Only in Britain did they leave any lasting impression on policy – and that in an unexpected form. For when Eden's account reached London on 28 April, the news from Vienna became a talking point among ministers. The cabinet considered its implications and, under the prime minister's lead, took a major decision: Pitt – like Thugut – assumed that Bernadotte's odd behaviour showed another Franco–Austrian War was imminent; if so, Emperor Francis should receive the naval support for which his ministers had been asking. Accordingly, four days after Eden's despatch was opened in the Foreign Office, the Admiralty ordered what nowadays would be called a 'task force' to leave the blockade of Cadiz and re-enter the Mediterranean. Nelson had already set out for Toulon with three ships of the line and some frigates, intrigued by reports of troop concentrations, but the revised orders from London turned a cruising squadron into a fleet. At the Nile he had under his command, not three battleships but a decisive thirteen. This margin of naval mastery won Nelson a peerage and left Napoleon's expedition marooned in Egypt. It was a strange consequence of allowing a tricolour flag to flutter over a Vienna sidestreet on the evening of Friday the Thirteenth.

Part II
Napoleon's Rival

Chapter 5
Sceaux and the Rue Cisalpine

'I WISH to enjoy the charms of a simple and quiet life', Bernadotte told the Minister of War in May 1798, when he turned
down the offer of a command in Strasbourg. After six years of
campaigning he was physically exhausted and needed a long spell
of leave, he explained. But where should he take it? A return to Pau
held no appeal for him: his sister Marie died in 1796, and he had
little contact with his mother and brother after failing to gain a
colonelcy in the Army of the Pyrenees. At Dourdan he owned a
farm which he had never seen; to put that in order would hardly
be a rest cure. A few weeks in Paris convinced him that it would be
foolish to cut himself off drastically from high society. For, although
he might despise the Directory's game of power politics, it was
always well to keep up with the state of play – which was, in that
summer, particularly fluid. Accordingly, on 19 June he took out a
three-year lease on a house in the Rue de la Lune at Sceaux, some
seven miles south of the capital. It was a pleasant place, looking out
across the parkland of a ruined château to wooded slopes around
Verrières.

There he settled with a small staff, retaining Captain Antoine
Maurin as his aide and continuing to educate himself by reading
widely. Like Napoleon at Passeriano, he felt impelled to improve
the minds of those around him, talking tediously at table about the
history of Malta, for example; and Maurin and his colleagues must
have been relieved that Sceaux was so near to Paris, for Bernadotte
often travelled into town that summer. He would be seen at Joseph
Bonaparte's fine mansion above Monceau or at the Luxembourg,
where the Directors lived in state amid the fading splendours of a
palace built for Henri IV's widowed queen. Long afterwards

Madame de Chastenay, who three years back had flirted briefly with Napoleon, recalled her first impression of Bernadotte among Paul Barras's guests at the Luxembourg Palace in June 1798: 'A tall figure, with black hair, dazzling white teeth, and no sparkle of wit about him whatsoever', she was to write; but she also added, 'He was a man you could not meet at a reception without taking notice of him and asking people who he was'.

The domesticity of rural retirement at Sceaux was broken by an unexpected intrusion from the past. He had last seen the Marquis d'Ambert heading out of Marseilles towards Piedmont in the heady early days of the Revolution. Now, eight years later, his former colonel was again in the news. For after the Fructidor Coup the republican majority on the Councils restored some of the repressive legislation of Jacobin times, one decree imposing the death penalty on any émigré who had slipped back to France secretly while his name was still on a proscribed list of traitors to the Revolution; and as ardent republicans began hunting down émigrés their attention was drawn to the *ci-devant* 'aristo' colonel from the Royal-la-Marine. While Bernadotte was in Vienna, d'Ambert rashly drew attention to his presence in France by a letter to the pro-government newspaper, *Ami des Lois*, in which he protested at the way in which he was being harried, denied he was ever an émigré traitor, and claimed credit for promoting the ambassador-general through the ranks of the Royal-la-Marine, thus making possible the victories with which his later career enriched the republican cause.

Bernadotte seems first to have heard of d'Ambert's latest folly when the newspapers reported his arrest in June. At once he called on Barras and, 'as the only price for my past services', asked that the Marquis might be freed. Barras claims that he wished to meet Bernadotte's request and have d'Ambert deported for his own good, but that Merlin de Douai, the Director responsible for internal order, insisted on fulfilling the letter of the law. There was, however, an easy way to thwart Republican justice, a ruse from which d'Antraigues and others had benefited over the past eighteen months; and Bernadotte gave d'Ambert every opportunity to follow their example. For, while the prisoner was on his way to a last appearance before the Military Tribunal, his guards managed to lose sight of him. Yet so insistent was d'Ambert on having his innocence established that he was too proud to escape. What more could Bernadotte have done? In the first week of July the Parisian press announced that the former Marquis d'Ambert had faced a firing squad in the Place de Grenelle.

By then a happier echo from his days in Marseilles was bringing back into Bernadotte's life the wealthy family of Clary, upon whom Colonel d'Ambert had allegedly sought to billet him nine years before. At one of Joseph Bonaparte's receptions he talked for the first time to Désirée Clary. In 1789 she had been a child of eleven; now she was a vivacious brunette of twenty, still unmarried, her spirit at once fascinated and repelled by the spontaneous combustion of Revolution around her. François Clary, her silk manufacturer father, had died in January 1794, fearful of the angry mood of the city in which he had built up the family fortune. Within a few weeks his widow, sons, and daughters were heavily indebted to Joseph Bonaparte who, finding them in danger from the Terror, afforded them sound Republican protection. Joseph himself fell in love with Désirée, only to be told by his brother Napoleon that her sister Julie – six years her senior – was a more suitable bride; and Joseph and Julie were married in August 1794. Napoleon was much attracted to Désirée, or Eugénie as he preferred to call her, and she reciprocated his feelings with starry-eyed intensity. In 1795 it seemed as if they, too, would marry; but, once he returned to Paris, Napoleon was soon captivated by the greater sophistication of the widowed Josephine de Beauharnais, and Désirée was left to look elsewhere for a husband.

In this search she received unsolicited help from the Bonapartes – an intrusion which, as a woman of spirit, she often resented. In November 1797, when Joseph Bonaparte was ambassador in Rome, Napoleon sent Brigadier General Duphot to him as a military aide: 'He will speak to you of his wish to marry your sister-in-law. I think that would be an advantageous alliance for her', Napoleon told Joseph. In later years Désirée herself said that Duphot, who had a lover and a son at Perpignan, did not measure up to her ideal as a suitor; but on 23 December she arrived in Rome, escorted by her mother and brother, Nicolas, to stay with Julie and Joseph at the embassy. Feeling was running high against the French in Rome at that time, largely because of tales of organised looting of church property throughout the peninsula. Four days after their arrival Madame Clary and her son were being shown the sights of Rome when rioting broke out. The sightseers returned safely to the embassy, only to find Désirée and Julie deeply distressed; in a skirmish close to the embassy Duphot had been mortally wounded. Within a couple of days the ambassador and his guests left for Genoa – and the crisis which brought Berthier to Rome with an army of occupation. While Mme Clary settled in Genoa, Désirée returned with Joseph and Julie to Paris.

Bernadotte had met Joseph and Julie in Milan in July, before either man became an ambassador. Over the next ten months their experiences in Rome and Vienna drew them together; while he was still at Rastatt, they began to exchange letters. After Napoleon left for Egypt in early May, Joseph and his brother Lucien Bonaparte found it easier to pursue careers of their own in Paris, even cultivating the friendship of men whom he distrusted as possible rivals. Bernadotte was made welcome by both Joseph and Lucien and it is not surprising if Désirée fell in love with so striking a newcomer to her brother-in-law's circle. For already she saw herself as a woman of destiny, fated to meet a hero whom she could proudly lionise, and Bernadotte fulfilled that role admirably. Long afterwards, she told her court chamberlain that she agreed to marry Bernadotte because he was a soldier capable of standing up to Napoleon. But her temperament responded to a more positive appeal: he was tall, with the piercing eyes of an eagle set in a clearly chiselled face which conveyed energy, drive and action. His presence projected all the confidence of a leader of men.

The nature of Désirée's appeal to Bernadotte is harder to assess. As yet there had been little romantic passion in the General's life, and such love letters as survive are stilted in style, ponderously conventional. Did he embark on a courtship of convenience, wooing a wealthy young woman already so closely linked to the Bonapartes that she was one of Jupiter's satellites? Yet he was not by nature a cold or calculating planner in his personal relationships. A good cross-section of the Republican officer corps seem, at one time or another, to have looked wistfully at that petite, well-rounded figure and caught the slightly mocking smile from those brown eyes. Why should not Bernadotte, too, have responded warmly to these charms? His temperament was Gascon in spirit, readily fired by the vigour of Désirée's naturalness – for she, also, was a southerner. Although he was fifteen years older than she, an easy relationship swiftly established itself between them, never so intense as to insulate their love from public affairs, but marked, a trifle unexpectedly, by mutual tolerance and understanding. Their union was firmly rooted in the ground; hence, no doubt, its resilience and durability.

No one knows precisely when they met or when they were betrothed. On 16 July 1798 the 'widow Clary' completed an affidavit at the French Consulate in Genoa recognising her youngest daughter's wish to marry General Jean Baptiste Bernadotte and giving her son-in-law, Joseph Bonaparte, full powers to represent her in all matters concerning the marriage. Two days later Bernadotte requested an extension of his leave for another three months, both to complete his recovery 'from six years of campaigning and because the happiness of his life (*le bonheur de sa vie*) would be ruined were he forced to go away at this time'. He also negotiated a loan of 50,000 francs (the equivalent of about £100,000 in modern terms) from Gabriel Ouvrard, the twenty-eight year old entrepreneur who, from concessions to supply food for the French and Spanish navies, had become the richest man in the republic. Although the loan did not allow Bernadotte to keep Désirée in the style to which she was accustomed at her sister's home, it lifted the level of life at Sceaux from a bachelor simplicity to the smart assertiveness of newly-weds on the fringe of high society.

Joseph and Julie were wedded secretly in church as well as in a civil ceremony. But for Bernadotte and Désirée, as for Napoleon and Josephine, the sanction of law was sufficient in itself; and on 17 August they married at the town hall of Sceaux-l'Unité. The contract of marriage, carefully prepared by Joseph and his notaries so as to safeguard Désirée's share of her father's wealth, shows the signature 'Bonaparte' four times, for Joseph, as principal witness, was supported not only by his wife Julie, but by his brother Lucien and by Christine, the inn-keeper's daughter whom Lucien had married at St Maximin three years before. Among other witnesses were Désirée's uncle, Victor Somis, and a sole representative from the bridegroom's 'military family', his twenty-six year old cavalry aide, Captain Antoine Maurin. Désirée was content for the honeymoon to be spent in the Rue de la Lune; there were, after all, many less romantically named streets.

The idyll did not last long. Sceaux may have been near enough to central Paris for her husband, but it was too distant for Désirée. Laure Junot, who claims to have been at Sceaux for the wedding ceremony, recalls their early married life in her racily waspish reminiscences:

She was, naturally enough, fond of her husband, but this affection became downright vexing to the poor Béarnais who, having no halo of romance in his make-up, was sometimes highly puzzled at her behaviour. She was constantly bursting into tears: when he had gone out, because he was away; when he was about to go out, more tears because he would soon be absent; and when he came home, further weeping because he might have to go away again – perhaps not for another week, but at sometime or other he would have to leave her.

No doubt this pen-portrait is overdrawn. Yet it is not implausible. For within nine weeks of their marriage, the Bernadottes left Sceaux and put down 19,300 francs for a small house on the Rue Cisalpine (now Rue de Monceau), not far from the town mansion of Joseph and Julie. With Bernadotte's long extended leave about to expire, Désirée was determined to be close to her sister and the whirling centre of Parisian society.

When Bernadotte's leave ended in mid-October, the house in the Rue Cisalpine was not ready, and Désirée stayed for several weeks with Julie and Joseph. While there, she discovered that she was pregnant and therefore less able to participate in Parisian social life – fashionable taste, inspired by Napoleon's expedition, was Egyptian in inspiration that winter, requiring a geometrical figure and, weather permitting, diaphanous drapery. She could, of course, have joined her husband, who had taken up a command in his old stamping-ground around Mainz, but he did not want her to leave Paris. For, although France was still at peace along the German frontier, another round of fighting against Austria seemed likely; far better for the child to be born in the capital, well away from all war zones.

Despite his close association with Paul Barras, Bernadotte remained highly critical of the Directory as an institution of government. In this attitude, he was not alone. A five-man team of self-centred politicians was ill-suited to face the emergencies of war. All over France garrison commanders complained of their inept leadership; armies were kept short of men, of equipment, of food and – most dangerously – of pay, for the Directors' failure to establish an acceptable system of taxation had left the Ministry of Finance with a deficit of nearly 120 million francs that summer. These grievances were exploited by royalist agents, who were subsidised by British secret service funds, and who therefore found it profitable to take seriously the wild talk which they themselves encouraged. One agent, unidentified, appears to have been active at Giessen, the university town in Hesse-Darmstadt where Bernadotte set up his headquarters on his return from leave.

On 3 November 1798 James Talbot, the British envoy to Switzerland, confidently informed his Foreign Secretary of unrest among French garrison commanders, especially along the Rhine. 'Our agents', he wrote to Lord Grenville, 'have made successful overtures to the military, and amongst others to General Bernadotte' who 'unfortunately is to have a command in Italy.' Three weeks later Talbot sent off another despatch: a rising in Paris was imminent, he claimed; several hundred officers were ready to storm the Luxembourg; and an agent had said that, if there were a coup in Paris, Bernadotte – 'upon whom he believes he can perfectly rely' – would forestall any march on the capital by a relief army sympathetic to the Directory. But Talbot had an exaggerated sense of the dramatic. Over the next two months nothing disturbed the tedium of political life in Paris, and by the end of January 1799 the Foreign Secretary had become impatient. In a sharp note to his envoy Grenville complained that Talbot was allowing himself to be hoodwinked by 'totally unrealistic' schemes.

After the Vienna episode, Bernadotte was so well-known outside France that any secret agent hoping for good money from London would take care to include his name when fabricating the latest fantasy; and Grenville was right not to give Talbot's reports greater credence. In 1798 Bernadotte was still too sound a republican to become another Dumouriez or Pichegru, working for a Bourbon restoration. His political beliefs were more sympathetic to the neo-Jacobin reaction which had spread across much of southern and south-western France in the summer and autumn. Yet on at least one count Talbot's informant scored a near miss. In the same week that Grenville sent off that reprimand to his envoy, Bernadotte was summoned back to Paris and offered command of the Army of Italy. Twelve months previously, he would have welcomed the post: now he was cautious. In a detailed memorandum he emphasised the shortage of troops capable of stemming an enemy advance into Lombardy from the Venetian fortresses in Austrian hands. He calculated that, with another 20,000 men as reinforcements, he could put into the field some 73,000 combatants and retain a reserve of 50,000 troops to safeguard communications and garrison the

Cisalpine Republic and Piedmont. To establish a smaller Army of Italy would be to court disaster.

If Barras's memoirs may be believed, then he, at least, recognised the truth behind Bernadotte's shrewd assessment. English subsidies were welding together a new coalition, uniting Austria, Britain, Russia, Turkey, Portugal and Naples; and the military balance in northern Italy was likely to be tilted sharply against the Republic and its dependencies. His fellow Directors, however, remained unconvinced. So, too, did General Scherer, the Minister of War. Indeed Scherer was so unimpressed by Bernadotte's reasoning that he rashly told the Directors he would himself lead the Army of Italy – and with no more talk of those reinforcements which the veteran of the Tagliamento and Gradisca had thought essential to hold Lombardy.

Bernadotte was sent back to the Rhine as general-in-chief of an 'Army of Observation', which was – like the executive body which invented it – a cumbersome creation, existing largely on paper. When, in March, war returned to the Rhine he found he was expected to advance into Germany with an army still more than 20,000 men short of the number assigned by the Ministry of War. 'Everything is in appalling chaos', he told Désirée in a note from Strasbourg on 25 February; 'You yourself, though a woman, would be astonished to see how weak are our existing resources.' The next six weeks were to add no lustre to his military reputation.

On every battle-front the war went badly for the French that spring. South of the Alps Scherer's Army of Italy was defeated by the Austrians outside Verona and again at Magnano; it could not prevent General Suvorov's Russian expeditionary force from entering Milan by the end of April and overthrowing Napoleon's impromptu Cisalpine Republic. Masséna, sent into Switzerland with the 'Army of Helvetia', was forced to abandon Zurich before establishing a strong defensive position southwest of the city. But the most unexpected blow fell north of the Alps where General Jourdan, having led his 'Army of the Danube' through the southern slopes of the Black Forest, was repulsed by the Archduke Charles at Stockach and driven back to the Rhine. Bernadotte fared little better. Although he sent General Ney to seize Mannheim, he did not have enough troops to draw the Austrians away from Jourdan by marching once more on Würzburg.

In this hour of crisis Bernadotte's health gave way. On 3 April he informed Jourdan, as overall commander on the German Front, that he had been 'spitting blood . . . for the last eight days'; Dr Franzenberg, his personal physician, stressed his patient's urgent need of rest. Jourdan at once authorised a term of sick leave but he insisted that the General should not tire himself by a long journey back home. It was agreed he should recuperate at Simmern, in the Hunsrück, as a guest of the father-in-law of one of his aides, Colonel Maison. In a letter to Désirée from Simmern on 26 April he complained that he was still 'spitting blood', hardly cheering news for a wife in her seventh month of pregnancy.

By then the enemy's offensive north of the Alps had lost its momentum. Jourdan himself left the Rhine in mid-April, handing over the so-called 'Army of the Danube' to Masséna. Technically Jourdan became Inspector-General of Infantry, but his principal desire was to get back to the capital. For, during the lull in the fighting, he was determined to alert the Directory to the needs of the armies along the frontiers before a second Russian corps came to support the Austrians. Nor was Jourdan alone in this objective. From Lombardy General Joubert also hurried back to the capital. In the last week of May the two generals received reinforcement. Four weeks of fretful boredom at Simmern was quite enough to convince Bernadotte he was fit again; Dr Franzenberg was browbeaten into allowing him to travel to Paris, and continue his convalescence at home in the Rue Cisalpine.

The political situation in the capital remained confused. The neo-Jacobins in the bicameral legislature demanded reasons for the series of defeats in Germany, Switzerland and Italy; they began to sniff out corruption, frauds by army contractors and financial wastage. Everyone could sense that a drastic re-ordering of the government was in the offing. As on the eve of 18 Fructidor two years before, there were constant rumours of a military coup. In 1797 Augereau had saved the triumvirate within the Directory from the crypto-royalists. Now Paul Barras, still anxious to safeguard his own position, was pursuing an even more devious policy: he was prepared to encourage the army to support the plans of the former Abbé Sieyès, whose appointment as a Director he had recently helped secure; for although he knew that Sieyès was a master craftsman among constitution makers and wished to replace the existing model by a smarter version, he was confident there would still be a place in it for himself. All Barras and Sieyès required in

June 1799 was a general who would help them force the other three Directors to resign in favour of nominees content to do just what they were told.

Bernadotte, having rashly boasted that he could sweep away those tiresome lawyers in the Luxembourg with a mere 'corporal's guard', seemed a natural choice. He could have not simply a detachment of troops, Barras told him, but the command of all the armed forces in the Paris region. The offer took Bernadotte by surprise, and he hesitated; his aides-de-camp, Maison and Maurin, urged him to seize the opportunity; so, it would seem, did Joseph and Lucien. Yet, however ambitious Bernadotte might appear, he remained at heart a cautious upholder of authority rather than a conspirator. Once again he let slip the initiative. On 18 June 1799 (30 Prairial, Year VII) Lucien Bonaparte, an adroit political manager, kept the Council of Five Hundred in permanent session until the three unpopular Directors resigned, while General Joubert took command of the Paris garrison, although without deploying troops around the Luxembourg. So, for the second time in two years, Bernadotte sat out a coup in the capital, one in which on this occasion the army and its commanding general remained off stage, watching and waiting in the wings.

Yet Bernadotte benefited from this Prairial transformation of government. His report on the needs of an Army in Italy four months back would have staved off disaster, had the Directors and Scherer accepted it, and now his services were belatedly recognised. Sieyès, prompted by the Bonaparte brothers, offered him the Ministry of War. To the consternation of his friends, he refused it. General Joubert rode out to the Rue Cisalpine and repeated the offer. It was again rejected. Only at the tearful insistence of both Julie and Désirée did he agree to become the Carnot of the new emergency. Even then he insisted on his own terms: no moving into the Minister's official residence, for he wished to continue living in the Rue Cisalpine, riding across Paris early each morning to his administrative office; and he would choose his own team, for although his brother-in-law Joseph kindly offered to supply him with a hand-picked secretariat, Bernadotte had no intention of surrounding himself with Corsicans on the make. As military secretary, he chose Major Rousselin, from the 'Army of Observation' (an officer whom a less egalitarian society would have styled the Count Rousselin de Corbeau de Saint-Albin). There were posts for

Bernadotte's old aides, Gérard, Maison and Maurin, and for General Sarrazin. Even the accommodating Doctor Franzenberg was found a convenient niche, as inspector of military hospitals. Yet none of these appointments was a sinecure, for the new Minister was a hard taskmaster. He accepted office on Tuesday, 2 July. So eager was he to take up his duties that, despite his recent illness, he arrived at the Ministry before four o'clock on Wednesday morning. Over the following nine weeks, he expected his staff to follow this example and work a fifteen or sixteen hour day.

The strict routine of business may well have been broken right at the start of Bernadotte's tenure of the War Ministry. For, at half-past eight on the Thursday morning, Désirée gave birth to a son, at home in the Rue Cisalpine. The boy was not baptised in infancy, but on the following Sunday the birth was formally recorded by the registrar of Paris, Arrondissement I, with Joseph Bonaparte and the family doctor, Jean Paroisse, as witnesses. His first names, François and Joseph, honoured his grandfather and his uncle; but he was always known by his third name, Oscar. It is this choice which has aroused most interest; for in exile on St Helena, Napoleon claimed responsibility for selecting so rare a name, having met it in his current favourite reading, a translation of the Ossian epic.

This familiar tale must almost certainly be a fabrication. Napoleon was in Egypt at the time; he may, of course, have written to Joseph on hearing that Désirée was expecting a child and offered to be the boy's godfather, provided he bore the name 'Oscar', but no such letter exists. Possibly the name was chosen by Joseph Bonaparte, who says in his Memoirs that he, rather than Napoleon, was the boy's sponsor. Joseph, too, admired the Ossian legends. Moreover when, two years later, Joseph and Julie had their first child to survive infancy, they called her 'Zenaïde', as rare and unfamiliar a choice in France as 'Oscar'. There is, however, no reason why Désirée should not herself have chosen the name by which she called her son; for during her confinement she, too, had been dutifully 'improving her mind' with much reading. A catalogue of books published in Paris at the end of the century shows the popularity of proto-Romantic melancholia and fable, a trend which may well have induced one Clary sister to look (like Mme de Staël) to the sagas of northern Europe, while the other sister found inspiration more exotically in Persian legend. Yet, whatever the origin of Oscar's name, it is clear that the birth of a child to Désirée gave the Bonapartes an opportunity to draw the Bernadottes more closely into their family circle. 'When the Minister returned home', Barras wrote in his Memoirs, 'he always found there, allegedly inquiring after Madame Bernadotte's health, the brothers Bonaparte, or at all events Joseph and his wife.'

If Joseph thought that through his brother-in-law he might use the Ministry of War as a mounting-block to help the Bonapartes into the saddle, he was mistaken. For Bernadotte soon showed that he was a natural war leader, with principles elevated above faction or family. His first insistence was that there should be no bureaucratic delay: 'nothing shall remain for more than twenty-four hours . . . unconsidered or unanswered', he ruled on taking up office. But his greatest concern was to weld the army together as an efficient unit once again. Over the 30,000 battle-hardened troops in Egypt, he had no control but, between northern Holland and southern Italy, there were 260,000 men, looking for leadership to Paris. In the absence of any generalissimo, much depended on the quality of individual army commanders. Bernadotte reinstated generals dis-credited over the previous twelve months because their political views had fallen out of favour and he threatened with court-martial garrison commanders lax in resisting the onslaught of Austrian or Russian troops. Falling morale was rallied, not simply with gusts of Gascon rhetoric, but by promises of food, clothing and back-pay which he then fought fiercely to fulfil. He became, momentarily, the nation's drill sergeant, checking the evasion of call-up and the high incidence of desertion, firing the ardour of new recruits with that parade-ground oratory which had lifted the Sambre-et-Meuse a few years before.

As printed in the fading columns of the *Moniteur* his speeches and proclamations recall the popular patriotism of Danton. But like so much of Bernadotte's work at the Ministry that summer, they seem also to point to the immediate future. For in style and character they anticipate the practice Napoleon was to institute in the Marengo campaign of sending to the official journal 'Bulletins of the Army', drafted as propaganda to boost morale. In August some six hundred veterans in the Paris region were so moved by Bernadotte's evocation of 'the spirit of '92' that they came to the Ministry of War and volunteered for service again. Such gestures were of value to his grand strategy, for he wished to strengthen the armies on the distant frontiers by raising two hundred new battalions, picked from the best of the conscripts and from high quality troops held to garrison Paris and other cities. He met a threat of insurrection from the nine bands of 'royalist brigands' in western France largely by bluff, leaving the National Guard and neo-Jacobins to stamp out the most serious uprising at Toulouse while further north he ordered the thinly-spread 'Army of England' to mount frequent patrols along the main routes, so as to create an impression of strength which it did not possess.

There was little new in Bernadotte's strategy for defeating the challenge from the East. Joubert, at thirty the ablest of the young generals, was sent to Liguria to revive the Army of Italy; Masséna, with whom Bernadotte had long been on bad terms, was ordered to go over to the offensive in Switzerland but to send 18,000 men northwards for a diversionary thrust into Germany from the Rhineland. Unfortunately on 15 August, before he could organise his new command, Joubert was attacked by the main Austro–Russian army corps at Novi, in the hills north of Genoa, and was killed leading a cavalry charge; his troops held out for sixteen hours, but were finally forced back into Liguria. Masséna moved more cautiously; he deeply resented the demand that he should release so many troops for the Rhine offensive; at one moment, he even sent the Minister his resignation, with a request for sick leave. The one-time convalescent of Simmern recognised this ploy: after telling Masséna that the movement of troops was postponed, Bernadotte drily commented, 'I know well enough your devotion to the Republic to believe that you have forgotten the state of your health'. A few weeks later Masséna's army inflicted a double defeat on the Russians and Austrians close to Zurich which tilted the balance of the war once more in France's favour. By then, however, Bernadotte was out of office.

His relations with other government ministers and with the Directors were often strained. In the last week of July he threatened the Minister of Finance with a drawn sword when told there was no money to pay the troops or their suppliers, although in a calmer mood the two men were able to negotiate a loan, on somewhat specious securities, from Genoese bankers. Two of the new Directors – Louis Gohier and General Jean-François Moulin – were impressed by Bernadotte's mastery of detail when he expounded grand strategy at the Luxembourg. Even Sieyès, who resented his blustering manner, commended the speed with which in August he found reinforcements to enable General Brune to defeat the ill-coordinated Anglo–Russian landings in the Netherlands. But the third new Director, Pierre Roger Ducos, thought Bernadotte too Jacobin in his sympathies and backed Sieyès in criticising the Minister's apparent cult of popularity. 'We count for nothing; nobody takes any notice of us', Sieyès was heard to complain early in September, 'it is the Minister of War who constitutes the government'; and after hearing the Minister in full rhetorical flight, he commented, 'There goes a thrush that thinks itself an eagle'.

Ultimately it was this conflict with Sieyès that led to Bernadotte's downfall. The ex-Abbé and Barras, both politically men of the Centre, were frightened by the resurgence of Jacobinism in the capital and the strength of its following in the Council of Five Hundred. Four days after Bernadotte became Minister of War a Jacobin Club, calling itself *La Réunion des Amis de la Liberté et de l'Egalité*, opened its doors in the *Manège*, the riding-hall next to the chamber of the Council of the Ancients; and by the end of the month it was claiming a membership of three thousand Parisians. On 16 August the Directory authorised Fouché, as Minister of Police, to clear the neo-Jacobins out of the *Manège* but the club survived, unofficially, in the Rue du Bac and received warm support from General Jourdan. Politically Bernadotte's sympathies inclined towards the club and especially with its championship of a vigorous prosecution of the war. He was too circumspect to set foot in the *Manège* or the new quarters in the Rue du Bac, but Fouché's agents noted every meeting which he held with Jourdan or other radical deputies; and Sieyès and Roger Ducos were willing to believe that the Minister of War was a crypto-Jacobin. On 1 September Bernadotte delivered one of his fiery speeches to young recruits outside the old barracks of the Swiss Guards, at Courbevoie, between Paris and St Germain; the parade became a great demonstration of loyalty to the ideal of the Republic as represented by its Minister of War. At the same time General Jourdan made it clear that he would shortly launch a scathing attack on the Directory in the Council of Five Hundred. Next day Fouché ordered the expulsion from the capital of sixty-six radical journalists; over the following week Sieyès, at the Luxembourg, began to urge his colleagues to get rid of their Minister of War before he got rid of them.

On Friday, 13 September, General Jourdan made an eloquent

speech in the Council of Five Hundred proposing that it should follow the example of the Assembly in July 1792 and declare 'The Country in Danger'. Such an action would mean the virtual suspension of the Constitution and permit administration by emergency decree until good patriots had routed the republic's enemies, outside and inside the state. Although the deputies refused to follow Jourdan's lead, the tone of the debate alarmed Sieyès. At eleven that night he met his fellow Directors at the Luxembourg and alleged that Jourdan and 'that Catiline Bernadotte' were in collusion, an accusation which Gohier, for one, found unconvincing. Next morning the Minister of War was himself summoned to the Luxembourg. 'Do you find the honour of being seated in a ministerial arm-chair as worthwhile as being up in the saddle at the head of an army?', Barras asked him. It was a curious question, to which Bernadotte cautiously replied that he would be happy to serve again with his old companions on the battlefield. After he had left, Barras insisted to Sieyès and Ducos that this cautious response showed the Minister's willingness to resign. Together they signed an official statement, accepting Bernadotte's resignation because of 'the wish, so frequently expressed, of resuming active service with the armies'. Director Moulin was away ill that Saturday and Director Gohier was receiving petitioners in a formal audience, already listed among his engagements. Their absence did not, however, prevent Sieyès from adding their names to the decree which recorded the Minister's resignation. A copy of the decree and a letter from Sieyès, as current chairman of the Directory, were sent to the Ministry of War before being released for publication in the *Moniteur*.

Predictably, Bernadotte went out fighting. He acknowledged receipt of the decree and the 'polite letter' and bluntly told Sieyès, 'You accept a resignation which I have not given'. But, provided that the public would be able to read in their newspapers that he had not voluntarily given up his post, he was ready to accept the verdict of the Directory and seek retirement on half-pay. 'After twenty years of uninterrupted labour', he wrote, 'I do not conceal from you that I stand in need of repose.'

At the Luxembourg itself there were two angry men on the day his retirement was made known. Both Louis Gohier and Jean-François Moulin were furious to find that their colleagues had assumed they would give their assent to Bernadotte's dismissal. When, a quarter of a century later, Gohier came to write his memoirs he was willing to attribute the whole change in the fortunes of war, between Masséna's victory at Zurich and Napoleon's triumph at Marengo, to the energy and patriotic zeal which Bernadotte showed in his ten weeks as a Minister. Nor was this judgment on his skill as an organiser of victory a well-matured historical afterthought, intended to win Gohier a reading public in Sweden. For, on that day of Bernadotte's resignation, both Gohier and Moulin resolved to assert their status as Executive Directors. If they could not re-instate him, they could at least pay tribute to his achievement.

That afternoon, arrayed in the full majesty of office, with scarlet cloaks, plumed hats and an escort of the presidential Guard, the two Directors rode out from the Luxembourg in a carriage of state and headed down the Rue du Tournon. They turned northwards over the Seine, crossed the great square where the guillotine had stood, trotted through the Faubourg St Honoré, and on for another three kilometres up the slope towards the Mousseaux parkland, where the breeze was beginning to shake chestnuts from the trees. At last the mounted cavalcade clattered into the quiet courtyard which separated the two wings of no. 291 Rue Cisalpine. Director Gohier and Director Moulin stepped down. They formally thanked the fallen Minister for his services to the Republic over the past ten weeks. 'We forgot nothing in ensuring that our demonstration was given an official character', Gohier recalled in his Memoirs. Carriage and horses then turned about, and as the sound of hooves on cobbles died away, the Rue Cisalpine and its most distinguished occupant sank back into the tranquillity of autumn. It had been a brief scene, little more perhaps than a curtain call; but it was without precedent in the tragi-comedy of the Directory. 'You made a pompous visit out to Bernadotte, then?', Sieyès remarked sarcastically to Gohier next day. 'The most pompous we could manage', came the answer. Never again did Bernadotte stand so high in the esteem of the capital.

Chapter 6
Brumaire and After

ON THE day the two Directors rode out to the Rue Cisalpine, four small vessels were sailing westwards across the Gulf of Tunis, a strong south-easterly filling their canvas. Aboard the frigate *Muiron* were Napoleon, his stepson Eugène Beauharnais, General Berthier, and Admiral Ganteaume; and in the frigate *Carrère* were Generals Murat, Marmont, Bessières and Lannes. They had embarked at Alexandria three weeks before, leaving 30,000 French troops in the Nile valley under the command of Kléber, who was not even told of his appointment or of Bonaparte's intention to return home until the *Muiron*, the *Carrère* and their two escorting corvettes were at sea. Northwesterlies for days on end, and the threat of interception by patrolling British warships, made the little squadron hug the North African coast, tediously lengthening the voyage. No one in France was informed of Napoleon's plans, nor did he know anything that had happened in Europe over the past three months. Who could tell by now which harbours were in enemy hands? When, soon after dawn on 30 September, the familiar limestone cliffs of Bonifacio loomed up to starboard Napoleon sent a corvette ahead to make sure a tricolour flag still flew over Ajaccio before he risked setting foot in his native city. A further change of wind delayed him for five more days, long enough for news of Jourdan's 'Country in Danger' call and Bernadotte's fall to reach him. 'I shall arrive too late', Napoleon chafed. At last, shortly after darkness fell on 6 October, the wind veered to the south and the four vessels slipped away from Corsica to head for the coast of Provence.

Some forty hours later the afternoon tranquillity of Paris was broken by the echo of saluting cannon from the Champs de Mars. A report from Alexandria confirmed Bonaparte's defeat of the Turks

91

at Aboukir on 25 July, a victory which consolidated the French hold on Egypt. The news was especially welcome, for recent despatches from the Army of the Orient had caused perplexity and dismay: it was hard to see what the Syrian expedition had achieved; the lists of dead, sick and wounded were growing painfully longer; and, most alarming of all, the bubonic plague was said to be sweeping through several regiments. Now it was good to know that the Bonaparte touch was still there, even if his victory was won against a remote enemy in another continent rather than over the Austrians. More news followed, four days later; and it was far more surprising. The field semaphore from the south let Paris know that General Bonaparte was back in France, having come ashore at St Raphael, near Director Sieyès's home town of Fréjus. If the *Muiron* and *Carrère* had berthed at Toulon or Marseilles quarantine officers would have thrown a cordon around ships' crews and passengers alike, detaining them for up to thirty days in a lazaretto. At a small port like St Raphael there was little risk of delay from the authorities. Less than six hours after being welcomed enthusiastically ashore, Napoleon was on his way to Avignon, Lyons and the capital.

Most members of the Parisian establishment heard of the *Muiron*'s landfall while they were at the Luxembourg, where both Gohier and Sieyès were holding receptions on the evening the news broke. Bernadotte, to his wife's annoyance, was not there; for since his resignation he had virtually cut himself off from high society. But he cannot have missed the general excitement that night since so many houses in the fashionable districts of the capital were illuminated in Napoleon's honour. Not, however, no. 291 Rue Cisalpine. For Bernadotte was astonished by the news. He argued that the returning army commander had committed two offences, both of which were punishable by court martial: he had deserted the troops he took to Egypt; and, although arriving in France from a plague-spot, he had failed to observe quarantine regulations, either at Ajaccio or St Raphael. The inference was that had Bernadotte still held office as Minister of War, he would have ordered Bonaparte's arrest. He even went so far as to urge this policy on Barras, receiving the characteristic response 'Let's wait and see'. There was sound sense in this advice, for it was unlikely any guards would have obeyed such an order. Barras knew from Fouché's reports how, at Aix and Avignon and Lyons, Napoleon had received the acclaim of a hero returning to save a nation from its enemies. 'Everyone waits impatiently for Bonaparte, because for everyone he brings fresh hope', one of the smaller Parisian newspapers, the *Messager du Soir*, declared:

He reached his home in the Rue de la Victoire at six in the morning of 16 October. Only a few hours later he paid a courtesy visit on Louis Gohier, who had succeeded Sieyès as president of the Directory three weeks before. *'Vive Bonaparte'*, the sentries shouted as they presented arms when the General reached the Luxembourg. But Gohier's account of their conversation suggests a certain frigidity:

> 'The news that reached us in Egypt was so alarming that I didn't hesitate to leave my army, but set out at once to come and share your perils', said Bonaparte, with some embarrassment. 'They were indeed great, General,' I replied, 'but by now we have gloriously overcome them. You have arrived in fine time to help us celebrate the numerous triumphs of your comrades-in-arms.'

Many comrades-in-arms, if not actually engaged against the enemy, hastened to pay their respects to Napoleon. Yet, despite pleas from Désirée and Julie and heavy-handed moves towards reconciliation by Joseph and Lucien, Bernadotte continued to stand aloof. He was incensed at the treatment accorded to Kléber, his old friend from Fleurus and the Sambre-et-Meuse: did he, one wonders, hear of the letter in which the new and reluctant commander-in-chief of the Army of the Orient complained to the Directory of the way in which his predecessor, 'that little bugger' (*ce petit bougre*), had set out across the Mediterranean without once briefing him on the problems of Egypt? The subsequent fate of Kléber, who was assassinated in Cairo by a Moslem fanatic in the following June, was to make Bernadotte's resentment at the flight from Egypt a lasting grievance in his complaints against Napoleon. When, in the third week of October 1799, two members of the Council of Five Hundred visited Bernadotte to seek his patronage for a 'welcome home' banquet, he advised them to postpone the celebrations until Bonaparte satisfactorily explained the reasons that had made him abandon his army; 'Besides', he added, thinking suddenly of that breach of quarantine, 'I don't care to sit down at dinner with someone carrying the plague'.

Gohier, however, had no such qualms. Perhaps, too, an instinct for survival made him regret his cool reception of Bonaparte. On

22 October he entertained Napoleon and Josephine to dinner and, to Mme Bonaparte's consternation, sat her husband next to Sieyès. 'What have you done!', she whispered urgently. 'There is no man he more detests than Sieyès. He is his *bête noire*.' Gohier patted her hand reassuringly – a favourite pastime that autumn – but he noticed that Napoleon ignored Sieyès completely, not even exchanging a word with him; he was uncertain of how he should handle the politicians. Later that evening, Moulin came over to Gohier's apartments with General Moreau, whom Napoleon had never met before. At once, however, he set about trying to win him as an ally, for he knew how deeply he was respected by officers who had served in the German campaigns. It was only through the mediation of his brother Joseph and Talleyrand that Napoleon began to recognise Sieyès's political value and seek his backing. Meanwhile Sieyès himself was prepared to learn a new role, to serve a militaristic government. To the amusement of Parisian society, by the end of the month the fifty-one year old ex-Abbé could be seen earnestly taking riding lessons in the parkland behind the Luxembourg.

It was harder for Napoleon to win over Bernadotte, who still harboured old resentments from the closing months of the Italian campaign. The immediate effect of his return from Egypt was to drive Bernadotte into close contact with dissident generals whom he had earlier treated with suspicion, notably the neo-Jacobin commanders, Jourdan and Augereau. But loyalties remained uncertain from day to day. Which way, for example, would Moreau jump if there was a political crisis, for he had been heard to criticise both the Directory and the ambitions of the Bonapartes? It was clear, too, that Désirée was fostering the sympathetic friendship between her husband and her brother-in-law, Joseph. And Jourdan, though suspicious of all the Bonapartes, believed it might be possible for Bernadotte, Moreau, Augereau and himself to work in close partnership with Napoleon, substituting rule by the army for the muddle-headed rule of Barras and his cronies. It was as much under pressure from Jourdan as from the entreaties of Désirée that, ten days after Napoleon's arrival in Paris, Bernadotte set off for no. 6, Rue de la Victoire, to see him for the first time since the peacemaking at Campo Formio.

The meeting was not a social success. Both men were ill at ease, as Josephine Bonaparte soon perceived. When Bernadotte, glaring fiercely at his host, expressed his conviction that the Republic 'will resist her enemies, both domestic and foreign', Josephine thought it tactful to intervene, soothing ruffled feelings once more, as at Passeriano under such different circumstances two years before. Nevertheless, at the prompting of Joseph and Désirée, a second visit followed next day. Once again the atmosphere was heavily charged, with Bernadotte resenting his host's tirade against the neo-Jacobins and their alleged follies. The following evening the two men met for a third time, a chance encounter in the foyer of the Théâtre Française. Napoleon asked if he might call on the Bernadottes next morning in the Rue Cisalpine, as both generals and their wives were invited to dine later that day with his eldest brother out at Mortefontaine, the country mansion which Joseph had purchased thirty miles north-east of Paris; and Bernadotte made it clear that Napoleon and his wife would be welcome to breakfast with them.

Napoleon and Désirée had not seen each other since he left Marseilles for Paris in May 1795 as her fiancé. Now, on 29 October, they met again, after four and a half years. Small wonder if, as two memoirists recall, Désirée made a greater fuss of her guests than Bernadotte thought the occasion warranted: she had never entertained Josephine before; and, in so far as she thought of politics at all, she would have liked to see her husband, her brother-in-law and her former fiancé working together as an extended family. The ladies are said that morning to have talked of roses, while Napoleon privately hinted to Bernadotte what hardly needed to be said: that, should he find himself at the head of a new government, he would favour the appointment to the highest commands of generals who had given him their support. The two men were joined by Lucien, who had been elected to the presidency of the Council of Five Hundred in the previous week, and was therefore in effect Speaker of the lower chamber in the Assembly, an influential post. Out at Mortefontaine the Bernadottes found that Joseph had invited over a dozen leading political figures, including Talleyrand and Pierre Roederer, the able journalist and economist. The guests talked to each other in small, secretive groups, going silent when Bernadotte moved among them, as if to emphasise that he was close to a conspiracy but not yet admitted to its secrets.

Next morning, back in Paris, he met Moreau, told him of his fears and received the confident answer, 'We shall stop him'. Tension continued throughout the following week. On 6 November – 14 Brumaire, Year VIII, by the revolutionary calendar – the banquet in honour of the returned hero was held at last, in the Temple de la Victoire, known in less godless times as the Church of St Sulpice. Under 'Speaker' Lucien's skilled management, the banquet had changed its character: for now it was to honour, not simply his brother, but the past victories of General Moreau, too. Napoleon stayed only an hour, taking little wine and hardly any food, perhaps because he feared it might be poisoned. During the banquet, glasses were raised to five toasts: 'To the French Republic!', proposed the presiding chairman of the Council of Ancients; 'To the continuing triumphs of French arms on land and at sea', said Lucien; 'To Peace', ventured Gohier; 'To the faithful allies of the Republic', offered the first honoured guest, Moreau; and finally, from Napoleon himself, 'To the union of the peoples of France'. Yet if his eye ran down the long tables, he would have spotted a gap in that unity around him. For, although more than six hundred people had subscribed to the St Sulpice banquet, there were absentees too: no Jourdan and no Augereau; and, to the principal guest's intense irritation, no Bernadotte either. Despite the pull of marriage and kinship, the ex-Minister of War was still resolutely determined not to be counted a Bonapartist.

In later years, when November 1799 was remembered as the grey dawn of the First Empire, Mme de Staël insisted that Bernadotte was the one person who might have saved the Republic on 18 Brumaire. This he could have done, however, only through intense activity on 16 and 17 Brumaire and an utter conviction in the wisdom and principles of his cause. He held no office, military or administrative; he had no large following of troops in the capital; and, although widely esteemed eight weeks before, he had become yesterday's hero once the Councils began to acclaim Moreau and Bonaparte. There was a rumour among the guests at the St Sulpice banquet that the three absent generals were in the Faubourg St Antoine that evening, trying to kindle Jacobin fire among artisans short of food and employment. This was nonsense; they lacked the verbal facility of revolutionary demagogues skilled in bringing the Paris mob on to the streets. Moreover, after a succession of coups d'état which left their life unchanged, most workers ignored the faction fights of generals and lawyers. A cynical apathy ran through the poorer faubourgs.

There was no decisive break between the three generals and Napoleon. Both Bernadotte and Jourdan were among thirty guests who lunched with him on 7 November (16 Brumaire). The table-talk that Thursday was reassuringly familiar: little on the inner political power struggle, but much on military matters, particularly the strategic need to wage war in enemy territory rather than stand on the defensive. Friday was Désirée's twenty-second birthday; late that evening Joseph called at no. 291 Rue Cisalpine on his way back to his town mansion in the Rue Rocher only to be told that Bernadotte had retired to bed; he left a message that he would return early in the morning and that the two men would then ride to the Rue de la Victoire for urgent consultation with Napoleon.

Paris on the morning of 18 Brumaire – Saturday, 9 November 1799 – was bitterly cold, a dank miasma hanging over streets from which fog was slow to lift. It seems to linger still in several accounts of what happened from hour to hour that day. Yet some moments stand out clearly enough. When Bernadotte reached no. 6, Rue de la Victoire with Joseph he found the house filled with senior officers in uniform, whereas he was in mufti:–

> 'How's this then?' Napoleon greeted him. 'Why are you not in uniform?'
> 'Because I am not on active duty,' Bernadotte replied.
> 'You soon will be!'
> 'I think not.'
> 'Go back; get into uniform. I cannot wait long. You will find me at the Tuileries, with all our other comrades in arms.'

But Bernadotte was obdurate; he would not take part in any rebellion or help to overthrow the constitution. He was prepared as a private citizen to do nothing to impede Napoleon; he would not incite troops or civilians to offer resistance, 'But if the legislature or the Directory order me to defend them, I will obey'. He then rode back to Joseph's home in the Rue Rocher for a protracted breakfast. Meanwhile supporters of Napoleon in a hastily convened emergency session of the Council of Ancients announced that there was a Jacobin conspiracy to seize power. In order to frustrate this evil design it was proposed that General Bonaparte should receive command of the Paris region and that the legislative councils should leave their improvised chambers in the Tuileries and meet the following day out at St Cloud, where they might more effectively be protected from a Jacobin mob. Napoleon arrived at the Council and gave a pledge of loyalty to the assembly.

When Bernadotte left the Rue Rocher, still in his civilian clothes, he rode into central Paris to discover what was happening. Had he, over the breakfast coffee, sat out yet another Paris coup? Or had Moreau fulfilled that boast he made eleven days before and put a stop to Napoleon and the trouble-makers? Brumaire, however, unlike Fructidor and Prairial, was a long drawn-out affair. By Saturday noon the outcome was still far from clear. In the Tuileries Gardens Bernadotte was recognised by veterans of the demi-brigade of which he had been colonel five years before. The officers, uncertain of their orders, were puzzled to find him out of uniform; but they left him in no doubt of their personal loyalty. He called on Jourdan, whom he found closeted with a group of angry deputies; they insisted that an emergency session of the Council, to which many members had not been summoned, had no authority to move the legislature out to St Cloud, some seven miles away. When Bernadotte arrived back at the Rue Cisalpine, an anxious Désirée told him that he had missed Moreau's aide-de-camp who brought a message inviting him to come in uniform, and join Generals Moreau and Bonaparte at the Tuileries. He ignored the message which, he assumed, confirmed his fear that Moreau, so far from stopping Napoleon, was now his ally. Later that Saturday, Bernadotte realised that allegiances were still shifting with disconcerting speed. For the same aide-de-camp arrived back at the Rue Cisalpine with another message from Moreau, who was guarding Gohier and Moulin, the two Directors not in the conspiracy. Now Moreau invited Bernadotte to come to the Luxembourg and discuss with him ways of preventing Napoleon becoming a dictator.

Bernadotte, however, feared a trap. He, at least, held consistently to his principles. Moreau was told that if he personally, with a detachment of the Directorial Guard, arrived in the Rue Cisalpine with orders from the supreme executive authority, then Bernadotte would get into uniform, accompany him back to the Tuileries and deliver so stirring a speech to the troops on duty that they would arrest General Bonaparte. The two Councils could then function normally again in Paris, rather than out at St Cloud. But Bernadotte emphasised that, without the presence of Moreau and the necessary orders, he would take no action. He was still waiting when the day ended; neither Moreau nor the orders ever came.

That night there was little sleep in the Rue Cisalpine. The candles burnt late: General Sarrazin, once Bernadotte's chief staff officer in Italy, arrived with a plea from Napoleon for a further meeting, only to find his old commander in deep consultation with Generals Jourdan and Augereau and several members of the Jacobin Club. Well before seven next morning the two Generals called again, this time with eight deputies on their way to the session of the Councils at St Cloud: Sieyès and Fouché were said to be ready to arrest, proscribe and deport any members of the Council who proposed Bernadotte as military commandant. The neo-Jacobin deputies urgently sought his advice and he gave it to them clearly, although with significant changes from the message he sent Moreau the previous evening: he recommended that one of the deputies should propose that 'General Bernadotte shall be the colleague of General Bonaparte . . . in maintaining the security of the nation'. He undertook to be at St Cloud, in full uniform and with his aides-de-camp, 'within twenty minutes' of hearing such a proposal had been carried; and he added that should Napoleon then become so defiant that it was essential to proclaim him 'an outlaw', the Council could depend on him, so that 'You will have at your side a general and at the very least a great proportion of the troops'.

Bernadotte, however, never went near St Cloud on that momentous Sunday, when Napoleon so nearly lost control of events. In their eagerness to get the Councils away from the Tuileries to a suburb where they could be intimidated in isolation, the makers of the coup overlooked a practical difficulty: palace rooms, long neglected, were ill-suited to serve as an improvised parliament house. For the Council of Ancients to gather, even in emergency session, without the full pomp of office – the decorated dais, the decorous figure of Minerva, all the stage-props of a confused classicism – was unthinkable. A long delay gave deputies a chance to discuss the crisis informally, gathering in small groups under the trees of Le Nôtre's landscaped hillside above the Seine. It taxed the nerves of Bonaparte and Sieyès, waiting in what had once been the apartments of Charles II's favourite sister, Henrietta-Anne ('Minette'); while, back at the Rue Cisalpine, the lack of news heightened Bernadotte's Gascon impatience. Not until half-past three did the Ancients, robed in their scarlet togas, file into the Galerie d'Apollon, hoping for a speedy session. They accepted letters of resignation from all the Directors except Sieyès and then invited the Council of Five Hundred to draw up a list of possible successors. At that point Napoleon illegally burst into the Galerie and harangued the Elders on the need for decisive action and the appointment of a provisional ruling committee to save the Republic from Jacobin extremism. He found, however, that the mood of the Ancients was turning against him, and he hurried off to the Orangery, where his brother Lucien was presiding over a stormy session of the Five Hundred. When, again illegally, Napoleon burst into the chamber, some deputies sought to eject him. He emerged with blood on his face from the manhandling they offered him. Lucien suspended the sitting and formally called on help from the troops outside. General Leclerc (who had married Pauline Bonaparte) and General Murat (who was about to marry her sister, Caroline) cleared the Orangery while Napoleon, astride a black cavalry charger in the courtyard, made certain that the Ancients, too, had suspended their sitting. That evening, at nine o'clock, a rump session of chosen deputies declared the Directory at an end and authorised Napoleon, Sieyès and Roger Ducos to serve as provisional consuls of the republic, pending the enactment of a new constitution. Just thirty-three days after stepping ashore at St Raphael Napoleon was effectively master of France.

Alarming rumours drifted back into Paris throughout the Sunday afternoon, especially after the troops ejected the Five Hundred from the Orangery. Army rule, it was feared, meant bloody repression. Several prominent Jacobins were arrested, others going into hiding. Jourdan was among those taken into protective custody, but Augereau is said to have congratulated Napoleon on his success and to have asked, with bland reproach, why the new consul had not sought his aid when making a coup. That night General Sarrazin rode out to his house at Villeneuve-St-Georges, a village ten miles up the Seine, where the Fontainebleau road skirted the forest of Senart. There, to his amazement, he found awaiting him Bernadotte and a young man who, on closer inspection, he recognised as the General's wife 'in boy's clothes'. The guillotine had been kept busy after Thermidor, the galleys had taken their prisoners off to Guiana after Fructidor. Who could tell what would follow Brumaire? Bernadotte and Désirée did not believe that Napoleon would institute a reign of terror, but they knew him well enough to fear his initial reactions, and they profoundly mistrusted the ex-Abbé who had become his partner in government. They therefore asked Sarrazin for sanctuary at his home, or at a hideout in the neighbouring woods, for they were sure that if Napoleon flew into a fit of rage against his opponents, he would soon calm down. Then, of course, they would return safely to Paris. It is not clear if Oscar was left with his nurses in the Rue Cisalpine, or had been taken by them to his aunt, Julie Bonaparte.

Next morning Sarrazin rode back to the Luxembourg, where there was much coming and going of senior officers. He was surprised to be greeted by the new Consul, who smilingly asked after Bernadotte: 'When you see him, tell him that I shall always be glad to number him among my friends', he added. Presumably Napoleon knew of the Bernadottes' movements through Joseph and Julie; although he kept silent about his immediate intentions, he planned to take no action against Joseph's brother-in-law and Lucien's close friend, for had not Lucien's initiative in the Orangery saved Brumaire from disaster? The Bernadottes, however, accepted Sarrazin's hospitality at Villeneuve for two more nights, until letters from Joseph assured them that it would be perfectly safe to return to the Rue Cisalpine. Even so, Bernadotte was slower than the other dissident generals to seek reconciliation with the First Consul, perhaps through embarrassed irritation that his flight with Désirée into the woods was so widely known. Gascon pride lay dented: it was hard to wait vainly in the wings for a hero's cue and end the day performing a modified *As You Like It* in some Parisian Arden.

The proscriptions following Brumaire were not so harsh as after Fructidor, for Napoleon genuinely wished to unite the factions in the Republic rather than perpetuate divisions. Most neo-Jacobins benefited from amnesties within three months of the coup. Jourdan, at first sentenced to banishment on the Isle of Oléron, was reinstated far sooner; he was serving as Inspector-General of Infantry again before the end of the year and Augereau was given command of French troops in the Netherlands on 28 December. Bernadotte remained on half-pay in the Rue Cisalpine, while the constitution of the Consulate was being drafted. Through Désirée he kept in close touch with Napoleon's brothers and sisters. On 20 January 1800 Bernadotte was at Mortefontaine, Joseph's huge country estate, for the civil wedding of Murat and Caroline Bonaparte; and his name appears in the marriage register as principal witness. The dashing extrovert, Joachim Murat, had served under him on the Tagliamento and in Austria, but the Bernadottes' prominence in the celebrations at Mortefontaine may well have owed more to the close friendship between Désirée and the bride, for Caroline had been with her in Rome when Duphot was murdered. The First Consul was too busy to come out to Mortefontaine for his youngest sister's wedding celebrations.

A few days later Bernadotte accepted the offer of a seat on the Council of State, the principal advisory body established by the new constitution for the Consulate. For three months he attended meetings of the Council's War Committee, discussing both the major issues of policy and pressing problems of logistics and manpower. It was depressing to find that, because of the breakdown of local government in the last months of the Directory, only a third of the conscripts ever reported for training at their barracks. Although there was a lull around the frontiers, France was still at war, a peace initiative by the First Consul at Christmas having been contemptuously and foolishly brushed aside by the British Government. While Bernadotte was prepared to argue with Napoleon and with Carnot (his Minister of War) over the relative merits of aggressive and defensive strategies, he had grown tired of Paris politics and hankered after a command in the field once more. Moreau was building up a new Army of the Rhine, ready for a spring offensive through Baden, Württemberg and Bavaria; and Berthier was concentrating a Reserve Army around Dijon which would cross the Alps as soon as the roads were clear and flood down into the north Italian plain. No one doubted Napoleon would lead the Reserve Army in the terrain where he had gained his earlier victories, but an ill-phrased constitutional safeguard forbade the First Consul to command an army within France's frontiers. Who better to take it across the Alps than Bernadotte, using the experience he had accumulated three years before? It was even reported in the Paris newspapers in the second week of March that he would become the Consul's principal lieutenant-general.

Napoleon, however, thought otherwise. Berthier was his natural choice as a deputy, although he was also troubled by claims from his sisters' husbands, Murat and Leclerc. The independent-minded Moreau, along the German frontier, was hard enough to handle; he could not manage Bernadotte in Italy as well. Moreover the structure of France's latest constitutional novelty, the Consulate, needed buttressing by a victory won by its chief executive in person, not a triumph he must share with some rival general on horseback. He therefore had no doubt where that hot-blooded Gascon should serve while he was in Italy. On 1 May, 1800 – five days before Napoleon set out for Dijon and the Alps – Bernadotte took command of the Army of the West, with headquarters at Rennes, the old capital of Brittany.

He believed he had been assigned an important mission. Soon, he thought, he would be called to repel a seaborne invasion. The frigates of the Royal Navy were close inshore from Ushant down to the Loire, spying out the coast and teasing the defending forces, while larger vessels patrolled out at sea. Yet when, soon after his arrival, British troops tried to seize Belle-Isle and land in Quiberon Bay, they were speedily driven back to their transports, which then wallowed in the Biscayan swells for over a month before being summoned back to Plymouth and Weymouth. Bernadotte's chief enemies became the royalist agents who over the past eighteen months had been stirring up resistance among the Chouannerie, insurgents who terrorised much of southern Brittany and Anjou. His immediate predecessor, General Guillame Brune, had instituted a system of repression, leaving townsfolk and peasantry cowed and frightened. Bernadotte continued to hunt down the Chouan leaders but tried to lessen their appeal to the Bretons by conciliatory gestures; in particular, he concentrated on re-establishing order along the roads, so that food and fodder could move freely. To Napoleon's chagrin, he failed to capture the ringleader, Georges Cadoudal, a Breton from the Morbihan peninsula; but by the autumn of 1800 he could claim – and did – that the west of France was at last pacified. For a man of Bernadotte's temperament police duties of this type remained a thankless task.

During his first two months at Rennes Bernadotte was conscious of a further responsibility, potentially greater than his immediate preoccupations. It had been set out for him by the First Consul in a message from Paris, sent on the eve of his departure for the Alps and Italy: 'Should I fall, you will find yourself with forty thousand men at the gates of Paris; and in your hands will be the fate of the Republic'. Despite the clash of principle which had kept them apart at Brumaire six months before, Napoleon seemed now to be recognising his recent antagonist as heir-apparent.

There was nothing strange about his succinct political testament. So long as Napoleon was alive and in the saddle he would not contemplate the possibility of defeat in Italy, but as a realist he remembered the fate of Joubert and his army in the previous year.

Another battle of Novi would throw Paris into political turmoil, and it was by no means clear where the sovereignty of the Republic should be entrusted. For within little more than a month after Brumaire Napoleon had encouraged the resignation of the experienced Sieyès and Roger Ducos in favour of a lawyer, Jean Jacques de Cambacérès, as Second Consul and a solidly reliable accountant, Charles Lebrun, as Third Consul. Whatever the qualities of these two newcomers, they could never maintain unity in the government without a dynamic soldier as First Consul. If Napoleon had not come back from the 1800 Campaign, either Carnot as Minister of War would have set up an interim dictatorship, or there would have been a dash for the capital by Bernadotte from Rennes or by Moreau from the lower Rhine, assuming he could disengage his troops from battle with the Austrians. That Napoleon would prefer such a race to be won by Bernadotte is hardly surprising. Throughout his life he possessed to the full a Corsican sense of family loyalty; and he felt certain he could rely on Joseph's brother-in-law to safeguard Bonaparte family interests, offering protection, not only to Joseph, Lucien and their sisters, but also to the formidable matriarch who had followed her sons from Corsica to Toulon, Marseilles and Paris. If Napoleon had met his death on the Lombard plain, a heavier burden than 'the fate of the Republic' would have weighed down Bernadotte's hands.

The First Consul was absent from Paris for a mere fifty-seven days of campaigning that summer. The decisive battle was fought on 14 June around the village of Marengo, outside Alessandria, barely ten miles from Novi. Like Waterloo, Marengo was a turning-point at which history almost swung the wrong way. Napoleon had underestimated Austrian strength, especially in guns and cavalry; he was saved from defeat only through the enterprise of Desaix who, from nine miles away, heard intense cannon fire and arrived with reinforcements at the crucial moment; he was to die hours later at the head of his cavalry. It is not surprising that Napoleon, although paying tribute to Desaix, kept silent over this narrow margin of victory when he sent a report of the battle to his fellow consuls. France wished to hear that Austria had been humbled at a single blow, and this was the news which delighted Paris later that week. Brumaire and the new constitution had aroused little interest outside Paris; only one and half million voters bothered to record their approval of the Consulate in the December plebiscite, less than half as many as its organisers hoped. But Marengo dispelled this long apathy. Victory in a new Italian campaign converted Brumaire in retrospect from a muddled farce to the curtain-raiser for a victorious peace.

The celebrations continued in the capital for two days; neither of the Bernadottes took part in them. At the start of June Désirée shut up their home in the Rue Cisalpine, left Oscar with her mother (by now living in the Faubourg St Honoré) and travelled west to join her husband in what had formerly been the bishop's palace at Rennes. At the weekend when Paris was going wild with delight at the news from Italy, the Bernadottes were visiting the garrison where, just eight years before, he served as a newly commissioned Lieutenant; and Désirée described in a letter to her brother the pride and pleasure of accompanying the 'Councillor of State, General-in-Chief' to St Malo to be greeted by the sound of cannon reverberating from the rocky promontories around the bay in his honour. Soon afterwards, back in Rennes, there were more artillery salutes, this time to let the people of Brittany know of Marengo. Officially the commander of the Army of the West shared the nation's delight at the First Consul's victory. Yet the news was bitter-sweet; not only was Napoleon back on a pedestal, but the young generals who had married into his family would be returning in triumph with their brother-in-law. No longer might Bernadotte claim to stand as heir-apparent of the Republic. The grey granite of Rennes seemed suddenly more distant from Paris. Belatedly he realised that in accepting the command in Brittany, he had stepped out of the public eye.

Chapter 7
'That Hot-headed Southerner'

ALTHOUGH Bernadotte was nominally in command of the Army of the West until the late spring of 1802, he found garrison life in Brittany vexatious and seized every opportunity to return to Paris, where he continued to sit on the Council of State. These were the years in which Napoleon left his most enduring mark on the institutions of France, through the Civil Code and a Law of Public Worship, which gave effect to his concordat with the papacy. At the same time he intensified the authoritarian character of his government until in August 1802 he became Life Consul, with the power to nominate a successor. Bernadotte remained a critic of the Consulate, deploring the spread of a thinly veiled dictatorship. So, indeed, was Lucien Bonaparte, whose initiative at St Cloud saved Brumaire from disaster. Lucien and Bernadotte had hoped that Napoleon would become France's George Washington, dedicated to 'the preservation of the sacred fire of liberty'; instead it seemed as if he were modelling himself on Lord Protector Cromwell, together with an active interest in internal security reminiscent of Cardinal Richelieu. He retained Joseph Fouché as Minister of Police, supplementing his activity by a gendarmerie, headed by General René Savary, and a network of private informers.

Bernadotte left Rennes for Paris on 10 October 1800 and did not return to Brittany for another six months. On that same day the Paris police arrested a Corsican, Joseph Aréna, in the foyer of the Théâtre de la République, where the First Consul was attending a performance of the opera *Horace* and the ballet *Pygmalion*. Napoleon had been warned of a plot to assassinate him that night and Aréna was found with an arsenal of offensive weapons, incompletely hidden on his person. Arrested with Aréna was his companion, the gifted sculptor, Giuseppe Ceracchi, who the police soon found was awaiting the payment of 720 francs from Bernadotte. Suspicion at once fell on the general and, while her husband was on his way up to the capital, Fouché's police cross-questioned Désirée, who was staying at her mother's home in the Rue d'Aguesseau.

Fouché, however, had acted precipitately. Désirée knew Ceracchi; but so, too, did Joseph Bonaparte and Eugène de Beauharnais (who was, by chance, in charge of his stepfather's bodyguard at the Théâtre de la République that night). For Ceracchi was a Roman from Trastevere, who three years before had taken refuge in the French embassy during the riot in which Duphot was killed. On that occasion he became so ill-disciplined that Eugène was forced to strike him 'several times with the flat of my sabre'. After this experience the sculptor settled in Paris, where he specialised in classical busts which transformed Directory worthies into look-alike Pompeys, Ciceros or Mark Antonys, tact making him stop short at laurel wreathed Caesars. Bernadotte had sat for Ceracchi in the previous spring, shortly before leaving for Rennes; he appears to have delayed settling the bill for 720 francs until he could come to Paris and see the bust for himself. The police accepted Désirée's explanation; a week later the First Consul invited a ruffled Bernadotte to ride beside him at a review outside Rocquenfort, and there were inspired leaks to the Press, suggesting he would receive a new and important army command. Aréna, Ceracchi and several alleged accomplices were found guilty of a Jacobin conspiracy and, after being held for sixteen weeks, went to the guillotine. The bust of Bernadotte survives in the museum at Pau.

During the investigations into the Aréna conspiracy, the Bernadottes were completing the purchase of a country estate. They sold their house in the Rue Cisalpine to General Laroche on 30 October at a slight profit and four weeks later became joint owners of La Grange la Prévôte, an estate twenty-two miles east of Paris off the road to Melun, at Savigny la Temple. Joseph and Julie had paid 258,000 francs for Mortefontaine, while the Bernadottes purchased La Grange for 200,000 francs (about £400,000 today), but it used up Désirée's dowry and sent her husband cap in hand to his wealthier friends for loans, which he seems to have repaid within a couple of years. La Grange was not so pleasantly sited as Mortefontaine, nor did the estate cover so many acres, but it included two farms, pastures and woodland as well as a château in need of much renovation. For the next three and a half years the Bernadottes owned no house in central Paris, often staying with Madame Clary and her son Nicolas at no. 23 Rue d'Aguesseau in the Faubourg St Honoré. Although Désirée may well have soon tired of the wind-swept countryside around Corbeil, La Grange remained Berna-dotte's favourite home for the next ten years.

A week before Bernadotte arrived back in Paris from Rennes his old antagonist General Berthier became Minister of War, an office he was to hold until September 1807. The two men clashed fre-quently in the Council of State, with Bernadotte complaining that the Army of the West was kept short of men and material. The war with Austria, suspended for protracted peace negotiations after Marengo, was renewed on 22 November 1800 and Bernadotte had hopes of a field command. It was, however a brief campaign: General Moreau was victorious at Hohenlinden on 3 December and by Christmas had advanced to within sixty-five miles of Vienna when Emperor Francis authorised an armistice. The Peace of Lunéville, in February 1801, re-established Napoleonic dominance in Italy and along the Rhine; and Bernadotte, finding the Army Topographical Department preparing maps of southern England, became interested in securing the command of a landing in Kent or Sussex. A few days after the peace celebrations in Paris he sent a letter to Lucien Bonaparte – then ambassador in Madrid – confiding to him that, were he disappointed over the English command, 'I shall set out for our lands over the seas to seek there the happiness denied me in my homeland by those who owe me justice and recognition'.

To complain of a denial of 'justice' was an exaggeration. He was, however, still regarded with some suspicion by Napoleon, even though it was clear that he knew nothing of the fumbled conspiracy of Aréna and Ceracchi. Plots, fomented for the most part by royalist agents, continued to threaten internal security. On 24 December 1800 the First Consul narrowly escaped assassination in the Rue Saint-Niçaise when a wagon, filled with gunpowder, exploded as he was on his way to the Opéra once again. Bernadotte was among the audience awaiting Napoleon's arrival at the Théâtre Française that night and, while alarming rumours were circulating, an agent of either Fouché or Savary noticed him hurry down the staircase; he had not returned to the theatre when the First Consul and his wife at last entered their box, and the agent appears to have lost track of his movements; it was easy for police reports to make the most natural reactions appear suspicious. Later, back at the Tuileries, Napoleon's family discussed what would have happened had the assassination succeeded. Would Moreau, the hero of Hohenlinden, have been called to the Consulate, as some believed? 'No', replied Napoleon wryly, 'it would have been General Bernadotte. Like Antony he would have presented to the excited people the blood-stained robe of Caesar.' This was a shrewd judgment: for, while Moreau was eight hundred miles away, Bernadotte was in Paris itself. Yet there was no suggestion that he was implicated in the assassination plot and he continued to possess considerable influence. When some eight weeks later, Madame Juliette Récamier's father, a postal official, was arrested and charged with allowing the circulation of royalist propaganda, Bernadotte intervened. He went at once to the Tuileries, saw the First Consul and soon secured the poor man's swift release. His initiative won him the lasting gratitude of the best listener and most attractive salon hostess in Paris.

By the end of April he was at last back in Brittany, despite rumours, which even reached London, that he was to command an invasion of England. He left Désirée in Paris and, over the next few months, sent her letters so full of tedious advice on the need to persevere with lessons in music and dancing that she complained he was treating her like a child; more accurately, perhaps, he was trying to create another Juliette Récamier, who was renowned for her gracious movement and musical voice. In her husband's absence Désirée was escorted in Parisian society by two of his friends: Admiral Laurent Truguet, a bachelor of forty-nine who had been an ambassador in Madrid and a Minister of Marine; and Ange Chiappe, a forty-one year old ex-deputy of both the Convention and the Council of Five Hundred. While the Admiral was politically sound and reliable, Chiappe was under frequent police surveillance, for he was an independently minded Corsican, with a low opinion of all Bonapartes. Bernadotte's friendship with Chiappe – and his own outspoken remarks – were politically injudicious. When Joseph urged Napoleon to find his brother-in-law an active field command, he received the sharp rejoinder, 'You can take it from me that if that hot-headed southerner (*cette mauvaise tête meridionale*) goes on flinging muck at what my government does, instead of giving him the command he wants, I'll have him shot in the Place du Carrousel.' 'Is that a message you want me to pass on to him?', asked Joseph. 'No', Napoleon replied, 'it's a hint I am giving you as his friend and brother-in-law, so that you can give him sound advice to be more sensible.'

In the autumn of 1801 it became clear that there would be no invasion of England: peace preliminaries were signed on 1 October, even though the Treaty of Amiens was not concluded until the following March. Bernadotte stayed on in Brittany until late November, and while he was still with the Army of the West he received yet another disappointment. He would have liked to command the expedition which was sent to the Caribbean to restore French sovereignty over San Domingo (Haiti). That honour went, however, to Pauline Bonaparte's husband, General Leclerc, and within a year cost him his life, for yellow fever was rampant on the island. No one in Paris anticipated such terrible losses from sickness and when Pauline and Leclerc travelled down to the Brittany coast, Bernadotte was still sore from having been passed over. After entertaining the couple to dinner he exchanged angry words with Leclerc, which were duly reported to the First Consul, further lengthening the list of Gascon indiscretions. Yet, even so, Napoleon continued to seek a suitable post for Bernadotte: ambassador in Constantinople? Governor-general of Guadeloupe? Both suggestions were firmly rejected. Earlier Bernadotte had claimed that he wished to find happiness 'over the seas'. By now the First Consul, too, wished to see good mileage, preferably oceanic, keeping Paris and that wrong-headed southerner well apart.

Yet for much of the spring of 1802 Bernadotte was within a carriage drive of the capital, travelling in frequently from La Grange. It was a period of renewed political apprehension. In late January a constitutional innovation enabled the Consuls to purge the legislature of a group of twenty liberals, the so-called *Idéologues*, and replace them by more accommodating nominees. Among the 'wets' thrown out in this way were Pierre Daunou and Benjamin Constant; both belonged to that intellectual circle associated with Mme de Staël, and much admired by Bernadotte. According to Germaine de Staël, there now formed around the General a party of army commanders and veteran politicians who encouraged him to protest at the drift towards dictatorship. Bernadotte invariably insisted that the critics of the Consulate should keep within the law; but General Savary's memoirs maintain that while he would not himself countenance any plan to assassinate the First Consul, the action of some of his supporters amounted to treason. There was widespread talk of conspiracies, most of which Napoleon seems to have discounted, but he increased the powers of General Davout, commandant of the grenadiers of the Consular Guard. From March 1802 onwards Davout, like Fouché and Savary, maintained his own police intelligence service, giving particular attention to the generals.

On Easter Day – 18 April 1802 – the church bells rang out again over a France which was now formally reconciled to the papacy. To celebrate the new concordat Napoleon and Josephine drove in royal state from the Tuileries to hear Pontifical High Mass at the cathedral of Notre Dame. While Archbishop Boisgelin, who had preached at Louis XVI's coronation in 1775, was making certain that his sermon was appropriate for the occasion, the First Consul had his troops pass in review; and at the most sacred moment in the service, the Elevation of the Host, four battalions of infantry packed into the Gothic cathedral solemnly presented arms. Bernadotte, an agnostic who had never failed to respect the Church and its institutions during his campaigns, was present that Sunday; he had come by carriage, with Generals Augereau, Masséna and Macdonald as his companions. Like him, they were ill at ease, nagged by a republican conscience and alarmed by the mounting evidence of Napoleon's imperial pretensions. In later years Bernadotte claimed that, on the way to Notre Dame, there was a moment when he stopped the carriage and suggested the four Generals should call on the troops in the streets to follow their lead, arrest the First Consul and restore the true liberties of the Republic. On reflection, however, none of the four stepped down from the carriage which, having held up the whole procession, then resumed its journey to the cathedral. Everything about this account is hard to credit, except the good sense of his three companions in not attempting anything so rash. No other record of the day's events mentions the stopped carriage. Nor is there independent confirmation of Bernadotte's further claim that when, during the long service, he beckoned to an orderly and sent him for a glass of water, the guards around the First Consul stood on the alert for fear he was signalling the start of a coup.

If Bernadotte's tale was a Gasconade it nevertheless caught the mood of the day; it simplified with dramatic gestures the complex emotions common to hundreds of officers in the capital that April. For many veterans of the Jacobin armies remained puzzled by the speed with which the war between Church and Revolution had come to an end and by the welcome offered that spring to returning exiles who had once fled the embrace of a nation in arms. Yet, however much individual officers might deplore Napoleon's determination to impose a hierarchic structure on his new society, their will to oppose him actively was paralysed by admiration for his past and by recognition that rewards were coming easily to those whose services merited his confidence. Had the First Consul imposed upon France a tyrannical oligarchy, narrowly based and inflexible in its composition, the plots and conspiracies of 1802–04 would have offered a more serious challenge to his plans. All four Generals grumbling their way by carriage to Notre Dame that Sunday became under the Empire proud bearers of Marshal's batons and recipients of the wealth and privilege accompanying such honour.

In that spring of 1802 the strongest hostility came from Moreau's Army of the Rhine, so recently heroes of the Hohenlinden campaign. They looked upon themselves as the true republicans, unsullied by the grandeur of Italy and Egypt and resenting the publicity given to Napoleon's passage of the Alps and that narrowly won victory at Marengo. General Moreau himself pointedly stayed away from the Easter church parade, preferring to exercise his horses at Grosbois, his estate on the hills above the Marne valley. Soon Moreau anecdotes were circulating in Paris; when the *Moniteur* announced that the First Consul was instituting a Legion of Honour, it was said that Moreau had derisively invested his dog with a new collar. Unlike Bernadotte, he remained outside the protective fringe of the Bonaparte family. Even so, he was too important a figure for Fouché or Savary to threaten directly. But Davout, eager to prove the value of the newest intelligence service, decided to strike at Moreau indirectly. On 7 May two cavalry colonels, friends of Moreau and veterans of his campaigns, were arrested for planning the First Consul's assassination.

There was no shred of evidence against Colonel Donnadieu or Colonel Fournier, and they were never charged. After a few (highly unpleasant) months of detention they were released and re-instated in their old ranks. But, as Davout anticipated, the incident created a sensation. Five days after the arrests Anthony Merry, Britain's acting chargé d'affaires in Paris, reported to the Foreign Office that he believed in the existence of a conspiracy of Generals, intent on preventing the First Consul from usurping even greater authority. Davout welcomed this air of expectation; fear and rumour would flush out the military dissidents, he hoped. Not only would the arrests curb Moreau's activities; they might also deter Bernadotte. In case the Gascon was slow to take the hint, Davout arranged for a police spy to watch him, somewhat ostentatiously.

Unfortunately either Fouché or Savary had already assigned an agent to keep Bernadotte under surveillance, although more discreetly. The rivals, unaware they had been given similar assignments, successfully fabricated evidence against each other, both having pretended when they met and entered into conversation that they believed Bernadotte was the only man capable of overthrowing the despot Bonaparte. This particular farce was to have a second act, too. For when Davout's agent began to trail Bernadotte, the General was using Mme Clary's home in the Rue d'Aguesseau; and her sons-in-law, Joseph as well as Bernadotte, were furious at spotting an incompetent spy keeping her house and garden under observation. There was a stormy scene at the Tuileries, with Napoleon forced on the defensive. This ludicrous misadventure had lasting repercussions: for Bernadotte never forgave Davout, and the enmity between the two Marshals was to leave a mark on the general history of Europe.

Bernadotte's name had emerged unsullied from both the Aréna conspiracy and the Donnadieu-Fournier affair. But soon another police official was hot on his trail. Louis Dubois, an attorney's assistant before the Revolution, became Prefect of Police for metropolitan Paris under the Consulate – a good advancement, although far lower down the social ladder than Fouché or Generals Savary and Davout. But in the last days of May 1802 Dubois had a lucky break: the mistress of a Captain in the Army of the West brought him a collection of seditious leaflets (*placards*) posted to her lover from Rennes; and one named 'Moreau, Bernadotte, Jourdan, Masséna, Macdonald' and three other generals as being opposed to that 'petty tyrant who dictates laws to us'. Prefect Dubois at once reported the matter to the Tuileries and found that his news was of interest to the First Consul in person, especially when the army authorities discovered the recipient of the leaflets was both a junior officer recently serving under Bernadotte and also the brother of Moreau's principal aide-de-camp. An elated Dubois was told to investigate the matter but keep it secret from Fouché, who was himself under suspicion of protecting Jacobin associates of his days in the Convention.

To conceal plots from Fouché was, of course, impossible. His henchmen, master craftsmen in unsealing the correspondence of others, already knew about the leaflets. Within a few days they had even tracked down the printer. Had they worked painstakingly at their own pace they might have produced a formidable dossier. But there was now furious competition between Dubois and Fouché, whose agents discovered that the seditious writings had been brought to the printer by a junior officer named Bertrand. More ominously Lieutenant Bertrand was acting on the orders of General Edouard François Simon, Chief of Staff of the Army of the West from February 1801 and therefore a daily companion of Bernadotte throughout the seven months he had spent in Brittany that year. Both Simon and Bertrand were arrested at Rennes on 25 June 1802, little more than a month after Moreau's two colonels.

Yet once again nobody was brought to public trial. Simon and Bertrand denied that Moreau or Bernadotte knew of their activities – which seem, indeed, to have been no worse than a protest against Napoleon's acceptance of a life consulship. Both men were formally disgraced by court martial in early August; Bertrand probably became a police informer, after a term of imprisonment; General Simon spent seventeen months under detention on the island of Oléron, off Rochefort and La Rochelle, but was pardoned in January 1804 and served with such distinction in Portugal and Spain that in 1811 he was created a Baron. But, at the time, the First Consul was extremely angry, with Moreau who had ridiculed the whole affair and even more with Bernadotte, since it was clear that his constant disparagement of Consular government had encouraged Simon to frame his protest. Neither for the first time nor the last, Napoleon was heard by his aides to remark that Bernadotte deserved to be shot for his rash talk. The General was advised to keep away from the Tuileries until the storm blew over. In September the Paris newspapers reported the presence of the Bernadottes at Plombières, where husband and wife were taking the spa waters. When Charles James Fox made his famous visit to France that autumn he met Bernadotte, not in the Bonaparte family circle at Malmaison, but among Madame Récamier's dinner guests at Clichy. And when Julie, as had become her custom, interceded with her husband's brother for her sister's husband, she found the family bond wearing so thin that she left the Consular presence in tears.

In calmer moments Napoleon still believed his wisest course would be to offer the hot-headed (and careless-tongued) Southerner exiled promotion overseas: had he not often expressed a longing for the limitless horizons of the New World? Bernadotte was tempted by a proposal that he should become Captain-General and Governor of Louisiana, the old Bourbon colony which, in 1801, was retroceded to France by Spain. To the French, Louisiana implied much more than a firm foothold on the American continent; the territory stretched from the mouth of the Mississippi to the Rocky Mountains, an area as large as the American Union itself. Rumours of the offer went the rounds of the Parisian salons. Anthony Merry was so certain the General would accept the Governorship that he warned the Foreign Office in London how, 'when Bernadotte proceeds to Louisiana (which will be as soon as the armaments can be prepared) he is to take possession, at the same time, of the Floridas'. But the plans were not so advanced as Merry believed. Bernadotte would not be hurried into new responsibilities from a sense of duty; he had suffered that experience in Vienna. Before setting down his terms for the Louisiana post he consulted Lafayette, who was among the émigrés welcomed back to Consular France. At Lafayette's prompting, he demanded guarantees that he could take across the Atlantic at least three thousand young settlers and another three thousand good troops. Napoleon was indignant; 'I wouldn't do that much for one of my brothers', he protested. The offer went instead to General Victor, who accepted the post. That Victor never sailed off across the Atlantic is hardly surprising; non-voyages were becoming common for eminent Frenchmen in Nelson's time.

By December 1802 the First Consul's patience was sorely tried, as Joseph, Julie and Désirée recognised. Talleyrand, as Foreign Minister, came to the rescue. If a governor's mansion in New Orleans did not appeal to Bernadotte, then he could carry the honour of France up the Potomac, where President Jefferson was awaiting a pioneer envoy from Paris in his half-built White House that looked out towards the undomed Capitol. On New Year's Eve it was formally announced in the Paris newspapers that General Bernadotte would be France's Minister to the United States. At La Grange the Bernadottes began to prepare for their mission: Colonel Etienne Gérard would once again serve as military attaché; Dr Franzenberg was to be both physician and secretary; and Ange Chiappe was also attached to the minister's personal staff. Bernadotte received written confirmation of his appointment on 21 January 1801, with a recommendation that he should leave Paris for an Atlantic port in the near future.

He was still at La Grange ten weeks later; and on 1 April an exasperated Napoleon sent a peremptory note to Talleyrand requiring the Minister to the United States to set out next day for the coast. This appears to have been interpreted as a notional order, for it was not until 19 April that farewells were exchanged with the Clary family. As the carriages headed westwards, the General sighed sadly: 'This is perhaps the last time I shall see our country home', he said. 'I don't believe a word of it', Colonel Gérard replied crisply.

Five years back Bernadotte and Gérard had hurried to Vienna at breakneck speed. Their return to diplomacy was sedate, not least because the new Minister was accompanied by Désirée and Oscar, who was not yet four; a long, lingering drive down the Loire, with comfortable halts at Orléans, Blois and Tours, brought them to La Rochelle nine days later. Of the frigate which was to carry them to America, there was no sign: it had sailed for Guadeloupe. Another vessel took aboard urgent supplies for San Domingo and could not accommodate the minister, his companions and their baggage. Dutifully Bernadotte rode down to Rochefort, where he found the frigate *Sibella* fitting out, but she could not possibly be ready for sea until the second week of June. That would mean a wait of two more weeks, staying in a tedious *auberge*, with Désirée – a poor sailor – looking out across the bay to the grey Atlantic with mounting apprehension.

The Bernadottes never boarded the *Sibella*. When he arrived back at La Rochelle the General heard from the Foreign Ministry that, after negotiations with the American Minister in Paris, the whole of French Louisiana had been sold to the United States, thereby diminishing the importance of his mission to Washington. He also received a back copy of the *Moniteur* from which he discovered that, in the second week of May, the Peace of Amiens had broken down; France was accordingly once more at war with Britain. He wrote at once to Talleyrand, resigning for a second time from the diplomatic service; he wrote also to the First Consul informing him that he assumed 'public events' had put an end to his mission to America and offering 'my services and my sword' to the Republic; and, at greater length, he wrote, too, to his brother-in-law Joseph, explaining that it was not his fault that two frigates had sailed without him, asking Joseph to intercede with

Napoleon, and hoping he would soon find himself again in the field with a military command. Next day, with a welcome burst of speed, the whole party set off for Paris. Eight weeks after his sad farewell to La Grange, Bernadotte was back home again.

There, to his surprise, he remained, inactive for eleven months. For the First Consul had no use for the sword Bernadotte offered the Republic. His most pressing need was for ships. Although he might fume at Bernadotte's casual assumption that 'events' had cancelled the American mission, at least the *Sibella* would now be free for other operations: along the whole Atlantic coastline only five warships were fit for sea in the week Bernadotte made his trip from La Rochelle to Rochefort, and all of them were based on Brest. The renewal of the struggle with Britain had come sooner than the Ministry of Marine, or the Ministry of War, anticipated. General Mortier struck a personal blow at King George III by occupying the Electorate of Hanover without encountering much opposition; and throughout the year England remained on the alert against a French invasion. An army was massed on the heights behind Boulogne, while Napoleon went into residence at Pont-de-Briques; he pored over maps of southern England with Berthier at his side, and on a windswept November afternoon looked out from the cliffs above Ambleteuse and observed 'houses and movement' on the Kentish coast as clearly as 'one sees the Calvary' on Mont Valérien 'from the Tuileries'. But still he did not summon to Boulogne those Generals who, in the past, had given most attention to planning a cross-Channel invasion: Augereau (who was at Brest, examining the prospects for a landing in Ireland), Masséna (rusticated to Rueil) and Bernadotte (landscaping his estate at La Grange). When New Year gales battered the Channel, the possibility that Napoleon and Berthier could ferry 150,000 men to Kent and reach London within a week became as remote as the tunnel on which English caricaturists depicted his engineers labouring day after day.

The British met the invasion challenge by vigorous action at sea and by reverting to the cloak-and-dagger conspiracies in which Windham and Stuart had placed such faith a few years before. Lord Whitworth, ambassador in Paris during the Peace of Amiens, returned to London predicting that, given encouragement and leadership, the French people would rise against the tyrant who had deluded them into believing the hardships of war were over; a triumvirate of Moreau, Masséna and Bernadotte seemed to him the most likely replacement for the Consulate, should Napoleon sustain some fatal accident. The British accordingly gave ready backing to every enterprise designed to topple the Consulate. In the third week of August 1803 Georges Cadoudal, the Breton royalist whom Bernadotte failed to capture three years before, was smuggled in a Spanish brig from Hastings to the Normandy coast, whence he made his way to Paris and went into hiding. Soon afterwards General Pichegru slipped back into France and was able to make contact with Moreau on his Grosbois estate, seeking the support of this hardened republican for a muddled constitutional royalism. But when rumours of renewed plotting reached La Grange, Bernadotte was far too cautious to burn his fingers. He met Moreau twice in early February 1804 but acted circumspectly, and with good reason; for Cadoudal, Pichegru and Moreau were trailed by police spies and, to some extent, duped by Fouché and his agents.

Soon after Moreau's talks with Bernadotte, Pichegru and Cadoudal were arrested in central Paris in quick succession and Moreau himself was seized on the road to Grosbois. In his prison cell Pichegru either committed suicide or was strangled; Cadoudal was brought to trial and eventually guillotined, along with seven other accomplices. General Moreau, however, posed a problem for Napoleon. His trial for treason merely emphasised his popularity: each time the prisoner was brought to court, the sentries presented arms in his honour. The judges cleared him of high treason but sentenced him to two years' imprisonment for lesser actions against the interests of state. But to save Moreau the suffering of incarceration, Napoleon offered him exile; he left France for the United States, and eventually settled at Morrisville, on the Delaware River.

Bernadotte was alarmed by the arrest of Moreau, although the two Generals had never been close companions. He was concerned by the extent to which the First Consul allowed police agents to play upon his own suspicions. In this spring of 1804 Napoleon corresponded more closely to the tyrant depicted by his enemies than at any other time in his career. While the storm over Moreau's arrest was still shaking Paris, a French task force raided Baden, kidnapped the royalist military commander, the Duc d'Enghien, and brought him back to Vincennes, where he was executed ten hours later after a military tribunal had found him guilty of treasonable links 'with England'. The Bonaparte family, too, experienced the full blasts of Napoleon's anger. Lucien Bonaparte had continued to criticise his brother's Caesarism, notably on visits to Mme Récamier; and, having been left a widower in 1800, Lucien subsequently married a woman of whom Napoleon disapproved. Accordingly he, too, was sent into exile, although in Italy rather than across the Atlantic. On the night before his departure from Paris – just ten days after d'Enghien's execution – Lucien was visited by Bernadotte, and the two men stayed talking until dawn broke over the city.

So late as April 1804, Bernadotte might therefore be reckoned among the dissident Generals critical of Napoleon. Désirée, however, had throughout the previous months been seeking to heal the rift between her husband and her one-time suitor. On 6 March, for example, she was among fifteen women who joined over a hundred male guests dining in the Tuileries, at a time when her husband was judiciously unwell and Napoleon anxiously testing opinion over the Moreau affair. Eight weeks later Bernadotte was summoned to the Tuileries for a private audience with the First Consul. He went with some trepidation but found Napoleon at his most gracious and persuasive. It was, he told Juliette Récamier soon afterwards, 'not quite what I expected; Bonaparte wished to propose to me a treaty of alliance'. The First Consul insisted that the Nation had shown it accepted his rule, he argued that France needed the support of 'all her children', and he therefore urged Bernadotte 'not to hold apart' but 'march forward with me and with France'. To an appeal of this nature, there could be only one answer. 'I did not promise him affection', Bernadotte told Mme Récamier, 'but I promised him loyal support, and I shall keep my word.'

By this accord Napoleon won the backing of the republican soldier whom he regarded as his most formidable rival, once Moreau's influence was liquidated. But for Bernadotte to have spoken of 'a treaty of alliance' and not simply a reconciliation suggests that he anticipated material gains from his pledge of loyalty, and a few days later his first advancement for five years was made public. On 14 May the Paris newspapers reported that General Bernadotte was returning to active service, as Governor and Commander-in-Chief in Hanover. This news, however, was soon followed by a more sensational announcement, although one which outside observers had predicted more than a year before: for, on 18 May 1804, a legislative decree modelled on the 'senatus consultum' of classical Rome declared the government of the Republic 'entrusted to an Emperor' and proclaimed that 'Napoleon Bonaparte, at present First

Consul of the Republic, is Emperor of the French'; an additional clause, the only one subsequently submitted for approval by popular plebiscite, resolved that 'the Imperial dignity be hereditary'. Having breached the constitution by resort to ancient Rome, the new Emperor at once reverted to a practice of the French monarchy. The title 'Marshal of France' went back to the earliest days of the Capetian kings, but the dignity had been abolished by the Convention in 1793. Now, on the day after accepting the imperial title, Napoleon I announced the creation of fourteen active and four honorary Marshals of the Empire: the seventh name was that of General Jean Baptiste Bernadotte. On the list were several of his personal adversaries, including Berthier and Davout, but some good sound republican names were there, too – among them Jourdan, Augereau, Masséna and the one-time colleague of Danton, Guillaume Brune. The Marshalate, like the Legion of Honour, was intended to draw all factions in fighting France together under the one Emperor.

With a pleasant historical irony, it was in the palace of St Cloud that Bernadotte and nine other Marshals in Paris met on 23 May to take an oath to the Emperor and thank him for the dignity bestowed on them. While some, who would have contentedly buried Caesar under the Consulate, now dutifully came to praise him, Bernadotte at least spoke out honestly: 'Sir, I long believed France could flourish only under a republican government. That conviction guided me until experience showed me the error of my ways. I beg your Majesty to rest assured of my eagerness to implement any measures you may desire me to carry out.' Warmly Napoleon shook the Marshal's hand. When Bernadotte stepped back into the crowd of senior officers in the audience chamber, General Sarrazin congratulated him in a whispered aside on his conversion to the imperial ideal. As Sarrazin had frequently heard Bernadotte disparage Napoleon in private conversation, there was in his remarks an undertone of cynical doubt over the Marshal's sincerity. But, however he may have felt on other occasions, Bernadotte believed in the sentiments he sought to convey that Wednesday morning at St Cloud. He turned on Sarrazin and, with a Gascon flourish, declared in tones loud enough for the other Marshals to hear, 'I swear to you that, from this day on, Bonaparte shall have no truer friend than Bernadotte'.

Chapter 8
The Marshals Go To War

AFTER nearly a year of bored rustication at La Grange, Bernadotte welcomed the opportunity of serving the new Emperor
as virtual viceroy in a German Electorate. He left Paris a fortnight
after the ceremony at St Cloud and on 17 June reached Hanover,
to be greeted by gun salutes, the pealing of church bells and a guard
of honour. He was well received by the townsfolk, too. Over the
past eighteen months, the prosperity of the city's merchants had
suffered considerably, from both the severing of links with London
and the burden of maintaining an army of occupation, numbering
almost 30,000 men. They anticipated a recovery, under the protection of their new Governor, for he was already respected in Germany
as a general who had restrained the rapacity of his soldiery in the
Rhineland.

In these hopes they were not disappointed. Bernadotte was an
improvement on General Mortier, whose troops had hustled the
Duke of Cambridge out of his father's Electorate a year before.
Mortier's nominee as commandant, General Schinner, was an Alsatian martinet hated throughout the city. In contrast to the arrogance
of Mortier and Schinner, the Marshal seemed gracious and generous
in manner. Within a few weeks he was giving assurances of just
administration, both to the civic authorities and to the University
of Göttingen; and by August the Emperor was so alarmed by
the reports reaching him from northern Germany that he sent
Bernadotte an anxious warning: the Hanoverian merchants were a
wily community; they would pull wry faces and give plausible
reasons for non-compliance whenever they were asked for money.
But the Marshal was meticulous over such matters. He gave orders
to prepare a careful survey of Hanover's resources and means of
raising revenue and was thus able to send convincing statistics to

Paris. By early November he even succeeded in persuading Napoleon to divert money raised elsewhere in Germany to bolster support for France in the Electorate; and in the spring he eased the threat of famine by securing the release of wheat held in French military depots. Not surprisingly, Bernadotte remained popular with the Hanoverians throughout his fourteen months in the city. The vice-regal experience was of lasting value to him. He was delighted by the spacious tranquillity of his official residence outside Hanover, where the landscaped limes and lindens and the cluster of playing fountains were even finer than the Emperor could enjoy at St Cloud. In later years at Stockholm, 300 miles further north, he sought to recapture this quiet elegance of Schloss Herrenhausen at Drottningholm palace and, on a far smaller scale, in his summer villa at Rosendal.

Since Hanover was the only territorial possession of George III to pass under French rule it is hardly surprising that the British Government closely scrutinised Bernadotte's activities. Their principal source of information for the first months of his governorship were the reports sent by Sir George Rumbold, an experienced diplomat who had served the Foreign Office as chargé d'affaires in the Hanse towns since 1801, with his formal residence beside the River Elbe, in the neutral Free City of Hamburg, a hundred miles north of Hanover itself. Napoleon's counter-intelligence service believed, not without reason, that Rumbold was Britain's chief spymaster in Germany, and in the second week of October Bernadotte received a letter from Fouché passing on an 'express order of the Emperor': Rumbold must be abducted and his personal papers seized.

Militarily this was a simple operation: French cavalrymen, in civilian clothes, snatched Rumbold from his villa on the night of 24–25 October and brought him to Hanover. His papers were sent to Paris – where nearly three hundred confiscated documents were still in the Archives Nationales more than 180 years later. The unfortunate Rumbold was received with courtesy by Bernadotte, who was able to assure him that he was not about to be executed. However, when he was conveyed to Paris, Sir George was imprisoned in the Temple; he was only released and repatriated on the intervention of King Frederick William III of Prussia, with whom both Napoleon and Bernadotte were seeking at that moment to improve their personal relations. The British made good propaganda out of the Marshal's 'brigandage' in abducting a diplomat from a neutral city. Privately, however, it was acknowledged that he treated his captive considerately.

Soon after Rumbold's abduction Bernadotte was summoned back to Paris for the Emperor's coronation. He was among the prominent dignitaries in Notre Dame on 2 December, the official painting of the ceremony by David showing him standing expressionless behind Cardinal Fesch and to the right of Caulaincourt, Eugène de Beauharnais, Talleyrand and Berthier. Other worthies, resident in Paris, enjoyed official status at the Imperial Court: thus Talleyrand was Great Chamberlain and Berthier Master of the Royal Hunt. Bernadotte, although not himself a functionary, was ceremonial bearer of the Imperial Collar in the coronation procession and was therefore resplendent in the new court dress: velvet cloak, knee breeches, silk stockings, high cravat and a large jabot together with a small cape with deep facings and a Troubadour hat, trimmed with ostrich feathers. This theatrical costume looked better on ex-Sergeant Belle-Jambe than on several colleagues of greater girth and smaller stature. Unlike Davout, Ney and other veteran campaigners, Bernadotte enjoyed the formality and improvised protocol of Court life. Désirée, too, revelled in the fêtes and receptions which accompanied the coronation. To board over the auditorium of the Opéra in order that the Marshals might give a ball in honour of their Emperor and Empress seemed to her a fine gesture, which was matched by the determination of the Legislative Assembly to have the galleries of the Tuileries filled with spring flowers – oleanders, lilies and lilacs forced into full blossom so as to defy the sleet and snow of those December days. For some older friends this transformation from a nominally egalitarian Republic into a hothouse Empire was unbearable; why, Désirée wondered from time to time, did they no longer hear from Ange Chiappe?

But although the Bernadottes may have lost the friendship of one Corsican, they continued throughout the winter to bask in the approbation of the island's most illustrious citizen. Napoleon gave lavish financial support to all his Marshals, granting endowments to supplement their high salaries as regular officers of the army. So generous were these gifts that, by 1809, they were bringing the Bernadottes a supplementary income of 292,000 francs, a considerable sum, even though barely a fifth of that enjoyed by Berthier. Nor were all these rewards purely financial. On New Year's Day in

1805 Fouché was instructed by the Emperor to arrange for the disposal of Moreau's former properties, for which the exiled General's family had received nominal compensation: the estate out at Grossbois would pass to Marshal Berthier; but Moreau's town house – 28, Rue d'Anjou – was to go to Marshal Bernadotte, with immediate possession.

This mansion in the Rue d'Anjou, once the Dutch embassy, was among the most splendid in the Faubourg Saint Honoré. Since the Empress Josephine had already purloined some of Moreau's furniture for Malmaison, the Emperor offered the Bernadottes a further 200,000 francs, which enabled Désirée to fit out their new possession with elegant simplicity. For the next eighteen years she looked upon 28, Rue d'Anjou, as her home. Half a century later, when she was a widowed Queen, long since settled in Sweden, the Emperor Napoleon III forbade the mansion's demolition in case she should wish to return to Paris. Only in the 1860s, after Désirée's death, was Baron Haussmann allowed to thrust the Boulevard Malesherbes across the site.

Bernadotte returned to Hanover in mid-February, 1805; but it was not until the early summer that Désirée travelled up through western Germany to join him in the Electorate. Like her husband, she was delighted by the Herrenhausen – where, on 15 June, she took part in a fancy-dress ball. But her sojourn in Hanover was brief. By the third week of August Napoleon, who spent much of the summer with his invasion army at Boulogne, had come to recognise that the Channel constituted a greater obstacle than a mere 'ditch which will be leaped'. He feared the machinations of London, for British funds were encouraging Russia, Austria and perhaps Prussia to come together in a Third Coalition and renew the war in Germany. Rather than wait for his enemies to strike at his empire, Napoleon ordered an about-turn for his newly-named Grande Armée. By 28 August the finest army ever raised by the French was trudging steadily eastwards towards the lower Rhine and the Danube. Next day Bernadotte was told that his army of occupation in Hanover would constitute I Corps of the Grande Armée; he was to march these 15,000 men to Würzburg, as unostentatiously as possible. There he would meet the main army of Napoleon's Bavarian ally; and the combined force would then be poised to descend on the enemy flank, cutting communications between Vienna, the Russian expeditionary force under General

Kutuzov, and the principal Austrian army in the field, nominally commanded by Archduke Ferdinand, with General Mack at his side.

It was six years since Bernadotte last went to war, and by 1805 he had become, at 42, the oldest of the six corps commanders in the campaign. Nevertheless he kept his men in as good order as on that long march from Coblenz to Milan eight years before. The I Corps entered Würzburg on 27 September, weary after ten days' foot slogging in full kit along 350 kilometres of dusty roads southwards from Göttingen. After five days of rest I Corps, together with more than 20,000 Bavarians, went forward again; they formed the outer rim of an encircling arc, pivoting upon Ulm so as to reach the Danube at Ingoldstadt. To reduce the length of the march the Marshal was ordered to cut across the territory of neutral Prussia at Ansbach ('Anspach' on the maps of the time). Once again the iron discipline which he maintained prevented any disturbances during this, much-publicised, violation of Prussian territory. 'I am leaving nothing undone to see that our passage through Anspach is as little burdensome as possible', Bernadotte reported to Berthier, the chief of staff of the Grande Armée. 'I am bivouacking only on lands where the harvest has been taken in, and I am paying for everything at full price with ready cash.' Within five days he was at Ingoldstadt. As yet, not a shot had been fired, nor any blood shed during the march.

Cautiously (and, by Berthier's reckoning, far too slowly) I Corps moved south of the Danube, with Bernadotte using his Bavarian troops as a vanguard to free their homeland from the Austrians. On 12 October Bernadotte entered Munich, which became his headquarters for the next fortnight. Briefly it seemed as if his return to active campaigning might pass without a major battle. For in that October Napoleon was to achieve the greatest triumph of purely strategic planning in his career: his enveloping movement cut off the principal Austrian army, around Ulm; and on 20 October General Mack surrendered, Archduke Ferdinand having slipped away northwards so as to avoid the humiliation of a Habsburg surrendering to a Bonaparte.

Mack's capitulation at Ulm prevented 50,000 crack troops in Emperor Francis's army from taking any further part in the war. So elated was Napoleon at this triumph that, on the eve of the surrender, he wrote to Bernadotte as if the whole campaign was almost over: of the main Austrian army, he said, 'nothing is left but debris'; and he poured scorn on the enemy concentrations still gathering in the east: 'What can an army of 30,000 Russians and 25,000 Austrians do against us today?' he asked, with a characteristic flourish of rhetoric. Should Kutuzov, or any Austrian army corps, come up from the East, 'the turn of your army and the Bavarians will come', Napoleon explained. This was an over-confident assessment: when Kutuzov reached Braunau on 23 October the combined strength of the Austro–Russian force along the River Inn was 58,000 men; and there were still four other Austrian armies in the field. Momentarily there was some hesitation over the next objective: Napoleon himself came up northwards through Munich to Linz, where he lingered with renewed uncertainty; Bernadotte seized Salzburg, which he entered on 30 October; and Murat, largely on his own initiative, pressed forward towards the tempting prize of Vienna.

Winter came exceptionally early that year. Driving sleet during much of the last week of October left the lower roads thick with mud and there was already heavy snow in the more mountainous districts. As the Austro–Russian vanguard began to fall back towards Moravia, Napoleon improvised a new strategic plan, seeking to catch Kutuzov, like Mack, by an enveloping manoeuvre. Murat and Lannes were to enter Vienna, seize the Danube bridge and form an outer arc, pivoting on St Polten; and Bernadotte was expected to bring I Corps hurriedly north-eastwards from Salzburg to Melk and then cross the Danube. Murat and Lannes were successful on 12 November, but it was impossible for Bernadotte to lead his men over some 120 miles of difficult terrain and cross the Danube beneath the fortified abbey of Melk without at least two days of preparation. River crossings were a familiar problem for the veteran of the Rhine and the Tagliamento. But, after the heavy rain and snow, the Danube was a broad and fast-flowing stream that month. There were no pontoons, only fourteen small boats, and a landing stage which collapsed under the unexpected weight of traffic. Napoleon had wanted Bernadotte and his corps north of the Danube by Thursday, 14 November, at the latest. The main body of men did not set out until the Friday night, with a strong icy cold wind blowing across the open land beneath the rock on which the abbey stood guard over the entrance to the Wachau defile. It was Saturday morning before Bernadotte led his forward troops north-eastwards away from the Danube and towards Moravia. Long before then the wily Kutuzov was clear of Napoleon's trap.

Relations between Bernadotte and his Emperor had remained amicable ever since the creation of the Marshalate. Now, however, after the Melk delay, they plunged to a new low. 'I am consoled by the knowledge that Your Majesty is well aware of the difficulty of getting an army across a river where there is no bridge', Bernadotte wrote, hopefully. But His Majesty was disinclined to make allowances: 'Bernadotte', he wrote to his brother Joseph, 'has made me lose a day, and on a day depends the destiny of the world.' He complained that 'the glory' of entering Munich and Salzburg had gone to Bernadotte's head: perhaps failing health was making him lethargic, Napoleon added. Berthier's comments on the delay at Melk were even more caustic and, suitably embellished, reached Bernadotte's ears.

Yet, once across the Danube, the Marshal wasted no time. He thrust northwards and established his headquarters at the town of Iglau (now Jihlava, in Czechoslovakia), for there was now little doubt that a decisive battle would be fought in Moravia, on the plateaux west of the wooded Carpathian foothills. By the end of November the Russians and Austrians had brought together an army of about 85,000 men, concentrated between Brünn (Brno) and Olmutz (Olomouc); Emperor Francis and the young Tsar Alexander I were with their troops; and it was Napoleon's intention to tempt the enemy to attack what they assumed was a numerically smaller force while summoning Davout's III Corps from Vienna and Bernadotte's I Corps from Iglau to provide such powerful reinforcements that the balance of battle would swing in favour of the French.

At mid-morning on Friday, 29 November, a courier from Napoleon reached Iglau with orders for Bernadotte. He was to leave the Bavarians to garrison Iglau and come forward at once with his French regiments, the original I Corps with whom he had set out from Hanover nine weeks before; and he was to let his men know that a great battle was imminent. By dusk on Saturday I Corps had marched fifty-six miles across a frozen countryside to the plateau beyond Brno, looking out towards Austerlitz, a small town now known as Slavkov, which had sprung up around the principal estate of the Kaunitz family. Napoleon had his headquarters on a knoll above the hamlet of Schlapanitz, about nine miles south-east of

Brno, and Bernadotte bivouacked some three miles to the north, close to the main road to Olomouc. When on Sunday morning Captain Lejeune, one of Berthier's staff officers, rode over to I Corps headquarters he was surprised and impressed to find Bernadotte, stripped to the waist despite the freezing temperature, vigorously working his way through routine gymnastic exercises. 'Mon cher ami', the Marshal explained, 'I am bracing myself up and taking a bath of good air' – a Gascon eccentricity duly relayed to those who had expressed concern about his health.

That Sunday – 1 December – was an anxious day for Napoleon. Despite a slight thaw the numerous ponds and lakes around Austerlitz were covered by a deceptively thin film of ice, while surface mud above the frozen ground made the tracks and primitive roads slippery and, in places, impassable. Austro–Russian movements confirmed Napoleon's assumption that the enemy would attack his right flank, enabling him to keep I Corps concealed behind high ground on his left flank, ready for a counter-attack. But, although Bernadotte had already brought I Corps to the arena of battle, there was still no news of Davout's III Corps, ten thousand men hurrying northwards in a fifty-hour forced march from Vienna. Not until dusk did the Emperor learn that his outer patrols were in contact with the vanguard of the III Corps. It was almost midnight before Davout reached Imperial Headquarters, where Napoleon had spent much of the evening in consultation with the six other Marshals on the battlefield – Bernadotte, Berthier, Bessières, Lannes, Murat, and Soult. All, including Davout, were around the Emperor next morning, the first anniversary of his coronation, for an eve of battle briefing, as they watched the sun break through the fog which shrouded the enemy positions away to the east. Count Ségur, who was present that morning, later recalled that when the Emperor gave his orders to Bernadotte, his tone became 'more clipped and more imperious'. It was as if he expected dissent, at a moment in the campaign when there was no time for argument.

The Russians and Austrians launched their main attack southwestwards across the French front line before seven in the morning so as to clear the high ground known as the Pratzen Heights in the fog; they planned to strike at Davout's tired men along the Vienna road and then wheel right to encircle the principal French force as it resisted a subsidiary attack along the Brno–Olomouc road. Napoleon allowed the Russians to push forward across the Pratzen

Heights, but at half-past eight ordered Soult to attack the enemy right flank with support from Bernadotte's I Corps on his left. Soon all the Russian and Austrian troops were falling back from the Heights on to the woods and pheasantries of Kaunitz's Austerlitz estate. Fighting in the centre of the line died away about half-past nine and the French brought up cannon and improvised a defensive position on the Pratzen slopes while the battle continued to be fiercely contested to the north and south of the Heights. In the early afternoon, as snow clouds blotted out the pale winter sun, a thousand horsemen of the Russian Imperial Guard launched a desperate assault against Soult's corps; they galloped up the slopes of the Pratzen, the sheer impetus of their charge breaking the French line. This was the critical moment of the battle. Bernadotte, away to the north, saw the French defenders waver and, on his own initiative, sent a division forward to take the pressure off Soult, who also received aid from Napoleon's Guard cavalry. It was this action which shifted the balance of the battle in Napoleon's favour; two of the finest regiments of the Russian army lost more than five hundred dead during that ghastly attempt to recover the Pratzen Heights. Bernadotte pursued the Russians eastwards – far too hesitantly, according to his later critics. Yet his caution made little difference to the outcome of the battle: by two o'clock in the afternoon there was no doubt that Austerlitz had given Napoleon the decisive victory he required to end the campaign.

While Tsar Alexander sought to pull his shattered army back across the frontier into Russian Poland, the Austrians requested an immediate armistice. Bernadotte established his headquarters ten miles south-east of Austerlitz, at Zaroviče, on the road to Hungary. Not far away the burnt-out shell of a windmill stood over a small depression in the Carpathian foothills and there, in the early afternoon of 4 December, he joined Soult in attendance on Napoleon. The two Marshals stood a few deferential paces behind the Emperor of the French as he condescended to receive the defeated 'Emperor of the Germans' – as Napoleon described Francis – and dictate his terms for peace with Austria. Bernadotte remained a silent witness of this humiliating episode in Habsburg history.

Napoleon was well satisfied with I Corps's contribution to his victory, despite the coolness he had shown towards their commander on the eve of battle. But the Marshal's immediate future was in doubt. He could not return to Hanover, for the Emperor Napoleon offered the Electorate to Prussia to induce King Frederick William III to accept a French alliance rather than enter the war on the side of Russia. Nevertheless, Frederick William agreed to cede the small province of Ansbach, the duchy whose neutrality Bernadotte had violated in his march to the Danube in the previous October; and, with a nice touch of irony, the Emperor now appointed the Marshal as Governor-General of Ansbach. The ducal *Residenz* was not so fine as Schloss Herrenhausen, but Bernadotte was able to entertain there in some style. Once again, he pleased the townsfolk by the apparent impartiality with which he raised taxes and imposed administrative reforms. In those early months of 1806 Napoleon was generous in ennobling his family and kinsfolk by marriage; and it was believed, not least by the Marshal himself, that Bernadotte would soon be created Duke of Ansbach.

This assumption misread Napoleon's intentions. Until the late summer of 1806, when the Emperor of the French became Protector of the Confederation of the Rhine, the political boundaries of the new Germany could only be drawn lightly and provisionally on the map. Already, however, the shape of Napoleonic Italy was sharply defined: the Emperor had been crowned King of Italy in Milan in the previous May and his stepson, Eugène de Beauharnais, installed as Viceroy a month later; and at the end of March 1806 Joseph Bonaparte was proclaimed King of Naples and Sicily. Napoleon originally proposed to Joseph that he should have with him in Naples those two southern hotheads, Bernadotte and Masséna, each with princely titles and endowments. Upon reflection, however, the Emperor hesitated over settling two such strong-minded and self-willed military commanders at the Court of a brother who did not always agree with his own policies. Masséna soon dropped out of the reckoning but Napoleon still looked upon Bernadotte as a potential rival, whose collaboration could best be assured by identifying him so closely with the new Imperial structure that no one would remember his former Republican sympathies. Two small papal states, Benevento and Ponte Corvo, were incorporated in Joseph's Kingdom: the Emperor 'converted them into two duchies' and proposed that Benevento should be assigned to his Foreign Minister, Talleyrand, while Ponte Corvo should go to Bernadotte. 'You understand', Napoleon told King Joseph, 'that when I bestow the title of Duke and Prince upon Bernadotte, it is out of consideration for your wife, for I have in my army Generals who have served me better and upon whose loyal attachment I can rely more confidently. But it seems to me appropriate that the brother-in-law of the Queen of Naples should have a distinguished rank at your Court'. On 6 July 1806 Marshal Bernadotte was formally created Prince and Duke of Ponte Corvo as 'testimony of our gratitude for the services he has rendered to our crown'. Désirée thereupon became 'Her Serene Highness the Princess of Ponte Corvo', a lower ranking than her sister, Queen Julie of Naples and Sicily, enjoyed but reasonable compensation for having not quite married General Bonaparte eleven years before.

Neither of their Serene Highnesses ever visited Ponte Corvo, a principality with barely half as many inhabitants as Désirée's birthplace, Marseilles; and its revenue was so small that Napoleon felt obliged to guarantee its endowment. But the princely honour excited envy; it is hard to escape the feeling that when the Marshals went to war for France, they also went to war with each other. Most of the Marshalate grudgingly recognised the merits of Berthier, the invaluable chief-of-staff who became Sovereign Prince of Neuchâtel in March 1806, and they were prepared to accept that Murat, as the Emperor's brother-in-law, had some claim to be created Grand Duke of Berg and Cleves. But why honour 'that miserable Ponte Corvo', as Davout called the new Serene Highness? Had he not been late in crossing the Danube and slow in pursuing the Russians after Austerlitz? No other dukedoms were bestowed on Napoleon's military commanders for two more years, an interlude in which feeling against Bernadotte ran so high that the disappointed status-seekers took delight in discrediting him. If in honouring Bernadotte the Emperor intended to raise him to eminent and unpopular isolation, he achieved his purpose. But there is no evidence that Napoleon's mind, however subtle, made a calculation so Machiavellian in design.

The Marshals were at war again by the autumn. The Napoleonic re-organisation of Germany in the summer of 1806 provoked Frederick William III of Prussia to send an ultimatum which reached Paris on 2 October. By then, however, Prussia's cumbersome mobilisation had been so meticulously observed by French intelligence agents that Napoleon was able to draw up his plans for a lightning campaign which would rout his newest enemy before Tsar Alexander could bring a Russian army to Frederick William's assistance. Bernadotte was ordered to take command of I Corps again: he would concentrate his 21,000 men at Nuremberg and, together with Murat's cavalry, form the vanguard of an advance north-eastwards through Saxony (Prussia's ally) on Leipzig and ultimately Berlin. Behind Bernadotte and Murat would follow Davout's III Corps. Six army corps would move closely together, each in theory ready to support the other, seeking to envelop and stifle the enemy, as at Ulm exactly a year before.

The vanguard crossed into Saxony on Wednesday, 8 October, advancing through the Thuringian Forest to take the town of Schleiz by dusk on Thursday, after a sharp battle with a small Prussian force. Over the following five days I Corps trudged north-eastwards through seventy-two miles of difficult wooded country, with Napoleon, Berthier and all the apparatus of military headquarters well behind them. Somewhere to the north of the forest was the Prussian army, with the Duke of Brunswick, Frederick the Great's nephew, once more serving as commander-in-chief, as in 1792. By Sunday Napoleon had clear information that the Duke had concentrated his forces around Weimar and Erfurt, further west than the Emperor had anticipated. This movement puzzled him, reports from outriders making him frequently modify his plans over the next days. He had no doubt, however, that the main body of his troops should change their line of march, wheeling to the left in as orderly manner as on a parade ground; Bernadotte's I Corps now became, not the spearhead of an advancing column, but the right flank of an enveloping crescent. Yet still Napoleon was uneasy. During Monday he dictated three sets of battle plans, each determined by fresh information about the enemy's movements. Unfortunately by now Bernadotte was so far ahead that there was a considerable lapse of time before orders could reach him. Moreover, perhaps because of Napoleon's tactical vacillation, the directives sent out by Berthier from headquarters were dangerously ambiguous. Here was a recipe for confusion, if not for disaster.

Napoleon's strategic assessment was sound: the French crescent formation closed in upon the weakly guarded Prussian left flank in the open, rolling countryside beyond the River Saale; and on Tuesday, 14 October, two battles were fought within thirteen miles of each other. On high ground to the north-west of the old university city of Jena Napoleon routed one section of the Prussian force while, on the plains of Auerstädt, Marshal Davout defeated the main body of Brunswick's army, a force almost twice as large as his own III

Corps. In a single day's fighting the Grande Armée wrecked what remained of Frederick the Great's antique war machine; the Duke of Brunswick himself was mortally wounded.

Bernadotte missed both battles, thereby incurring the sternest censure from his Emperor, and with good reason. Early on the previous afternoon – Monday, 13 October – Murat and Bernadotte entered Naumburg, a small city on the right bank of the River Saale, within sight of the battlefield of Rossbach where, six years before the Marshal was born, Frederick had (as he wrote) 'saved the reputation and honour of the nation' by a great victory over the French. The two Marshals knew that Napoleon anticipated a battle in the same region of Saxony, although not until Wednesday. Some three hours after reaching Naumburg Murat received orders to bring his cavalry as swiftly as possible south-westwards to Dornburg, sixteen miles away, with Bernadotte's slower moving infantry and artillery following him. Murat left almost immediately and, at six o'clock on Monday evening, Bernadotte sent a message to Berthier informing him that, as his men were weary from their five days of marching, he would set out in half an hour, make the journey in easy stages and be at Dornburg by daybreak. Neither Imperial Headquarters nor the two Marshals themselves appreciated the difficulties of the rocky terrain, especially around Dornburg, an overgrown village, dominated by three separate hilltop castles. Murat's cavalry did not reach the battlefield of Jena until after midday on Tuesday.

Yet if Bernadotte had adhered to the timetable he outlined to Berthier, all would have been well, even though the battle was fought a day earlier than anticipated. However, shortly before eight o'clock on Monday evening, he received a visit from Davout, who was bivouacked four miles away, near the bridge across the Saale at Kosen. There had been a change of plan, Davout informed him: fresh orders would be sent from headquarters in the morning. Bernadotte therefore decided 'to halt my troops where they are and await further commands', as he wrote to Berthier. At 3 A.M. Davout heard from Imperial Headquarters that he was to cross the Saale and take the road for Apolda, where he could fall on the enemy's rear should the Prussians pull back from Jena: 'If Marshal Bernadotte is to be found with you, you might march together. But the Emperor hopes that he will be in the position which he has indicated to him at Dornburg', wrote Berthier, ambiguously. Davout rode over to

I Corps headquarters again but Bernadotte firmly rejected any suggestion they should 'march together'. He reverted to the original plan of a (somewhat belated) night-march down the Dornburg road, for his men were already astride this route which, if left uncovered by troops, might have provided the retreating Prussians with a line of escape to Leipzig. Strategically it made good sense for Davout's III Corps to cover the left bank on the Apolda Road and Bernadotte's I Corps to guard the right bank.

No one could foresee on that foggy morning how, after marching a mere five miles from his bivouac, Davout would stumble across the main Prussian army at Auerstädt. Nor could anyone anticipate that Bernadotte would have such difficulty in getting I Corps through the narrow Saale defiles that he did not reach Dornburg until eleven o'clock. By then Napoleon was heavily engaged at Jena, and Davout in danger of defeat on his left flank at Auerstädt. Subsequently Davout complained that 'the wretched Ponte Corvo' had deliberately rejected his appeals for reinforcements. It is clear from the map that when the first cannon opened up at Auerstädt Bernadotte's troops were already so far south on the Camberg–Dornburg road that they were separated from III Corps by two rivers, each flowing through rocky ravines. Nevertheless, it would have been possible to detach his cavalry division, sending it over the Saale bridge at Camberg and across the River Ilm at Sulza, and it could then have taken Blücher's corps at Auerstädt on the right flank by midday. Yet rather than send troops to aid a Marshal with whom he remained on extremely bad terms in what he thought was strategically a sideshow engagement, Bernadotte kept his Corps intact for service with the Emperor – for, like everyone else (including Napoleon), he assumed that the decisive battlefield was outside Jena. Not a shot was fired by I Corps that day, although Bernadotte could rightly claim that in the mopping up operations his troops captured five cannon intact and took over a thousand Prussian and Saxon prisoners.

Although too proud to admit his error, Bernadotte soon realised that he had gravely misunderstood Napoleon's intentions that Monday night. At once he sought to save his reputation, leading the pursuit of the shattered Prussians in collaboration with two other Marshals who had not been heavily engaged at Jena-Auerstädt, Soult and Murat. On Friday, 17 October, he stormed the walled fortress of Halle, fighting desperately with inferior numbers and that impulsive valour that had won him Gradisca nearly ten years before. 'Bernadotte stops at nothing. Some day that Gascon will get caught', Napoleon commented enigmatically when he reached Halle on Sunday.

By then 'that Gascon' was in full pursuit of the enemy, thrusting deep into old Prussia and covering a hundred miles in the first week after Jena-Auerstädt. He crossed the Elbe by a bridge of boats at Barby on 22 October, took the city of Brandenburg three days later, and was soon chasing his main quarry, General Blücher, in a huge arc across the plains of northern Germany. Meanwhile, further to the east, Potsdam, Spandau, Kustrin and Stettin surrendered to the French with little resistance; and, on 27 October, in recognition of his victory at Auerstädt thirteen days before, Napoleon granted Marshal Davout the honour of leading the first triumphant entry of foreign troops into Berlin. By the last day of the month Blücher's weakly armed corps of 22,000 men was the sole Prussian force capable of offering co-ordinated resistance to the invader.

On several occasions Bernadotte called on Blücher to surrender; but in vain. At last, on 5 November, the old Prussian fox took refuge in the free city of Lübeck, with I Corps and Soult and Murat close behind. Next day the French forced their way into Lübeck, Bernadotte struggling desperately to prevent his troops from sacking the city. Only then did Blücher agree to capitulate; he had, he claimed, run out of ammunition. On the afternoon of 7 November he surrendered to Bernadotte: it was a moment of humiliation which, even during his last frenzied years of adulation, Prussia's great military hero could never wipe from his mind.

Bernadotte's triumphant pursuit of Blücher and the prompt despatch of more than fifty captured regimental standards at least wrung from the Emperor a letter of lukewarm praise. If reminiscences from St Helena may be believed, immediately after Jena Napoleon had given his signed approval for the Marshal's court-martial when he changed his mind on thinking of the distress it would cause Désirée, Julie and Joseph. Gradually the tension died away. Bernadotte, who did not meet Napoleon personally between 9 October and 8 December, still had personal enemies at headquarters – notably Davout and Berthier – but he had his champions, too. He could count on support from Marshal Lefebvre and Bessières, from Augereau (whose VII Corps had been in the thick of the fighting at Jena) and, on this occasion, from Murat as well. Nevertheless it remained hard for him to shake off a reputation for tardiness in offering assistance to those members of the Marshalate whom he considered his juniors in standing; and the feud with Davout dragged on until the fall of the Empire.

The assault on Lübeck lasted no more than a day. Yet ultimately it had a deeper significance in Bernadotte's life than any earlier episode of his military career. For the Prussians were not the only enemy troops occupying the city; among the regimental colours which Bernadotte sent as trophies to Napoleon were the first Swedish banners captured by the Grande Armée. Although King Gustav IV Adolf joined the Third Coalition against France in 1805, Sweden had so far taken little part in a war which remained distant from her lands. The collapse of the Prussian army created an unexpected power vacuum in northern Europe. French troops suddenly swept northwards to threaten not so much mainland Sweden as the borders of Swedish Pomerania, that coastal region around Stralsund and Peenemünde which for almost two centuries gave the Swedes a foothold south of the Baltic. There was a rapid realignment of Sweden's expeditionary force, which had been deployed in Lauenburg, and by the first week of November 1500 troops – mostly from the province of Ostergotland, around Norrköping – were in Lübeck awaiting vessels to take them to the island of Rugen or to Stralsund. It was as a generous custodian of these prisoners that Bernadotte made his entry into Swedish history.

Generals taken captive were never subjected to the indignities of close arrest as prisoners of war, and the Marshal arranged for the Swedish commander, Count Gustav Mörner, to be lodged with him and with some distinguished French exiles in one of the fine gabled houses of the old Hanseatic city. Never before had Bernadotte found an opportunity to converse with an officer from Sweden and, as Mörner's contemporary account shows, he was genuinely interested in the country's affairs. Perhaps he remembered that the only other Béarnais to win a Marshal's baton, Jean de Gassion, had served alongside the greatest of Sweden's soldier kings. Yet it is probable that, at the time, he was training his mind to serve Napoleon in future military operations along the shores of the western Baltic or the Kattegat, for there was no military expert on Scandinavia at French headquarters. 'Was it not more natural for Norway to be joined to Sweden than to Denmark?', Mörner reported his host as having asked at table on one occasion. Whatever the motive for the Marshal's desire for enlightenment on Baltic problems, Count Mörner was deeply impressed. So, too, were the Swedish soldiers who, on the Marshal's orders, were well fed and repatriated to Ostergotland. They carried back home with them tales of the Lübeckers' satisfaction at the Prince of Ponte Corvo's fair-mindedness in maintaining order within their port and city: why otherwise would the Council of Lübeck have presented Bernadotte with six saddle horses on the eve of his departure, in the hope that a 'benefactor whose remembrance shall ever be dear to us' would return 'as an honoured guest' in time of peace? Such sentiments went beyond the formal courtesies of a City Corporation thankful to be rid of a conquering soldier. His behaviour in Lübeck ensured that Bernadotte became a living legend in Ostergotland more than two years before a palace revolution in Stockholm first threw in doubt the succession to the Swedish throne.

Chapter 9
Changing Fortunes

B ERNADOTTE'S first encounter with Swedish troops soon
became for him no more than a passing incident in an unexpectedly protracted winter campaign. Napoleon had hoped his lightning
war on Prussia would give France a decisive victory in the East so
speedily that Tsar Alexander would not risk putting a Russian army
in the field. But French conduct in occupied Berlin incensed the
Tsar; he was especially outraged by Napoleon's publication of royal
letters captured in Charlottenburg Palace, including Alexander's
own correspondence with Queen Louise. The Tsar announced that
Russia would wage war against the French 'for the finest and most
just of causes' (unspecified); he planned to augment his regular
troops by conscripted serfs so as to oppose France by a front-line army
of 600,000 men. Napoleon, hastily revising his plans to go at once
into winter quarters, ordered an advance on the Vistula so as to
secure Warsaw and a north-eastwards thrust from Berlin against the
garrison city of Thorn (Torun). Bernadotte was ordered to leave
Lübeck and bring I Corps to Posen (Poznan) as soon as possible.
Despite heavy rain and sleet Bernadotte spurred his men forward
until they had covered 120 miles in thirty-five hours. At Posen, in the
second week of December, he found Napoleon amicably disposed
towards him but puzzled by reports that General Levin Bennigsen,
a Hanoverian in Russian service, was already forming a large army
east of the Vistula. Bernadotte was given command of the left wing
of the Grand Army, with Marshals Ney and Bessières subordinate
to him. Murat had the honour of taking Warsaw, with Davout,
Soult and Lannes in support.

For two and a half months Bernadotte sought to wage war in
what he described to his brother-in-law, Joseph, as 'the vilest place
in the world': an open rolling countryside in which there were no

proper roads, only tracks so inconspicuous that it was impossible to tell if they led to the next town or merely to the outlying granges of some huge estate. The weather, too, was unpredictable: heavy rain and sleet would be followed by a sudden thaw and then by another cycle of storms and snow. All this part of Prussian Poland was criss-crossed by swollen streams feeding the great Vistula and there were numerous lakes and marshes which by January were treacherously covered by three or four feet of snow, making them indistinguishable from the fields between the villages. Even before Bernadotte reached Posen he heard how Duroc's carriage had overturned on black ice, leaving the General – Napoleon's Grand Marshal of the Palace – with a broken collarbone. The opposing armies stumbled against each other as much by chance as by design.

Bernadotte distinguished himself in a series of actions along the ill-defined road from Thorn to Grodno (Grudziaz) in the week before Christmas. By early January 1807 his troops were short of food; he complained that he could not expect his men to fight under these conditions if they had gone twenty-six hours with nothing to eat; and, like every other corps commander, he urged Napoleon to call a halt to the fighting and go into winter quarters. But Bennigsen was a wily antagonist, exploiting the inability of the French commanders to keep in touch with each other. He inflicted severe losses on Marshal Lannes's V Corps at Pultusk on 26 December and, profiting from an error by Ney, threatened to break through the scattered French positions west of the Masurian Lakes and raid I Corps's advanced base at Osterode (Ostroda) in the last week of January. Bernadotte's quick response to reports of marauding Russian patrols enabled him to check Bennigsen's troops at Mohrungen (Morag), even though much of his baggage train was destroyed by the Cossacks.

Napoleon now sought to lure Bennigsen into a trap. He ordered Ney to retire southwards and Bernadotte to pull back beyond Osterode towards Thorn; he was sure Bennigsen would go forward in hot pursuit, hoping to exploit what would seem to him to be a widening gap between the two Marshals. At the same time Murat, with three divisions of infantry and three brigades of light cavalry, would assemble at Willenburg (Wielbark), sixty miles north of Warsaw, ready to launch an assault on Bennigsen's left flank, which would coincide with a surprise counter-attack by Bernadotte: 'It is essential that no move should be made obvious', Napoleon's directive insisted. He was himself at Willenburg and anticipated that a decisive battle would be fought on 2 February at Allenstein (Olsztyn), thirty-five miles to his north and about the same distance from Bernadotte's I Corps, south of Osterode. Hurriedly Berthier prepared copies of the orders which were to go out to each of the eight Marshals who commanded units of the Grand Army.

In northern Italy or Austria a general-in-chief could tell his staff to prepare copies of his operational plans and have them sent safely by courier to the commanders in the field. But a winter campaign in Poland posed new hazards. It was difficult for field commanders to keep in touch with each other: Berthier had already received complaints from Bernadotte of the tardiness with which orders from the Emperor reached I Corps headquarters. Accordingly Berthier entrusted an early copy of this latest battle plan to the first keen and young horseman he could find, who rode off towards Osterode with the despatches (which were not in code and could be understood by anyone who spoke French). Unfortunately the courier was a subaltern, fresh from the military academy: he lost his way in the unfamiliar wintry terrain of Poland; and, on being surprised by a Cossack patrol, he had no time to destroy the vital papers. The orders to Bernadotte were soon being studied by General Bagration, commander of the Russian vanguard, and then forwarded to Bennigsen. On the day Bernadotte should have mounted his counter-attack the whole of Napoleon's plan was in Bennigsen's hands. As one of his staff-officers later wrote, Bennigsen at once realised 'he was riding blindly to destruction'. He called off the pursuit of Bernadotte and began to retire north-eastwards towards Königsberg (Kaliningrad). Meanwhile Bagration had sent out patrols to search for other contacts between Napoleon's headquarters and I Corps. The Cossacks intercepted seven more couriers. Not a single order from headquarters reached Bernadotte between Wednesday, 28 January, and the following Tuesday, 3 February.

The breakdown in communications and the loss of the couriers made Bernadotte miss yet another setpiece Napoleonic clash of arms, the battle of Eylau on 7–8 February. Napoleon had belatedly realised on the Tuesday morning that the Russians had somehow acquired a shrewd knowledge of his intentions. There was no battle near Allenstein, as Napoleon had anticipated, only a sharp clash later that Tuesday near Ionkovo which ended indecisively because of the early nightfall. The French remained in close pursuit of the

Russians until Bennigsen took up defensive positions around the town of Eylau on Friday evening. By then Bernadotte was again in touch with headquarters; but he was two days' march away, with heavy snow falling on a frozen wasteland.

Eylau was a good battle to miss – an even bloodier encounter than Austerlitz, with one in three of the French killed or wounded. Napoleon's official bulletin claimed a victory, for it was the Russians and Prussians who withdrew rather than the severely battered Grand Army; but no attempt was made to renew contact with Bennigsen as he fell back on Königsberg. 'What a massacre! And with no result!' exclaimed Ney, when he first saw the contorted heaps of frozen corpses next morning. In the immediate aftermath of the fighting Napoleon claimed that had Bernadotte been at Eylau he would have won the battle with the loss of fewer men and horses; and in later years, too, he made the absent Marshal a scapegoat for his failure to gain a decisive victory. But, so long as the campaign continued, it was recognised at Imperial Headquarters that Bernadotte was not to blame for I Corps's absence: Berthier should not have entrusted despatches to inexperienced subalterns. A fortnight after Eylau Napoleon wrote in flattering terms to Bernadotte praising his gift of inspiring I Corps with 'that love of glory and zeal for the honour of my army by which you are yourself animated'. When the Grand Army fell back to winter quarters and the general-in-chief was ruling his Empire again, a personal letter from Napoleon to the Prince of Ponte Corvo informed him that the Emperor had bestowed a pension on his hard-working brother down in Pau and appointed him a member of the Legion of Honour. Outwardly Napoleon seemed prepared to look benignly on all Bernadottes, great and small.

Désirée had seen nothing of her husband for more than eighteen months. But when, early in March, he established headquarters at Schlobitten Castle she unexpectedly set out from Paris as soon as she could and travelled eight hundred miles across France and Germany to Prussian Poland, completing her journey before the spring thaw began to make daily life easier in the lower Vistulan plain. Her presence might well have posed an embarrassing problem for Napoleon. For most of April and May he was at Finckenstein Castle, about thirty-five miles south-west of Schlobitten, dallying contentedly with Marie Walewska, the loveliest of his mistresses, while hotly denying in every letter to Josephine the 'malicious rumours' which he knew to be circulating in the salons of Paris. Shortly before Désirée arrived at Schlobitten, he had written to Josephine forbidding her, for a second time, to come to Poland: an Empress, he explained, 'could not do the round of bivouacs and taverns'. Désirée, having spent much of the winter in Paris with her sister Julie, was well-versed in court gossip. But if she hoped to meet Marie Walewska she was disappointed; no invitation for her to visit Finckenstein reached Schlobitten. Characteristically, Napoleon put her socially in the wrong. In a letter to Bernadotte, sent some weeks after her arrival, he lapsed into the affectionate big-brotherly tone which he customarily used with Désirée and reproached her for not having written to him 'with news hot-foot from Paris' as soon as she reached Poland; but she need not make excuses until they next met face to face, he added with playful magnanimity.

She was still at Schlobitten in the first week of June when Bennigsen attacked I Corps positions along the River Pasteka, east of Elbing (Elblag). Bernadotte hurried forward to Spanden, where I Corps beat off a series of Russian assaults on 4 June. Next morning, when the Russians came forward again, Bernadotte was hit in the neck by a musketball as he rallied the defenders of the French bridgehead and he fell wounded from his horse. It was an astonishing escape from death. Although he clambered back into the saddle and wished to continue directing operations, the task was beyond him; he handed over command of I Corps to General Victor (once Claude-Victor Perrin of the Grenoble Artillery Regiment). Bernadotte was brought back by ambulance wagon to Marienburg (Malbork), where a hospital had been set up in what was once the principal residence of the Grand Master of the Teutonic Knights. It was a painful journey over terrible roads and so bad was the Marshal's condition when he reached Marienburg that the chief surgeon feared the ball was embedded near the base of the cranium; it might, he informed Napoleon, have affected the Marshal's brain. But this was an excessively gloomy prognosis and he was soon out of danger. Désirée helped nurse him back to health at Marienburg but, before he was wounded, he had arranged for her to travel with one of the couriers back to Berlin and on to Paris. Husband and wife duly parted again at the end of the month.

His convalescence meant that Bernadotte missed the battle of Friedland on 14 June, a clash of arms in which Napoleon showed all his old skill as an artillery specialist in defeating Bennigsen. And, to Bernadotte's chagrin, he could not join the grandees along the banks of the River Niemen when, after the first meetings between the French and Russian Emperors on a raft at Tilsit had ended the Polish campaign, Napoleon showed off his army to Tsar Alexander in a succession of reviews. But Bernadotte was well enough to take part in the festivities which celebrated Napoleon's final diplomatic triumph, the Treaty of Tilsit, with its astonishing reversal of alliances. He was, so he wrote to Désirée, warmly received; he could even report a long, cordial conversation with Berthier.

Napoleon reached the apogee of his power at Tilsit. He had no need to trouble himself over the easily ruffled sensibilities of Bernadotte or any other of his Marshals. When the Emperor stopped at Königsberg on his way back from Tilsit, he offered the Prince of Ponte Corvo, not a field command, but the Governorship of the Hanseatic Towns, with headquarters in Hamburg; and Bernadotte welcomed his new responsibilities. But the timing of the announcement of his appointment revealed more to him of the Emperor's inner feelings than all the smooth small-talk at Imperial headquarters that week. Although Bernadotte knew he would be made Governor of the Hanseatic Towns as early as 10 July the news was not announced until 14 July. And before then the public had a new hero to honour. On 13 July, for the first time since the revival of the Marshalate in 1804, Napoleon bestowed a baton on one of his Generals. As a recipient of this honour he chose Claude-Victor Perrin. For General Victor had not only ensured that I Corps reached Friedland in time for the battle, but made certain that the twenty thousand men Bernadotte had kept together throughout the harsh winter spearheaded the decisive French counter-attack, an action fought immediately beneath the Emperor's field headquarters. Never again did Bernadotte receive the command of crack French troops.

He remained Governor of the Hanseatic Towns – Hamburg, Bremen, Lübeck – for twenty months. Napoleon assigned him a threefold task: to bring northern Germany into the Continental System, closing the Hanseatic harbours to all commerce with Britain while encouraging new trade links with France; to prevent the British from establishing a foothold in Denmark; and to prepare for a possible invasion of Sweden, if King Gustav IV Adolf received further subsidies from London. Bernadotte soon saw that rigid enforcement of the Continental System would destroy the Hanseatic Towns; illicit trading continued, through neutral shipping which called at the smaller ports in neighbouring Holstein rather than at Hamburg. The Hanse merchants were grateful to their Governor for so wisely understanding their needs.

Tact, too, was required in handling the Danish Question. The surprise British naval assault on Copenhagen in the first week of September 1807 came less than five weeks after Bernadotte arrived in Hamburg; and he had not by then drawn up any plans to counter the British attack, nor indeed did he have any trained French troops he might have sent to the Regent of Denmark's assistance. A formal alliance treaty between France and Denmark at the end of October made his task easier; he moved a Dutch contingent into Jutland and several thousand Spanish troops into Fyn (Fünen), Denmark's second largest island. Briefly in early February 1808 it looked as if Bernadotte would be leading a combined force of Spanish, Dutch, French and Danish troops across the Sound and into the Swedish province of Skane for, at Tilsit, Napoleon had promised support to Tsar Alexander if he sought to wrest Finland from the Swedes. Yet, although Sweden and Russia were at war from 21 February 1808 until 17 December 1809, Bernadotte's expeditionary force never left the Danish islands. Napoleon did not want Sweden defeated too speedily. To have Russia engaged in a conflict north of the Gulf of Finland suited him well, for it would prevent Tsar Alexander from actively opposing his plans south of the Baltic, where he was re-drawing the map of northern Germany and Poland. From his letters to Berthier, Bernadotte appeared confident that he could cross the Sound successfully, penetrate southern Sweden and 'perhaps even take Stockholm'. Nevertheless it is clear from other correspondence that Bernadotte was relieved to be spared the invasion of Sweden: he could not count on the loyalty of the Spanish contingent in his motley army; and he saw no reason for increasing the burden of French commitments by carrying war into Scandinavia. Throughout his term as Governor of the Hanseatic Towns, he kept himself well-informed over Swedish affairs. There was, he told Napoleon as his invasion force waited on the shores of Zealand, an influential faction among the nobility which was sympathetic to France but filled with hatred towards Denmark; for the French to enter Scandinavian politics as patrons of the Danes would be a grave miscalculation.

A hero of the First French Republic: Brigadier-General
Bernadotte of the Army of Sambre-et-Meuse.

Bernadotte's birthplace. The Maison Balagué at Pau in the early years of the twentieth century. The Bernadotte apartments were upstairs, with the room in which he was born on the second floor.

Jean-Baptiste Kléber (1753–1800), Bernadotte's commanding officer at Fleurus and Maastricht and subsequently his close friend and adviser.

Francois Marceau (1769–96), Major-General in the Army of Sambre-et-Meuse. Marceau, an infantryman from Chartres before the Revolution, gained rapid promotion and was Bernadotte's companion-in-arms in 1795–6 during the campaigns along the Rhine and Moselle.

General Marceau was only twenty-seven when, in September 1796, he was wounded by an Austrian sniper at Altenkirchen. His death two days later was commemorated by several stylised prints. In *Childe Harold's Pilgrimage* Byron wrote:

> By Coblenz, in a gentle rise of ground,
> There is a small and simple pyramid,
> Crowning the summit of a verdant mound; Beneath its base are
> hero's ashes hid.
> Our enemy – but let not that forbid
> Honour to Marceau!

The young Désirée Bernadotte, painted by François Gerard.

The battle of Austerlitz, 2 December 1805. In the centre the cavalry of Bernadotte and Soult attack the Russian positions on the Pratzen plateau.

The entry of Napoleon into the Austrian capital in November 1805 as depicted by Antoine Vernet. Bernadotte was already familiar with Vienna from his short period there as ambassador seven years before.

A contemporary print of 'the flight of the French from Leipzig' in
1813 gives a good impression of the scale of the 'Battle of the
Nations'.

(*above*) This British representation of Bernadotte as 'Crown Prince
of Sweden' was readily on sale in London in the winter of 1813–14
together with prints of other allied leaders, notably Blücher and
Tsar Alexander I.

Queen Desideria of
Sweden and Norway,
shortly after her coronation
in 1829.

A modern view of
the royal palace in
Stockholm and
(centre left of the
palace colonnades)
the sixteenth-
century Storkyrkan
church. The
spire of the
Riddarholmskyrkan,
where Charles XIV,
John and Desideria
are buried, stands
out against the
background of the
Malaren lake.

Bernadotte as Prince Royal of Sweden and Norway; a
lithograph by von Delpech.

At first Bernadotte lived mainly in Hamburg but often travelling out to Lübeck and Travemünde. When his troops moved into Denmark he frequently stayed, too, at Odense and Désirée joined him there in March 1808, bringing with her their son Oscar, by now approaching his ninth birthday. But springtime in Denmark was far too cold for Désirée; she thought Odense a dull town and complained of a shortage of green vegetables and olive oil which would have made the food palatable. All in all, she was glad to return to Paris at the end of May. Four months later, however, she again travelled north, settling this time outside Hamburg, with Oscar, his tutor and his governess, the widowed Élise de Flotte, Désirée's close companion.

The Princess of Ponte Corvo, as Hanse society formally addressed 'Madame la Maréchale', found the countryside around Hamburg 'charming'. She liked the merchant families of the great northern port, which seemed to her wealthier than Marseilles of old, despite the strain of the Continental System. Unexpectedly she remained in Hamburg throughout the winter: the social life was elegant, with a season of French plays and 'superb ballets' gracefully presented, despite a principal dancer 'with legs like barrels and arms like spindles'. That winter Désirée was Hamburg's uncrowned Queen, treated indulgently by her husband and flattered by the City Senators. In France she had rediscovered her old Corsican friend, Chiappe, with whom she occasionally corresponded, but she was also still pampered by the greatest of his compatriots. When Napoleon received Alexander at the Erfurt Congress in the last days of September, the Tsar presented him with three magnificent fur pelisses: one sable Napoleon retained for himself; one he sent to his favourite sister, Pauline (whom he had recently allowed to separate from her husband, Prince Borghese); the third he gave to Désirée. One wonders why she had preference over the Empress Josephine, over Napoleon's sisters, or over her own sister, Julie, by now titular Queen of Spain. Sentimental affection, perhaps? Or a gesture of gratitude for discreet silence in the Paris salons after her visit to Poland the year before?

Bernadotte, too, was treated generously; to his earlier endowments could now be added revenue from estates in Poland, Westphalia and Hanover. Yet by November 1808 he was restless and in low spirits. Three months previously the Marquis de la Romana, commander of the Spanish contingent stationed in Denmark, had defected, secretly arranging for British ships to embark 10,000 men and transport them to Santander where they joined the Spanish national insurrection against Bonapartist rule. Bernadotte suspected that his personal enemies exploited this humiliating episode so that when Napoleon set out on his Spanish campaign he chose Davout, rather than himself, as commander-in-chief of a reconstituted 'Army of the Rhine'. This appointment ensured that Davout, who had been created Duke of Auerstädt in March, was virtually master of Germany, with 90,000 predominantly French troops under his command. By contrast Bernadotte, up in the narrow neck of land between the mouths of the Weser and the Trave, had less than 12,000 men to guard the north German and Danish coasts. Of this force only one under-strength division was French. The running feud between the two Marshals was soon renewed, with Bernadotte complaining that Davout was opening letters addressed to him from Paris. Both Joseph Bonaparte and Julie urged Napoleon to show his confidence in Bernadotte by making him a Grand Dignitary at Court. They argued that if Murat, now King of Naples, was titular Grand Admiral of the Empire why should not Bernadotte, as defender of the Baltic coasts, be created Vice Grand Admiral? But Napoleon, obsessed with the military problems of planting Joseph firmly on the throne in Madrid, understandably showed no interest in such matters.

By February 1809 Bernadotte's sense of frustration and incipient paranoia were undermining his health. He began spitting blood again, the worst attack since Jourdan ordered him to recuperate in the Hünsruck ten years before. Désirée was seriously alarmed and, at the end of the month, encouraged him to take to his bed. This illness of the Marshal coincided with a new threat of war in central Europe. For Count Stadion, Austria's Foreign Minister over the last three years, believed that Napoleon's preoccupation with Spanish affairs gave Emperor Francis an opportunity to avenge Austerlitz with a war of liberation, a campaign intended to 'break the chains which have bound down our German brothers'. Throughout the second half of February reports of Austrian war preparations reached Paris, much of the information gathered by the excellent intelligence network established by Davout, against which Bernadotte so frequently railed. The mounting crisis caused Imperial headquarters to improvise new military formations, calling up conscripts ahead of their time and hurriedly despatching marching orders to garrisons north and west of the Rhine. Accordingly, to Bernadotte's surprise, even while he was still confined to his bed in Hamburg, he received orders to set out for Hanover with General Dupas's French division. Bernadotte would then cut across Germany to Dresden, leaving Dupas to march southwards to the Danube more slowly. In Dresden Bernadotte would take command of a Saxon army, which – together with Dupas's Division – would constitute IX Corps in a new 'Grand Army of Germany'.

He challenged these orders on two counts: his poor health; and his reluctance to accept responsibility for a German contingent, after the misunderstandings with the Bavarians which had hampered his movements in the Ulm–Austerlitz Campaign four years before. His objections were ignored in Paris and in mid-March he considered himself sufficiently fit to set out for Hanover and Saxony. Despite his poor health he covered 320 miles from Hanover to Dresden in six days. Yet when, on 22 March, he reached the Saxon capital he found that nobody was expecting him; the King of Saxony had not even been informed of his appointment. Confirmation of his new responsibilities arrived soon afterwards, in despatches from Berthier. But Bernadotte was convinced that his 'personal enemies' at Imperial Headquarters outside Strasbourg were determined to discredit him; he was furious to discover that instructions to him were being sent in the first instance to Davout's headquarters, and sent forward by his couriers. A fortnight passed before Bernadotte received further orders from Strasbourg. Long before then he was anxious to resign his command, petitioning the Emperor either to allow him to retire to his estates or to send him 'on some distant mission, where my enemies would no longer be interested in persecuting me'. Napoleon ignored his Marshal's request.

Bernadotte may well have exaggerated the hostility shown towards him by Berthier and Davout. In 1809 he was a victim, not so much of jealousies and intrigue, as of mounting incompetence, an extension of the confusion which allowed battle plans to fall into Russian hands on the eve of Friedland. Because the war led within thirteen weeks to a humiliating defeat for the Habsburg Empire, it seems in retrospect yet another predestined triumph for Napoleon, his fourth against Emperor Francis's army. But it was a muddled episode, with errors of strategic judgment which seemed momentarily to leave hanging in the balance the fate of the whole campaign, perhaps even the fate of the French Empire. On 21–22 May an over-confident Napoleon, who had entered Vienna nine days before, suffered a major setback when the Archduke Charles prevented him from securing a bridgehead across the Danube at Aspern, four miles east of the Austrian capital. And, having summoned Bernadotte to bring his IX Corps – with 16,000 Saxon troops – southwards into the Austrian Empire, Napoleon then left Dresden defenceless. The city was raided by an Austrian force from Bohemia less than a fortnight after IX Corps's departure; the King of Saxony fled, with his court, to Frankfurt.

Knowledge that their homeland had been attacked in their absence lowered morale drastically among Bernadotte's Saxons, by then on the Danube forty miles west of Vienna. At last Napoleon gave some attention to Bernadotte's reiterated complaints, his conviction that the Saxon officers and men were so inexperienced that they would be unreliable in battle unless IX Corps had a good leavening of French veterans. Imperial Headquarters confirmed that General Dupas, who had led his division from Hamburg to Hanover and then rejoined Bernadotte at Linz, was to serve as IX Corps's tactical reserve. And, in a further gesture of goodwill, Napoleon invited Bernadotte to leave his troops at St Polten and join him in residence at Schönbrunn. The two men had not met since July 1807, when Napoleon passed through Königsberg on his way back to Paris from Tilsit.

Bernadotte arrived at Schönbrunn on Tuesday, 6 June, expecting to spend only one night at the palace. He remained there until the following Sunday. Each morning, as he was preparing to return to St Polten, Napoleon urged him to stay longer, and Bernadotte willingly obliged his Emperor. Napoleon was in the best of tempers. Despite the rebuff at Aspern, the French still held the Danube island of Lobau which he was preparing to use as the springboard for an assault on the Archduke Charles's positions in the Marchfeld plain. He was pleased with progress on the pontoon bridge which the engineers were building for him day by day. Reinforcements were coming from Italy. So long as the Archduke remained on the defensive, Napoleon could afford to wait and allow Bernadotte to let off steam, perhaps even overcoming the resentful suspicion which he so frequently showed towards his brother Marshals. Bernadotte was easy to flatter and on this occasion he found Napoleon a surprisingly sympathetic listener, perhaps because each evening he enjoyed the relaxed company of Marie Walewska, who was discreetly housed in one of the villas within Schönbrunn Park. When Bernadotte returned to St Polten he was pleased with his reception. Napoleon had brushed aside his objections to commanding the Saxons: Bernadotte might not speak German, but he could always show by encouraging gestures what should be done; and there was no need to augment IX Corps with French regiments for the Emperor was sure that his Marshal's own renown was in itself enough to lift the fighting ardour of the troops to the highest level. The fulsome phrases rang with welcome conviction in Gascon ears.

Planning for the earlier phases of the campaign had often been dangerously slipshod. But not so the preparations for the decisive encounter with the Archduke, when the Grand Army would cross from Lobau Island and fan out into the Marchfeld, isolating the Austrian corps commanders in a succession of enveloping movements to left and right of the central thrust around the village of Wagram. Napoleon was determined that this setpiece battle – in which he commanded nearly twice as many men and three times as many guns as at Austerlitz – should be meticulously planned. He left Schönbrunn Palace for Lobau at four in the morning on Saturday, 1 July, establishing his field headquarters under the shade of the tall poplars which spread back from the banks of the island as if they were chestnuts or oaks. Final orders went out to Bernadotte to bring the Saxons up from St Polten on Monday and cross the newly built bridges to Lobau under cover of darkness in the small hours of Tuesday morning, ready for Wednesday's great battle, in which more troops were to be engaged than ever before.

Austerlitz and Eylau were wintry clashes of arms, fought in snow-covered landscapes: Wagram was a summer battle which was decided, not under a blistering sun as in the engagements of the Friedland campaign, but during respites from thunderstorms and squalls of such heavy rain that momentarily it was hard to see far across the fields. The storms delayed IX Corps as it moved up from St Polten, making Imperial Headquarters complain that Bernadotte's men were, as usual, marching well behind the clock; and dawn had broken that Tuesday before the Saxons crossed the bridge into Lobau Island. Their arrival was observed by Archduke Charles who at once put his troops on the alert, along a ring of fifteen miles of fortified defences. There followed a long pause, however, for it was not until half-past nine in the evening that Napoleon sent IX Corps forward. Under yet another thunderstorm they reached the north bank of the Danube with few casualties. Next morning (Wednesday, 5 July) they advanced across the Marchfeld and captured the village of Raasdorf. By two o'clock on Wednesday afternoon Bernadotte could report that his troops had reached their first objective on the left centre of the French line. They were four miles beyond the bridgehead, in the tiny village of Aderklaa. On a slight incline ahead of them and across the Russbach, a marshy tree-lined stream, was the larger village of Wagram, the centre of the Archduke's defensive arc.

During the evening Napoleon made two attempts to break the Austrian position. Soon after seven o'clock Davout's corps and Oudinot's corps attacked the Austrians to the east of Wagram, only to be thrown back in confusion; and in the fading light Bernadotte's Saxons were ordered forward across the Russbach stream. They, too, were repulsed, their commander keeping them together with great difficulty. Moreover when Bernadotte sent for General Dupas's division, the reserve which should have strengthened the Saxons, he found that Berthier had ordered Dupas to support Oudinot, leaving IX Corps without any support troops whatsoever. Not surprisingly, by nightfall on Wednesday, 5 July, the Austrian positions were hardly dented, despite the fury of the assault.

When Bernadotte returned to Aderklaa that evening, he expressed himself forcefully to General Matthieu Dumas, a senior staff officer. He complained bitterly of the way in which Berthier had poached his reserves but he also criticised the Emperor's ruthless insistence on mounting a frontal assault. Had he been commander-in-chief, so he boasted to Matthieu Dumas, the Archduke would have been made to sue for peace by means of a 'scientific manoeuvre' rather than by throwing waves of infantry against prepared positions. Soon a version of Bernadotte's remarks was to reach his Emperor.

After thirteen years of intermittent campaigning against the Archduke, Bernadotte possessed a shrewder understanding of his military mind than did Napoleon. He was convinced that next morning Charles would seek to open a gap between IX Corps and Masséna's IV Corps to its left and thereby thrust due southwards towards Aspern, so as to cut Napoleon off from his bridgehead. Accordingly, soon after three o'clock in the morning, Bernadotte pulled IX Corps back one mile from the village of Aderklaa and thereby shortened the line, drawing closer both to Masséna's corps and to Eugène's

'Army of Italy', on his right; but he did not inform Imperial Headquarters of his action.

Sure enough, as the Marshal had anticipated, soon after daybreak Archduke Charles threw two Austrian corps at the pivotal point between Masséna and Bernadotte. Heavy cannon fire made IX Corps waver, but once again Bernadotte kept them together. By now Napoleon had heard of what he interpreted as the Marshal's insubordination, in abandoning Aderklaa, and he ordered both Masséna and Bernadotte to stem the Austrian thrust with a joint counter-attack to recover the village. Here, for half an hour, the Saxons were successful, duly re-entering Aderklaa under heavy fire. But, with Austrian light cavalry threatening their left flank, they found it impossible to hold the village. Suddenly the Saxons broke and began to fall back, far beyond the positions they had left that morning. A near-panic among inexperienced troops was, for Bernadotte, an old phenomenon: he responded to the crisis as at Rulzheim in 1793 and on the Sambre in the following spring; with drawn sword, he galloped behind them and then swung his horse across their ranks, his gestures urging them back into the line. At that point the Marshal came face to face with Napoleon. There was an angry exchange in which Napoleon is alleged to have asked sarcastically if this was one of the 'scientific manoeuvres' with which he was to force the Archduke to lay down his arms. The most inventive of memoir-writers, Baron de Marbot, declares that Napoleon thereupon dismissed Bernadotte from the Grand Army and ordered him to set off for Paris within twenty-four hours. But this dramatic tale is clearly a fabrication, for Bernadotte was still in command of the Saxons three days later. Nevertheless there is no doubt that relations between the Emperor and Bernadotte had again sunk to a low level of bitter recrimination.

Supporting cross-fire from massed French batteries halted the Austrian counter-attack and steadied the Saxons, who had suffered heavy casualties. Soon after midday Davout began to turn the left of the Austrian position while the French artillery, pounding Wagram village into ruins, forced the Archduke to withdraw. Napoleon had gained his victory by nightfall on Thursday, 6 July but, once again, at a heavy cost. One in five of the Grand Army lay dead or wounded on the battlefield. Among the casualties were more than a third of the Saxons in IX Corps.

There was no pursuit of the Austrians, who retired eastwards into Hungary and sued for an armistice on 12 July. Bernadotte, angered by what he regarded as Napoleon's callousness, spent two days after the battle with IX Corps at Leopoldau, seeking greater care for the wounded; he even urged the military governor of Vienna to commandeer every cab (*fiacre*) in the city so that casualties could receive the urgent treatment which they needed. Before the battle he had consistently begged the Emperor to relieve him from the burden of commanding such inexperienced troops. But after Wagram Bernadotte became their great champion. Since he considered that Napoleon had ignored their contribution to the Imperial victory in the official bulletins, he issued his own Order of the Day from Leopoldau on 7 July. It praised the valour of the Saxons in piercing the Austrian lines on the first day of the battle and the courage with which they renewed the combat next morning: 'Amidst the ravages of enemy artillery, your living columns remained as motionless as bronze. The great Napoleon witnessed your devotion; he numbers you among his braves', Bernadotte added. But 'the great Napoleon' made it clear to his Marshals that he had seen nothing of the sort and that no corps commander had the right to single out individual units as meriting the highest praise. Bernadotte was officially informed of the Emperor's displeasure. At the start of the following week Napoleon gave him permission to return home, 'for reasons of health'. By 25 July he was back in France, with Désirée and Oscar at La Grange la Prévôte, a Marshal on half-pay.

He was not unemployed for long. For, three days after his homecoming, observers on the cliffs near Boulogne sighted nearly fifty warships and over a hundred transports sailing northwards in close formation and with a following wind from the Downs, the anchorage between the Goodwin Sands and the North and South Foreland. That night this curious armada reached the estuary of the Scheldt. Soon the semaphore stations of the French Military Telegraph Service were signalling back to Paris reports of an invasion; the British were about to land a huge army on either side of the Scheldt, with Antwerp as the first objective.

In the Emperor's absence the news created a near-panic among his Ministers in Paris. It also prompted an urgent appeal from his brother Louis, King of Holland, for the despatch of a Marshal of the Empire who could put Antwerp's defences in order. By 2 August Fouché, as Minister of Police and the Interior, had assumed responsibility for levying the National Guard in the fifteen *Départe-*

ments of the North (which included Belgium). And it was Fouché who announced that the Prince of Ponte Corvo would defend the Empire from invasion. Next day Bernadotte arrived at the Ministry of War, 'booted and spurred', ready to meet the challenge. Despite their recent differences, Napoleon soon telegraphed his approval of the emergency measures and confirmed Bernadotte's appointment as commander of the Army of Antwerp; he had fought the English before in the Netherlands; and he knew well how to get the best out of National Guardsmen suddenly called to the colours. By 15 August – when cannon in Paris and Vienna saluted Napoleon's fortieth birthday – Bernadotte was on the outskirts of Antwerp, conferring with the King of Holland on how to defend the city.

Although Bernadotte improvised extensive defences they were never put to the test. No invading force came within fifteen miles of Antwerp, for the expedition was a fiasco. The British had sent 40,000 men under Lord Chatham in large vessels which could not navigate the difficult channels of the Scheldt estuary and dared not risk sailing close inshore while there were enemy batteries on the islands of Walcheren and South Beverland. The most Chatham attempted was the bombardment and occupation of Flushing (Vlissingen), the principal port of Walcheren. Bernadotte, of course, had no doubt that it was the spirited response to his call to arms that deterred the British from an advance on Antwerp. On 31 August he published another flamboyant Order of the Day, which carried Dantonesque echoes of the patriotic Republican oratory of 1794: he praised the courage of the National Guard in rallying to the colours; comrades in arms were coming from all directions to stand beside them and force the enemy's 'formidable expedition' to withdraw. Ultimately the invaders were defeated by another enemy: a local form of malaria wrought terrible havoc; and at the end of September Lord Chatham re-embarked his force, leaving behind the bodies of 106 men killed in action and 4000 dead from disease. But by then Bernadotte had been summoned back from the Netherlands.

When reports of this second Order of the Day reached Schönbrunn, Napoleon was once more irritated by his Marshal's flow of Gascon rhetoric. He was already angry that Bernadotte had circulated his original Leopoldau Order of the Day to newspapers in both Dresden and Paris and he became highly suspicious of the Marshal's motives in flattering troops under his command. As in 1802, the Emperor was overfed with sensationalist reports from rival intelligence services, most of which he had learnt by now to discount. Savary and Davout wished to discredit both Fouché, as Minister of Police, and Bernadotte, with whom so many of the Marshals maintained a running feud. Savary induced Napoleon to send a personal aide-de-camp, Honoré Reille, to Antwerp to spy on Bernadotte: 'You may write to me every day to let me know what is going on', he instructed General Reille. When the Emperor discovered that Fouché had reconstituted the National Guard in Paris itself, he began to take seriously the agents' tales of a Fouché–Bernadotte conspiracy. He incorporated Bernadotte's newly raised troops into a specially created Army of the North, led by Marshal Bessières, and soon after Bernadotte arrived back in Paris from Antwerp ordered him to come immediately to Vienna for consultation. The unfortunate Bernadotte – officially on sick leave so as to take the waters at a German spa – was forced yet again to cover the 820 miles separating the French and Austrian capitals. He left Paris in the small hours of 30 September. By 9 October he was once more at Schönbrunn.

This time he was received in audience by an Emperor who coldly sought explanations for his recent conduct. Why had he circulated the Leopoldau Order of the Day? Why had he drawn up another Order of the Day at Antwerp, despite the Emperor's insistence that he alone had the right to issue such proclamations? Why had he consorted in Paris with people whom Napoleon well knew to be political intriguers? Did he not realise that he could not see a man or receive a letter without his Emperor learning of it? Why did he, a Marshal and a Prince of the Empire, persistently follow independent policies of his own choosing? Later embellishment gives to this scene a dramatic quality which it may not have possessed at the time. Yet some of the words in a script which was clearly written later have a ring of authenticity. 'What sentiments do the French people feel towards me?', Napoleon allegedly asked Bernadotte. 'The admiration which your astounding successes command', he replied quickly (and, no doubt, accurately). The Emperor was mollified. Playfully he patted the Marshal's forehead: 'What a head!', he exclaimed. And swiftly came the response, 'You might add, Sire, what a heart! What spirit!'

By the end of the audience Bernadotte's affability had disarmed the Emperor. As on earlier occasions, Napoleon planned to neutralise the Marshal's political danger by an outward promotion which would carry him well out of reach of the would-be conspirators in Paris. Bernadotte had appreciated palace life at the Herrenhausen in Hanover, and he clearly enjoyed being in residence at Schönbrunn. Why should he not go to Rome, as Governor-General of the second city in Napoleon's Empire? Since Pope Pius VII was by now interned at Savona, Bernadotte could have his pick of palaces, together with two million francs for his expenses. Yet, to Napoleon's surprise, Bernadotte did not welcome the offer. His reasons are not clear; he may well have sensed the unpopularity of a French Governor imposed upon a city from which the Pope had been sent into exile; probably he knew, as Napoleon clearly did not, that Désirée retained horrified memories of her one visit to French-occupied Rome. Tactfully Bernadotte did not turn down the offer out of hand. All he sought at the moment was a period of rest and recuperation, not in Paris, but at a spa.

He left Schönbrunn on 21 October with Napoleon's permission for an extended sick-leave. The Emperor had suggested he might travel to Italy and visit his princely possessions in Ponte Corvo. But Italy did not appeal to him. The frail dynastic foundations of the Empire were becoming more and more apparent. Even while he was at Schönbrunn an anarchistic student lunged at Napoleon with a knife. Rumours of the Emperor's pending divorce and his search for a new bride were current both in Vienna and Paris. This was no time to settle far from the heart of the Empire. Bernadotte might, he thought, take Désirée to Plombières; the waters would be of benefit to them both. Then he would re-establish himself unobtrusively at La Grange. It was well out of sight of the Emperor, but within a few hours' ride of St Cloud and the Tuileries, should France call again on his services. That it was also twelve hundred miles from Stockholm as yet meant nothing to him. For there was no reason to suppose, in this late autumn of 1809, that when next the leaves were falling Bernadotte would set out northwards, as heir to a Scandinavian throne.

Part III
Napoleon's Enemy

Chapter 10
The Making of a Prince Royal

T HE winter of 1809–10 was deceptively quiet in Paris, a lull in
the campaigns to consolidate the new Empire. Napoleon was
concerned with dynastic questions; in particular, the need to father
a legitimate son to succeed him as Emperor. On 16 December he
divorced Josephine and in the first week of April married Marie
Louise, daughter of Emperor Francis of Austria; by July it was
known she was pregnant. The Bernadottes came into residence at
the Rue d'Anjou for the wedding celebrations – which were marred
by heavy rain – but took no part in public affairs. Although the war
simmered in Spain and Portugal, it never came to the boil that
winter. Only five of the twenty Marshals of the Empire heard guns
fired in anger; even Berthier went to Vienna on a diplomatic mission.
Often during these months of divorce and re-marriage Napoleon
allowed vital letters from his brothers, the King of Spain and the
King of Holland, to wait unanswered – only to blame Joseph and
Louis later in the year for rash displays of independence. Yet the
problems of one part of Europe could not be ignored. Napoleon
and his Foreign Minister, Champagny, found that they had to give
increasing attention to the map of the Baltic, a region the Emperor
scarcely knew.

By the Treaty of Tilsit Tsar Alexander had adhered to the
Continental System, thus cutting off the Russians from their great
market for hemp and flax and tallow in England. But so serious was
the loss to Russia's exports that within two years Alexander was
contemplating a reversal of commercial policy so as to re-open
Russia's Baltic ports. If Russia was going to break loose, it was
essential for France to find an alternative supporter in northern
Europe and in the first week of January 1810 Swedish diplomats
concluded a treaty in Paris by which their country joined the

Continental System in return for French evacuation of Sweden's small segment of territory south of the Baltic, in Pomerania. Thereafter, for almost two years, the possibility of using Sweden as a favoured client and ally against Russia made a strong appeal to Napoleon. Hitherto he had taken little note of the political storms which had raged in Stockholm over the past two decades. Now their reverberations held his interest.

There was good precedent for Franco–Swedish collaboration, going back to the diplomacy of Richelieu in the Thirty Years' War. Despite the great distance separating Sweden from France and barriers of language and religion a close affinity linked the Vasa and Bourbon dynasties in the eighteenth century. Swedish princes and nobles at court visited Paris and, on their return, gave their patronage to cultural institutions based on French models, and encouraged French scholars, scientists, singers, dancers and actors to travel north. Outside Europe a Régiment Royal-Suédois, mercenaries led by officers from some of the best families in Sweden, fought for the Bourbons in the Indies and North America; and beneficial trade treaties made the French connection, which was favoured by their sovereigns, readily acceptable to merchant communities in Stockholm, Malmö and Gothenburg.

The greatest of Sweden's Francophile rulers was Gustav III, the gifted dilettante whose delight was the theatre, as playwright, producer, and designer. His critics complained that Gustav made all life a play; he turned his twenty-one year reign into a masquerade whose artificiality his poorer subjects failed to perceive. But it was not Gustav who directed the dramatic scenes with which the reign was to open and close. He was away from Sweden at the time of his accession, visiting France with his two brothers, the elder of whom was to become King Charles XIII, many years later. Louis XV was entertaining the Swedish princes at Versailles in February 1771 when they received grave news from Stockholm: their father was dead, having supped one evening off oysters, sticky buns, sauerkraut, lobster and champagne and not survived till morning. The brothers returned home, King Gustav III resolved to strengthen the powers of the monarchy; he would brush aside the Four Estates of parliament (the Riksdag), in which rival factions of 'Hats' and 'Caps' were beginning to resemble the Whigs and Tories of England. In August 1772, with the approval and encouragement of his friends in France, he carried through a royal coup: party names were banned as 'hated abominations'; the selfishness of the aristocracy was denounced; and Gustav imposed a balanced constitution, paying lip-service to the ideas of Montesquieu. The Riksdag was retained, although with little authority over foreign affairs. Otherwise the King ruled as an enlightened despot supported by his people who, it seemed, would be content with wise, efficient administration. From Paris Gustav received a contribution to his exchequer of 300,000 livres; Louis XV was certain that if he needed a Baltic ally against Russia or Prussia he could count on Sweden. A revised Franco–Swedish alliance treaty was signed six months after Gustav's coup.

Eleven years later, still only 38, Gustav III was back in Paris, travelling incognito as the Count de Haga so that he could enjoy frivolities inappropriate to an earnest Lutheran king. It was June 1784: Grenadier Bernadotte was with the Royal-la-Marine at Besançon; Cadet Napoleon, at Brienne, was urging Joseph to persevere with his plans to become a priest and a bishop rather than 'enter the King's service'; while, at Versailles, Queen Marie Antoinette was entertaining Gustav, a full suite of 'Swedish gentlemen' and over a hundred other guests at the Trianon to an opera with balletic interludes, a supper with the choice of sixty-four main dishes and, for those who wished it, boating on a lake festooned with fairy-lights grouped around the Temple of Love. Gustav – a homosexual whose relationship with his wife, Sofia Magdalena, was unhappily tense – remained entranced by Marie Antoinette for months afterwards. Like him, she possessed the visual imagination to create a fastidious paradise in which to play out the private theatricals of Court. He returned to Sweden, full of admiration for the King and Queen of France and intent on embellishing still further his summer palaces. Earlier rulers translated the grandeur of Versailles into their own architectural vernacular; Gustav III sought to transplant the exquisite delicacy of Marie Antoinette's Trianon to the wooded islands around Stockholm.

Gustav also brought back from Paris Sweden's first trading post in the western hemisphere, Saint-Barthélemy, in the Leeward Islands of the Caribbean, a personal possession of the Kings of France for over a century. The subsequent foundation by Gustav of the Swedish West Indies Company to some extent placated merchants who grumbled that, in exchange for Saint-Barthélemy, he had granted the French new privileges in the port of Gothenburg.

Mounting resentment at Gustav's autocratic rule at home induced him to embark on an expansionist foreign policy, culminating in a rash attack on Russia across the frontier of Swedish-held Finland in the summer of 1788 and a planned naval assault on St Petersburg. Reality fell far short of Gustav's intentions; he was forced on the defensive and threatened with a major rebellion by a group of officers. In December 1788, like his friend Louis XVI four months before, he decided to summon the Estates in a Riksdag, convinced he could strengthen his own position by playing off one class against another. Whereas Louis's States-General could not come together until early May, Gustav's Riksdag met in early February; by the middle of the month he had isolated the nobility through constitutional reforms which enlarged the privileges of the lower classes – and, less conspicuously, of the King, too. Thus by the historic summer days of 1789 when Louis and Marie Antoinette became captives of 'the nation', Gustav III had won his political struggle and was hailed as Sweden's war leader against the Russians, their Danish allies and a handful of allegedly treacherous officers. Although he could not defeat Russia on land, he secured a naval victory – in which he himself participated – off Svenskund in July 1790 followed by a satisfactory peace a month later. Almost immediately he began to urge his fellow sovereigns to unite against revolutionary France and rescue Louis and Marie Antoinette from the constraints imposed upon them in the Tuileries.

Gustav was well-informed about the situation in France from Count Axel von Fersen, former commander of the Régiment Royal-Suédois and a close personal friend of Louis and, even more, of Marie Antoinette. Fersen was responsible for the meticulous planning which, on 20 June 1791, enabled the royal family to escape from Paris and head for the frontier. Had Louis allowed Fersen to accompany them eastwards beyond the outskirts of Paris, it is probable that they would not have been intercepted and turned back at Varennes. Waiting at Aachen was Gustav III himself; there he received a report from Fersen and eventually 'Monsieur' – the King's brother, later Louis XVIII – who, with the Swede's help, had left Paris on the same day but headed north for Mons.

Gustav, soon back in Sweden, continued for another nine months to sketch out plans for dramatic rescues or crusades to restore the dignity of monarchy. Behind these projects there lay that same element of fantasy with which his mind would play in his theatres at Gripsholm and Drottningholm. Inequitable taxation and rapid inflation led to further discontent; and Gustav summoned yet another Riskdag where he relied on splitting the opposition once again. Against him, however, was a strange coalition of nobles whom he had offended, of libertarians hostile to any despot however enlightened, and of regicide fanatics. Gustav, as elated as any actor by the warm reception he received at each of his well-staged public spectacles, discounted the strength of the Opposition. On 16 March 1792, at one of the opera masquerades in which he so delighted, he was shot from behind by a former Guards officer. Gustav died from his wounds within a fortnight – on the day that J. B. Bernadotte was commissioned in France's 36th Infantry Regiment.

The new king, Gustav IV Adolf, was only thirteen at his father's death. For over four years his uncle, the Duke of Sodermanland, ruled as Regent. When Gustav IV at last began to shape a policy of his own, he turned for friendship to Tsar Paul of Russia. At St Petersburg in December 1800 he achieved the personal success his father had known in Paris; Gustav's queen, Frederica, was a sister-in-law of the Tsar's eldest son Alexander; and there was a rare display of family cordiality at the Russian Court. Tsar Paul even showed his visitor the new Mikhailovsky Palace, with its elaborate security arrangements. Two months later the Tsar moved into the Mikhailovsky for the first time; within five weeks he was murdered there, by officers whom Gustav IV had met and as part of a conspiracy of which Alexander had known in advance. The fate of Tsar Paul, together with memories of Gustav III's last days, left the King morbidly suspicious of any gathering of officers, and disinclined to trust his wife's brother-in-law, by now Tsar Alexander I. When, in February 1808, Alexander followed Napoleon's advice at Tilsit and launched a surprise attack on Swedish-held Finland, Gustav IV Adolf's mistrust of Alexander seemed fully justified.

The Finnish War was a disaster: a third of Sweden's territory was lost to Russia. Gustav IV Adolf had already shown his military ineptitude in the Third Coalition, when the French Marshals – Bernadotte among them – ejected his troops from Swedish Pomerania. In the Finnish campaign he had no strategic plan of defence whatsoever, local victories by Swedish–Finnish troops remaining unexploited. The King fought in the Åland Islands, where he made the mistake of dismissing veteran Guards officers as incompetent and then failing to show any understanding of tactics himself, returning to Stockholm shaken and dispirited. Rumours spread that he was not, in fact, his father's son; similar tales circulated in St Petersburg before Tsar Paul's murder. The threat of a Danish attack in alliance with the Russians, and in particular an advance into Sweden from Danish-held Norway, convinced the army officers that Gustav IV Adolf must go. On 13 March 1809 General Adlercreutz and six officers burst into his room in the palace and arrested him; Gustav, remembering the fate of Tsar Paul, escaped down a secret passage, convinced he would be murdered. The officers recaptured him, and he was taken, terrified and screaming, to Gripsholm Castle, where he was interned in an upper room and forced to abdicate. Several months later he was hustled out of the country, a forgotten man, sick in mind and body.

Sweden's Revolution of 1809 remained bloodless. The Duke of Södermanland became Protector of the Realm while the officers and their political allies worked out an acceptable form of government. The resultant Constitution of June 1809 survived, with appropriate modifications to enlarge the franchise and create a bi-cameral parliament, until 1975: the King retained executive power, exercised through a Council of State appointed by himself; the Riksdag – still of Four Estates – was to meet at least once every five years and should have the sole right of taxation; laws should be jointly made and amended by the sovereign and the Crown; and there was a separate judiciary, comprising not only a High Court (of which the King was a *de jure* member) but an institutional novelty, the *Justitie-Ombudsman*, an official who would arbitrate where harsh decisions by the State created individual acts of injustice. The Constitution was enacted on 6 June; and on the same day the sixty-one-year-old Duke of Södermanland was proclaimed King Charles XIII. He was amiable, kindly and simple-minded, a prince so long accustomed to observing the fitful brilliance of his royal brother that he became tired by any action more strenuous than the signing of his name. He was also childless.

There was no firm line of succession in the Swedish royal house. The Vasa dynasty had been elected to a vacant throne in the early sixteenth century after a successful revolt against Danish rule, but the last true Vasa was Queen Christina who had abdicated in favour of her cousin, Charles X, a Wittelsbach from the Palatinate. Similarly, although both Gustav III and the new ruler, Charles XIII, had been born in Sweden, their father was a German Prince, from the House of Holstein-Gottorp, elected in succession to Sweden's childless King Frederick I because he could claim descent from the Vasas through female lines. In 1809 the Royal Council was following historical tradition in proposing that the Riksdag elect a foreigner as Prince Royal, heir to the Vasa throne. Yet the first choice was a curious one. Prince Christian August of Schleswig-Holstein was Charles XIII's cousin, but he was also commanding General of the Danish–Norwegian army along Sweden's western frontier. He was duly recognised by Charles as his heir and eventual successor in July 1809. But on 28 May 1810 Christian August was inspecting Swedish troops in the southern province of Skane when he suddenly fell from his horse in an apoplectic fit. Within half an hour he was dead.

Four days later the King agreed to summon a Riksdag to choose another Prince Royal. Front-runner was the Duke of Augustenburg, Christian August's brother, even though he was widely regarded as an absolute blockhead with even less to commend him than the deposed Gustav IV. By now, however, King and Council were acutely conscious of French power in northern Europe; Charles XIII had sent General Wrede to Paris as his personal representative at the marriage festivities of Marie Louise and, both from Wrede and from the Swedish envoy in Paris, Gustav Lagerbielke, the Council knew of the deterioration in Franco–Russian relations over the previous twelve months. Accordingly, as early as 2 June, Charles XIII wrote to Napoleon seeking his advice. Would Augustenburg be acceptable to the Emperor? Or had he another candidate to propose?

In the previous year the election was rushed through under threat of an invasion. But in 1810 the contending factions refused to be stampeded. The deposed Gustav IV still had his champions. One group, weary of Sweden's endless cavalcade of unstable princelings, wished to look instead for an eminent Frenchman, one of Napoleon's family, perhaps, or a Marshal who stood out as a leader of men. Among these Francophile officers was Baron Otto Mörner, a twenty-nine-year-old lieutenant in the Uppland Infantry Regiment who was about to marry the sister of the Swedish Chancellor, Gustav Wetterstedt. It was natural for Mörner to seek out his prospective brother-in-law and discuss the succession crisis. Although he was a cousin of the Count Mörner whom Bernadotte had treated so chivalrously at Lübeck, he did not specifically canvas on behalf of the Prince of Ponte Corvo at this stage; the merits of other Marshals seem to have come under discussion. Mörner suggested that, as there were only seven weeks until the Riksdag met and couriers travelled slowly between Sweden and France, he might go to Paris with duplicates of Charles XIII's message to Napoleon and press on Lagerbielke the urgency of informing Stockholm of the Emperor's views. He knew Paris well, claimed a close friendship with a senior staff officer, and persuaded Wetterstedt how useful he could be as a personal envoy, supplementing Lagerbielke's official diplomacy. Wetterstedt may have suspected Mörner of boasting, but he saw nothing to lose in letting him set out on this, somewhat ill-defined, special mission to the French capital.

The courier beat him by a single day. When, on 20 June, Mörner reached Paris, Lagerbielke was at St Cloud, pacing the parkland beside the Emperor, as Napoleon gave the considered judgment which Charles XIII had sought. The wisest solution, Napoleon declared, would be to recognise the King of Denmark as heir to the Swedish throne as a first step towards the union of Scandinavia in a single kingdom. Such an arrangement admirably suited France's general strategy: it would bind the Scandinavian states together against Britain and ensure that all the ports of the Baltic were linked firmly within the Continental System. Lagerbielke was dismayed; the prospect of eventual Danish Succession might unite the Opposition groups in Stockholm, he insisted. Napoleon did not press his point; but in the letter he wrote to Charles XIII four days later he again stressed the advantages of binding links between Danes, Norwegians and Swedes; Frederick VI of Denmark was his man.

Meanwhile Mörner, having discovered that his duplicate letter from the King was no longer needed, was acting independently. Within twenty-four hours of reaching Paris he met his staff officer friend, Pierre Lapié – who was, in fact, no higher than a Captain in the Topographical Section. But through Lapié, Mörner had talks with two Generals, Guilleminot and Grimoard, and sounded them out on possible French candidates for the Succession: Masséna? Macdonald? Eugène de Beauharnais? Bernadotte? Eugène, the Viceroy of Italy and son-in-law of the King of Bavaria, had a higher princely standing than any of the Marshals. But Bernadotte was already known and respected in Sweden, a legendary figure in Ostergotland. Moreover he was militarily unemployed and at leisure in Paris. The Marshal had received a Swedish Major at Dresden soon after the deposition of Gustav IV Adolf and, without reference to Napoleon, arranged for a suspension of hostilities along the Baltic coast during Sweden's internal crisis. At the end of February he had joined Champagny (Napoleon's Foreign Minister) in talks with Lagerbielke over Swedish affairs; and more recently he had exchanged pleasantries with General Wrede, asking in particular about his Lübeck prisoner, Count Mörner. It was therefore easy for young Mörner to obtain an invitation to meet the Marshal, at the Rue d'Anjou on 25 June, at midday.

The conversation went well. When Mörner insisted to Bernadotte that there was a pro-French lobby in Stockholm favouring his election, he was flattered. But he was also mistrustful. For why had these supporters sent as their emissary a mere infantry Lieutenant, not yet thirty? He could not, he explained to Mörner, become a candidate without the approval of Napoleon and of King Charles XIII; but he did not rule out the possibility of his name going forward. A powerful reinforcement followed the young Lieutenant next day. General Wrede, interested in Mörner's account of his visit, came to the Rue d'Anjou and confirmed that there was a French Party at Stockholm. He pointed out, however, that Bernadotte had three weaknesses as a candidate: he was not a Lutheran; he did not speak Swedish; he was allegedly out of favour with Napoleon. Wrede's comments provoked Bernadotte to a more positive response: language difficulties could, no doubt, be overcome and tales of disagreement with the Emperor were much exaggerated; as for religious allegiance, that presented no problem to someone 'born in the country of Henri IV'. Soon after Wrede left a former French merchant in Gothenburg called at the Rue d'Anjou; Jean Antoine Fournier, who had lived in Sweden for sixteen years, had been told by the Swedish Consul that the Marshal might find his services of value. Bernadotte, who had known Fournier in Hamburg, took note of his offer. Next morning, as already planned, he set out with Désirée for Plombières once more. For three weeks he remained in the Vosges, well away from the capital.

From Bernadotte's correspondence it seems he may have mentioned Mörner's initial approach to Napoleon at St Cloud a few hours before Wrede called on him. If so, neither he nor the Emperor took the matter seriously. But Wrede's visit confirmed that a group of Swedish nobles was looking for a French candidate: and, before leaving La Grange for Plombières, Bernadotte sent a report to the

Emperor. He informed him that Wrede had said that the will of the Swedish nation would be in his favour, should Napoleon approve of his candidature; and he also enclosed the first letter he had received from Mörner.

Napoleon was puzzled. Lagerbielke had said nothing about a French candidate; he was still insisting that the Swedish nation backed the Duke of Augustenburg. If there was, indeed, a French lobby in Stockholm, the Emperor was far from convinced that Bernadotte should be their nominee. On the day the Bernadottes reached Plombières, Napoleon sent his Grand Marshal of the Palace to the Elysée, where Eugène was in residence, to ask if the Viceroy of Italy wished for Napoleon's backing in the Swedish Succession contest. Eugène, taken by surprise, asked for twenty-four hours to consult his wife. He then turned the proposals down. His reasons were not entirely convincing – religion, kinship between his wife and the deposed Gustav IV's consort, etc. Almost certainly, as his step-father well knew, Eugène's chief consideration was a reluctance to leave the French Empire so long as his divorced mother might need his powerful backing. 'I am so sorry; I should have been much pleased; but I daresay you were right', Napoleon remarked to Eugène, a few days later.

The unfortunate Lagerbielke still knew nothing about any of this proto-canvassing in Paris. But General Wrede sent Mörner back to Stockholm and, after his departure, took Lagerbielke into his confidence. Understandably the accredited diplomatic representative of Sweden was highly indignant: 'In my long experience I have witnessed the occurrence of many extraordinary events, and have perceived with alarm the spirit of madness and political folly which possesses some young Swedes, but I admit to being stupefied by the incredible audacity of Baron Mörner', he wrote to the Swedish Foreign Minister on Saturday, 30 June. Nevertheless, Lagerbielke was fair; he knew Bernadotte personally and commended his qualities; but he begged to be informed whom he was to back. As yet he had seen nothing of Champagny since learning of Mörner's activities; on Sunday the whole diplomatic corps would be at a ball to honour Napoleon and Marie Louise, given by the Austrian ambassador; Lagerbielke intended to raise the matter that evening.

They had hardly begun their conversational sparring, in a small room at the Embassy, when fire swept through the improvised wooden ballroom outside. Fifteen hundred guests fled for their lives. Among them were Napoleon and Marie Louise, Metternich (Austria's Foreign Minister) and his wife, the Viceroy and Vicereine of Italy, and Caroline Murat, Queen of Naples, who suffered a miscarriage. Although Napoleon personally directed the fire-fighting, many had already perished or were badly scarred in a tragedy without precedent in Parisian society. For several days thereafter it was impossible for Lagerbielke to see Champagny. By the time that they did meet, news had reached Paris of another strange twist to events in Sweden and Napoleon was in no hurry to commit himself. If he backed Bernadotte, and the Riksdag failed to elect him, France would suffer a diplomatic rebuff. If the Marshal went ahead with his candidature independent of French support and was defeated, then the humiliation would wound Bernadotte's pride rather than the prestige of France. In his talks with Lagerbielke Champagny remained splendidly evasive; and Savary, who had succeeded Fouché as Minister of Police and had no love for Berna-dotte, made a belated effort to interest Lagerbielke in another Marshal: Berthier, perhaps? Masséna? or why not Davout?

The news from Sweden which had surprised Paris arose from an incident on 20 June, the day on which Mörner arrived in Paris and Lagerbielke went to St Cloud to discuss the Succession with Napoleon. For on that Wednesday the state funeral of Christian August took place in Stockholm amid rumours, encouraged by anonymous pamphlets, that the Prince had been poisoned by Gusta-vians. Their leader was said to be the highest of the Court dignitaries, Count Fersen, Marie Antoinette's old admirer, now Marshal of the Realm. There were no grounds for this canard, but during the funeral procession a section of the crowd began to stone Fersen's carriage. When he stepped down and sought cover, he was seized by the mob and slowly beaten to death, with soldiers and gendarmerie doing nothing to save him, as if conniving at lynch law in their streets. An uglier mood prevailed in Stockholm than in the bloodless revolution a year before.

Charles XIII and his Council, horrified by a crime whose motive seemed hard to determine, gave orders for the Riksdag to be summoned to Örebro Castle, over a hundred miles south-west of Stockholm. But tension remained high. When Lieutenant Mörner arrived home on 12 July, prematurely claiming that the French would back Bernadotte, the news 'burst like a bomb' on an over-excited capital. Partly for his own protection, Mörner was silenced by being placed under arrest and hustled off to his regimental depot at Uppsala. Yet by the time General Wrede returned – exactly a week later – the Francophiles were well-organised, with the Lieutenant's cousin, Count Gustave Mörner, as their influential spokesman. Wrede warmly supported them: Bernadotte's 'private life is a model for our days (*un exemple pour notre époque*)', he wrote, 'A good husband, a good father, a good friend, a good leader, he is loved by all around him'.

Meanwhile at Plombières this paragon was discussing his future plans with Désirée and her sister, Julie. What was agreed among them may only be deduced from contemporary letters – which the writers knew would be intercepted by the Emperor's spies – and from occasional remarks in later letters, generally inserted in moments of reminiscent self-justification. There seems no doubt, however, about three points: that Bernadotte was backed by his wife and his sister-in-law; that (as he wrote two years later) he was at that moment 'resolved to follow the Emperor's system'; and that, however much he might affect an air of leisured detachment, he regarded himself as a serious contestant with every intention of becoming Prince Royal. Despite his apparent isolation in the Vosges he was able to arrange his own information service: Hamburg merchants, grateful to him for past assistance, kept him well posted with news 'from the North' brought by express messengers travelling to Frankfurt and on to Strasbourg. On 21 July – the Saturday Charles XIII arrived at Örebro Castle for the elective Riksdag – Bernadotte was back in Paris, where he surprised Napoleon by his knowledge of events in Sweden.

At Stockholm and in Ostergotland popular feeling seemed on his side. But Charles XIII still backed the Duke of Augustenburg; King Frederick VI of Denmark enjoyed some support in the Riksdag; and Tsar Alexander I also had a runner – his brother-in-law, George of Oldenburg. Bernadotte, recognising that he needed an election agent, turned to Fournier, who had remained on hand in Paris. He was well-briefed, supplied with prints of the Marshal himself, of Désirée and of Oscar, authorised to speak generously of Bernadotte's accumulated wealth, and sent off post-haste to Örebro, with a diplomatic passport from Champagny. Fournier was a natural Public Relations man, with some journalistic skills. He seems to have drafted pamphlets of his own, printed in Swedish and in the form of convincing dialogues, to prove that no one was better suited to the nation's needs than this unseen Marshal awaiting a summons from over the sea. Under Fournier's management the Bernadotte-for-Prince-Royal campaign more closely anticipated a modern US Presidential trail than did Mr Madison's gentlemanly appeals to American voters two years before.

Had Bernadotte been required at Örebro in person then the Diet would almost certainly have become one more historic occasion he narrowly missed. Fournier, however, moved swiftly, leaving Paris on 26 July and reaching Örebro on Friday, 10 August: 'Two days more and he would have arrived too late', Lars Engestrom, the Swedish Foreign Minister, wrote at the end of the following week. Since foreign diplomats were barred from Örebro itself, Fournier stayed at an inn on the outskirts and sent a message to Count Engestrom emphasising his status as a private envoy, not in government service. But when the Count received him on Saturday morning, Fournier showed a verbal dexterity with half-truths that even Talleyrand might have envied. He claimed that Bernadotte could count on the Emperor's backing, but that Napoleon was maintaining a general silence as he did not wish to appear as intimidating the Swedes. To objections that a French Marshal would bring with him compatriots eager for lucrative posts in Sweden, Fournier insisted that Bernadotte had no wish to impose outsiders on the country that honoured him. From his considerable wealth, Fournier added, he would advance eight million francs at four per cent, adding that he would also settle outstanding claims by Swedish merchants and landowners for losses inflicted by the French in recent years. Count Engestrom was suitably impressed.

Throughout the fortnight Fournier was hurrying north, the elective Riksdag (generally called 'the Örebro Diet') had been in session. A special committee of twelve was appointed to examine the credentials of four candidates: Augustenburg; Frederick of Denmark; George of Oldenburg; and Bernadotte. When the committee decided in favour of a contestant, his name would be passed to the Council and then to the Riksdag as a whole, with the King finally giving his approval. On Wednesday, 8 August, eleven members of the Committee were agreed on Augustenburg; General Wrede was the only dissentient. Reports of Fournier's conversation with Engestrom on the following Saturday enabled Chancellor Wetterstedt to persuade the Council to delay further voting until Thursday. In his talks, Fournier enlarged still further on Bernadotte's considerable fortune and his qualities of military leadership. Members of the Diet who wished might see at General Wrede's lodgings an attractive portrait of an eleven-year-old boy, his hand confidently resting on the buckle of his father's sabre. 'Everybody is running to Count Wrede's to see the portrait of the little Oscar', Charles XIII was told by his aide-de-camp a few days later.

News that Napoleon had dismissed his acting ambassador in Stockholm for having opposed Bernadotte's candidature convinced waverers that Fournier's claims were justified and that the Emperor would aid Sweden if his Marshal became heir to the throne. When the committee next met, on Thursday 16 August, it gave ten votes to Bernadotte and two votes to Augustenburg. On Thursday the King recognised that he could stand out no longer against the obvious enthusiasm of Stockholm for the Marshal; and on the following Tuesday (21 August) – a mere eleven days after Fournier reached Örebro – the Diet voted unanimously in favour of Berna-dotte. Paris learnt the news on 3 September, although a muddled report led Napoleon to believe at first that the Swedes had chosen young Oscar, with his father as Protector. Next morning, however, Count Gustav Mörner arrived and presented Marshal the Prince of Ponte Corvo with a letter from King Charles XIII informing him of his election as Prince Royal of Sweden.

Guests dining with the Bernadottes on the evening that the news broke thought the Prince Royal seemed sad and sombre, while Désirée was ecstatically excited. He did not believe Napoleon would allow him to go to Sweden; she had no doubts on that score but failed to appreciate the difference between the decision of the Örebro Diet and the family conference at Bayonne two years before, which made Julie consort of a new 'King of Spain and the Indies'. If Queen Julie spent most of her time at Mortefontaine and in Paris, then Désirée saw no reason why a Princess Royal of Sweden need abandon her homes and friends in France. Napoleon, too, affected to see the Örebro Election as simply an extension of his own form of kingmaking: brothers Joseph, Louis and Jerome were found crowns; so was brother-in-law Murat; and now a Prince from the outer ring of the family would stand on the steps of yet another throne. The electoral victory of one of his Marshals at Örebro was 'An honourable monument to my reign and an extension of my glory', Napoleon declared at Court, taking care that his remarks reached Lagerbielke's ears. The Emperor assured Bernadotte verbally of his approval on 5 September, confirming his acceptance of the Örebro decision in a letter to the King of Sweden that same Wednesday. At the end of the week, however, there was a flurry of diplomatic activity. Metternich, Austria's Foreign Minister, had been in France since April and was in Napoleon's confidence throughout the discussions over the Swedish Succession; but it was essential to reassure Tsar Alexander, and the Russian ambassador in Paris was repeatedly told that Napoleon would have preferred one of the other candidates to have won the election. At the same time, Napoleon sought to impose fetters on Bernadotte's freedom of action. When, in 1700, Louis XIV created his grandson King of Spain he had insisted that the Letters Patent should contain a clause by which the new sovereign undertook never to bear arms against France. On Monday, 10 September, Bernadotte was told Napoleon would insert a similar clause in the Letters Patent permitting him to accept his Swedish elevation.

The Prince Royal-elect protested vigorously against this restraint; it would, he argued, bind a future Swedish King in vassalage to France. Napoleon tried to mollify him: 'Give the Prince of Ponte Corvo a million francs out of public funds (*sur la caisse de service*). That will be regularised straight away', ran a note from the Emperor to his Minister of the Treasury that Thursday. But Bernadotte, though prepared to accept funds as compensation for the endowment he was losing in France, remained adamant. On the following Thursday Napoleon received him at St Cloud for the last of those stormy interviews which had enlivened the relationship of the two soldiers over the past thirteen years. This time Bernadotte had his way: 'Sire', he demanded, 'would you make me a greater man than yourself by requiring me to refuse a crown?' 'Very well, then, go; and let our destinies be fulfilled', Napoleon replied. Nor was this his only concession: Bernadotte might have until the following May to assess the economic needs of his new country and decide if Sweden should become fully integrated in the Continental System. 'But then you must declare yourself – friend or foe!' Napoleon warned.

They met twice more. The Emperor and Empress invited the Prince and Princess Royal of Sweden to dine with them at the Tuileries on Sunday, 23 September; and on the Monday Bernadotte, in Swedish uniform, formally said farewell to Napoleon and his brother Marshals at St Cloud. He left La Grange on the following

Thursday, took Désirée and Oscar to Julie at Mortefontaine and, on the last day of the month, set out for Sweden, with Count Gustav Mörner travelling with him in his carriage. They stopped briefly at Cassel, where King Jerome of Westphalia was their host, spent three days in Hamburg and, at Fredericksborg, they were guests of an unsuccessful contestant at Örebro, King Frederick VI of Denmark. 'Everywhere I have been welcomed with great distinction', he wrote to Désirée, 'civic officials, soldiers, people, all seem to be competing with each other for the pleasure of greeting me.' Then, on 19 October, to Elsinore, with the Swedish coastline only three miles distant across the Sound.

At Elsinore that Friday morning, in the presence of the Archbishop of Uppsala, Bernadotte publicly affirmed his adherence to Lutheranism. It was a faith 'to which I have for a long time past been secretly drawn', he said, a reference to conversations he had held with Lutheran pastors in Hesse, Hanover and Hamburg. Next day he crossed the Sound aboard a Swedish gunboat and in mid-afternoon set foot on Swedish soil at Hälsingborg, to salutes from a naval squadron, from the cannon of the fort and from a cavalry regiment along the quay. Chancellor Wetterstedt and other dignitaries welcomed the Prince Royal. Before he left Hälsingborg he received a special envoy from the King with his commission as Supreme Commander of Sweden's Armed Forces. He had already been well briefed by Count Mörner; now his political education continued as his carriage sped on through cheering towns and villages across the plains of southern Sweden. In foreign affairs his companions believed they were moulding him to be, not the heir of Charles XIII, but the successor of Gustav III. At last, four weeks and a day after his farewell to Désirée, he reached Drottningholm, unostentatiously. It was agreed that he should meet the royal family privately before his ceremonial entry into the capital.

Charles XIII awaited his coming with apprehension. Ought he to have defied his Councillors, ignored popular sentiment, and refused to recognise the election of a Prince Royal until the Örebro Diet chose a royal prince? He had staked the future of monarchy in Sweden on the acclaim accorded to a foreign soldier by a small section of his own nobility. Had he acted foolishly? At sixty-two Charles was prematurely old, a dull intelligence drifting rapidly into senility. But he could remember vividly the social elegance of Louis XV's France, where men and women of quality practised the art of living. Now he was expected to welcome, both as heir to his throne and as his adopted son, a former sergeant who, at the time he was fêted in Versailles, was a day-pupil of the monks in Béarn. King and Prince Royal met in an ante-room of the palace and, after a few minutes, Queen Hedvig Charlotte joined them. No one, of course, knows what was said; but it is clear that, from the first, Bernadotte easily gained their admiration by the courtesy and charm of which he was already so skilled a practitioner. That same evening the King confided genially to his aide-de-camp, in a happy stage-whisper: 'My dear General, I have gambled rashly – but I think I have won.'

Bernadotte had already agreed to accept a historic first name which would associate him with the reigning sovereign and with soldier kings cherished in legend. It was therefore as Prince Carl Johan (Charles John) that he was presented to the four Estates of the Riksdag a week after his arrival in Stockholm. His address of thanks, delivered in French with Gascon rhetoric and subsequently read for him in Swedish, struck the right note, with its emphasis both on national pride and on the virtues of an enduring and just peace. To the surprise of foreign diplomats the Prince Royal seemed unable to put a foot wrong, in those first months in Sweden. Even poor Sofia Magdalena, Gustav's widow and mother of the deposed king, was heard to praise the newcomer as 'a happy choice, a Prince who was in every way obliging', one who was bringing back to the Swedish Court the old refinements of French life she had known in younger days.

There was, however, one disappointment for Stockholm's high society that November: Charles John had arrived without the new Princess Royal or the boy with the Nordic name whose portrait had aroused such interest at Count Wrede's in August. But as soon as Désirée received news of her husband's welcome in Sweden, she prepared to set out to join him. With Oscar, her friend Élise de Flotte and two nephews who were junior officers to serve as escort, Désirée left Paris for Hamburg in the third week of November. It was a bitter winter and the small group of three carriages made slow progress across Germany. By 5 December, when they reached Hamburg, Désirée was miserably cold; Christmas at Copenhagen and Elsinore brought little comfort. Messages from Stockholm emphasised a mounting crisis in Franco–Swedish relations and it seemed unlikely that Bernadotte could travel south to greet his wife. The Swedish coast, beyond the Sound, was wrapped in fog and she waited for several days before it was possible to cross so narrow a stretch of water.

When Désirée's cavalcade eventually reached Stockholm, at nearly ten o'clock at night on 6 January 1811, the temperature had fallen to −24°C (11°F). The city was illuminated in her honour; a salute of 256 guns greeted her; and there was a small crowd of wellwishers outside the palace, despite the ice and snow. But the reception meant little to her; she had a bad cold in the head and acute gingivitis. Unlike her husband, she found the first days in the barrack-like palace depressing, and she was not accustomed to hiding her feelings. Her insistence on retaining her Catholic faith alarmed the Lutherans around her. 'The Princess is small, not pretty and with no figure whatsoever', Queen Hedvig Charlotte noted severely in her journal. 'Her timidity makes her brusque . . . A spoilt child, but sweet, kind and compassionate.' However, the King and Queen had nothing but praise for Oscar; and as Charles John – at forty-eight – celebrated his first birthday with his extended family, all Stockholm's political factions still spoke highly of what had been achieved at Örebro. Sweden, it seemed, had found in this hot-headed Southerner a soldier-statesman capable of keeping Crown and People united. But was it to be in peace or in war? Did the Emperor he had served see the kingdom he would rule as partner, vassal or foe? Ought the Prince Royal to look to Britain or Russia rather than to France for support? Once the ice and fog began to recede in the Baltic and shipping could move freely again such imponderables of policy would demand swift solution. The long days of summer were to be Charles John's testing time.

Chapter 11
Whose Ally?

'THERE is nothing of the parvenu about him, not a gesture that is wrong or out of place', the Tsar's envoy, General Chernyshev, reported back to Alexander a month after Bernadotte's arrival in Stockholm. The comment was patronising, but apt. For the Prince Royal was totally at ease in his new role. During these first weeks he observed much and, uncharacteristically, kept his silence. Charles XIII suffered a stroke less than a month after Bernadotte's arrival. It was clear that, although the King was only in his sixty-third year and delighted in the presence of an adopted son and grandson, his mind frequently drifted away from the day-to-day business of government. Soon the Prince Royal would be called to act with all the decisiveness of a Regent. It was essential for him to learn Sweden's needs and understand Swedish ways rapidly.

Here, however, he was at a disadvantage. As an outsider it should have been possible for him to stand impartially above faction. In reality, he was dependent upon those members of the nobility who not only spoke French fluently, but could understand him – for, as an émigré commented during the Leipzig campaign, 'the Prince would busy himself dictating orders in Gascon'. He leant heavily on Count Mörner, on the soldier-diplomat brothers Carl and Gustav Löwenhielm, and on Chancellor Wetterstedt, who had been Gustav IV's private secretary. Count Engestrom, the earnest and scholarly Foreign Minister, puzzled him. Although judiciously detached over most questions, Engestrom was at heart a Russophobe and he found the newcomer's apparent self-confidence brash and disturbing; but he remained scrupulously loyal to the Prince, who retained him in office for fourteen years.

Some bonds linking Bernadotte to the Swedish nobility were

masonic, for the practice of Freemasonry was widespread among the officer corps; Charles XIII, having verified that the Prince was already initiated in the lower grades of a French lodge, in May 1811 conferred upon him the highest order of Swedish freemasonry, a decoration named after the King himself. But, quite apart from the brotherhood of freemasonry, Bernadotte had little difficulty in establishing good relations with the most respected army commanders, notably General Carl Adlercreutz, who had arrested Gustav IV. He also went out of his way to flatter General Count Stedingk, a soldier and diplomat of great experience. Stedingk was ambassador at St Petersburg when Bernadotte landed in Sweden; he was summoned back to Stockholm and, in 1811, created a Field-Marshal, a rare honour in the Swedish army. The Count, who was sixty-five when he received his Marshal's baton, had served under the unfortunate Fersen in the Régiment Royal-Suédois and retained sentimental memories of Marie Antoinette at Versailles, but he also knew the Russian army and its leaders intimately. He respected Bernadotte even if he had little patience with the Gascon rhetoric with which the Prince would, from time to time, seek to inspire decision making around a council table.

At first Bernadotte made every attempt to learn Swedish. Peter Adam Wallmark, a highly respected librarian and newspaper editor, came to the palace each day in those early weeks of 1811 so as to spend one hour teaching the Prince Royal his future subjects' language. Bernadotte was not a good pupil; formal tuition of this kind was alien to him. Like Napoleon at Passeriano, he wished to display his own erudition, secretly conning a subject in detail before Wallmark's arrival so as to overwhelm his tutor with knowledge of the distant past and passages quoted from France's greatest authors. Wallmark was, indeed, impressed; from him Swedish academics discovered, with surprise, that the Prince Royal was not merely a soldier of distinction and charm, but a deep reader who knew his Corneille and Racine, could cite Montesquieu, Rousseau and the great Encyclopedists, and was able to speak with authority of Alaric, the Visigoths and the Vandal Kingdoms of the Mediterranean. Such scholarship deserved honoured recognition at Uppsala University; it did not, however, help acquire a mastery of basic Swedish, and the Prince Royal's one attempt to read a speech in the language proved disastrous. Wallmark's daily hour of tuition was shared jointly by Bernadotte, Désirée and Oscar in February. By the spring the Prince Royal had cut his daily tuition time down to fifteen minutes; in the summer he gave up the attempt altogether. Only Oscar persevered; he mastered the unfamiliar tongue before he was thirteen. Bernadotte was able to make his needs known in Swedish to his servants, and it is possible he understood more that was said around him than he found it convenient to admit. But French was spoken in the Royal Council in Stockholm and at military conferences during his later campaigns. Poor Wallmark fell from grace in 1813 when an article in his newspaper, reviewing a propaganda pamphlet with rare impartiality, unwittingly revealed more of Bernadotte's military thinking than his royal pupil wished the world to know.

With Napoleon's permission, Bernadotte and Désirée retained in Stockholm a suite of between thirty and forty Frenchmen and Frenchwomen: military aides-de-camp, granted special leave of absence; secretaries and couriers; valets and maids; a hairdresser; a chandler, who was also a specialist in the use of wax for sealing documents; a dentist and a doctor. Bernadotte, knowing that the military aides would be recalled to French service, sent for two old companions: Colonel Louis Camps, a boyhood friend who enlisted in the Régiment Royal-la-Marine and who, since 1805, had served intermittently with Bernadotte; and Jean Gré, who had known Camps and Bernadotte in his childhood at Pau. Both men flourished in Sweden: Gré, after acting as a secret agent in Copenhagen, became the Prince's personal secretary; and Camps remained the Prince's close confidant, master-craftsman of his secret service with the rank of General and a large estate on Värmdö island.

Not every old friend of the Prince Royal could be sure of a welcome. General Sarrazin, who had given Bernadotte and Désirée sanctuary after Brumaire, survived a fever-ridden campaign in Haiti to become commandant to Boulogne but, with little advancement in ten years, he turned into a sour, disappointed man in constant conflict with his seniors. So deep was this rift that one night in June 1810 Sarrazin slipped away from Boulogne in a small boat to join Napoleon's enemies in London. Five months later a court-martial at Lille condemned him to death in absentia for desertion. Sarrazin's vitriolic attacks on the Emperor may have impressed the British Foreign Office but they did not at that moment endear him to his old commander; and, though Sarrazin set out on the long journey to Gothenburg, it was soon made clear to him that his presence in

Sweden would be an embarrassment and he was turned back to England. Five years after Bernadotte came to the throne, he acknowledged his debt to Sarrazin with the grant of a pension, but in 1811–12 the Prince Royal had to behave circumspectly. At Örebro Fournier had taken pains to dispel a widespread fear that a French Marshal would bring to Sweden a set of down-at-the-elbows old comrades, grasping for lucrative posts; and against this risk Bernadotte stood naturally on his guard. Even Fournier himself was rewarded discreetly and encouraged to return to France, despite his mastery of the Swedish language.

During his first year in Sweden Bernadotte had no intention of antagonising Napoleon by providing his personal enemies with sanctuary. Indeed, technically he was Generalissimo of an army serving in alliance with the French Empire. When Bernadotte arrived in Stockholm he had found Franco–Swedish relations strained by a fresh demand from the Emperor: Sweden must enforce the Continental System rigidly and, so as to make certain that there was no trade with London, must declare war on Britain. The Council decided that Sweden was still too weak from the disastrous Finnish War and too isolated diplomatically to risk challenging Napoleon; on 18 November 1810 Engestrom informed the French ambassador that Sweden would meet his demands. There was, however, no clash of arms between Swedish warships in the Baltic and the Royal Navy; ships flying neutral flags sailed into Gothenburg, maintaining secret commercial links with Britain; and the small ports in Swedish Pomerania continued to prosper, thanks to enterprising sea-captains who smuggled British manufactured goods into a continent eager to receive them. 'They are laughing at Sweden's declaration of war in London, and I even see a smile on Swedish faces in Stockholm', Baron Alquier, the French ambassador, informed Paris.

Napoleon was, however, prepared to allow Bernadotte the six months' grace he had promised so dramatically at their interview in September. There were cordial exchanges over the winter months: felicitations in March, when Marie Louise gave Napoleon the legitimate son for whom he had so long craved; and, as Bernadotte was at that time acting as Regent, the bestowal on the infant King of Rome of a blue ribbon, the highest decoration in Swedish chivalry, the Order of the Seraphim. Napoleon, too, was generous; a ring containing miniature portraits of the Emperor, Empress and their son was sent by special courier to Stockholm. More appreciated, perhaps, was the settlement of some of Bernadotte's claims over his lost estates. For Fournier, in letting the Örebro Diet believe that Bernadotte possessed a personal fortune, had unintentionally prompted the Estates to allow the Prince Royal a much smaller sum from the Civil List than his predecessors enjoyed. Compensation for the loss of a Marshal's pension and privileges was therefore welcome. A sum of 11,764 francs outstanding from the revenues of Ponte Corvo was even awarded, at Bernadotte's suggestion, to his brother in Pau, whom the Emperor had raised to the dignity of a Baron in the previous autumn. Amid the borrowed splendour of his adoptive family in Sweden, the Prince Royal was occasionally troubled by a pang of conscience for his kinsfolk seventeen hundred miles away in Béarn.

Graver matters of general policy took far longer to resolve. Many of Bernadotte's original supporters in Sweden assumed that he would lead the army forward in a war against Russia, aimed at recovering Finland. But a campaign of this nature held little appeal for the Prince Royal; it would turn Sweden eastwards in what might well become a cycle of conflicts with a powerful neighbour, for if Sweden regained Finland, there was no guarantee Russia would accept the loss of the Grand Duchy as final. Even before landing at Hälsingborg, Bernadotte was inclined to support a different policy, one favoured briefly by Gustav III, which would turn Sweden's interests westwards, towards the Atlantic and the maritime commerce of the greater oceans, not merely the Baltic. Bernadotte strongly favoured a Scandinavian union, binding Sweden and Norway together and perhaps straddling the Kattegat, with a foothold on one of the greater Danish islands, too. But since Norway was, in 1810, part of Denmark, an active ally of Napoleon, Bernadotte arrived in Sweden with greater hopes of achieving this change of policy in partnership with Russia rather than with France.

At the time of the Örebro Diet Tsar Alexander and the Emperor Napoleon were still paying lip-service to the friendship they had professed ever since their meeting at Tilsit three years before. Adhesion to the Continental System was, however, inflicting even greater damage on Russian commerce than on Sweden's merchants, who had the advantage of a longer ice-free coastline along which to defy French patrol boats. The Tsar also deplored Napoleon's expansionist policies within Germany and, in the last months of

1810, he particularly resented the incorporation into metropolitan France of the Duchy of Oldenburg, whose ruler had dynastic links with the Russian Imperial Family (and also with the Vasas in Sweden). On the last day of the year 1810 Alexander published a tariff decree which finally took Russia out of the Continental System: a heavy duty was clamped on goods coming overland, while restrictions on imports and exports by sea were virtually removed. News of the Tsar's tariff decree aroused cautious interest in Stockholm, although Alexander personally remained bitterly distrusted because of his annexation of Finland.

Tsar Alexander had already taken the first steps towards securing Bernadotte's co-operation. In a note written in his own hand twelve days before the tariff decree, he asked the Prince Royal for his 'friendship and confidence', assuring him that the preservation of the Swedish kingdom was in Russia's own interest. More subtly the Tsar, who in his boyhood had been tutored by the Swiss republican Frédéric La Harpe, flattered Bernadotte as a soldier rather than as an elected Prince. 'My admiration for you goes back a long way, to the time when you were still a General', the Tsar wrote. 'Since I was myself brought up as a Republican, I like to value a man for himself rather than by his titles.' Both Alexander and Bernadotte – and, in some respects, Napoleon too – followed their impulses, placing an artless emphasis on personal relationships in public affairs which was alien to more sophisticated sovereigns and statesmen. In a reply sent after news of the tariff decree had reached Stockholm, the Prince Royal showed a little more restraint: he did not mention France, Napoleon or tariffs but he emphasised his intention of upholding Swedish independence. Even so, at one point in his letter Bernadotte lapsed into the curiously emotive terms which Alexander affected: 'Yes, Sire, I shall be Your Majesty's friend, since you are so kind as to say that you wish that with all your heart.'

Meanwhile Napoleon was testing the loyalties of his former Marshal. Why not revive the tradition by which Swedish volunteers formed a regiment within the French Army? Might not 2000 Swedish sailors gain seagoing experience on the wider oceans if they were seconded for service with the French fleet at Brest? Both proposals were firmly rejected in Stockholm. But the Prince Royal was perplexed by the manoeuvrings of the Tilsit allies. If Napoleon was prepared to make Sweden, rather than Denmark, his favoured client in Scandinavia and help the Swedes to acquire Norway,

Bernadotte would take no step which would cut him off from France. At the end of January 1811 Captain Gentil Saint-Alphonse, one of his most trusted aides, was sent home to Paris, with detailed verbal assurances which he was to pass on to the Emperor. Bernadotte had every intention of establishing a messenger service of his own, more personal and direct than the ambassador could provide.

Napoleon received Gentil Saint-Alphonse at the Tuileries on 10 February. 'The Emperor listened attentively to everything I told him about Sweden's military resources and about the favours which Your Excellency was hoping to do for him one day', Gentil reported nine days later. Over Norway he was not helpful, but he showed such interest in Finland that 'his questions left me in no doubt over what was about to take place, even though he carefully changed the subject as soon as I mentioned Russia. "You are always talking about the Russians", he said. "Should it happen – well, let's wait and see. Right now one ought only to be making war on England".' Gentil explained that the Swedes were 'hoping to make common cause with France', but 'needed time to put their forces in order'; they would, he thought, 'be ready for employment by June'. These verbal assurances already went further than any previous Swedish commitment, but Gentil had still not delivered all he was told. He now developed sweeping generalisations made to him by Bernadotte in which the Prince had apparently envisaged a pincer movement on St Petersburg; 'I passed on what Your Excellency had told me about the left and right flanks of the Grand Army, which seemed to please him', Gentil reported back to Stockholm, somewhat enigmatically. It is hardly surprising if, despite Napoleon's lingering mistrust of his former Marshal, he began to believe that Sweden might, after all, become a loyal ally. Throughout the spring and well into the summer of 1811 Bernadotte passed on useful titbits of information gathered by Swedish agents: the disposition of the Tsar's army across Finland; the size of the Russian garrison in Riga; the comings and goings of secret British emissaries to St Petersburg. With such evidence of goodwill, Napoleon had no fear of any Russo–Swedish combination against him.

Outwardly relations between Sweden and France were far better in the early summer than in November, when Désirée had travelled north to join her husband. The coming of longer days and the clear Baltic sunshine lifted her spirits. Yet the daily round of life in Stockholm bored her. She found court-etiquette exasperating, especially when it imposed barriers which excluded Élise de Flotte, her close companion, from her company. The Clarys had always been a close-knit family, and Désirée was eager to see her sister, Julie, and her mother again. Since Julie had continued to live at Mortefontaine for most of the years she was a titular Queen, Désirée saw no reason why she should not spend a few months away from Sweden, on a visit home. She recognised that Oscar would have to remain in Sweden, for he was now Duke of Södermanland and was being educated as the nation's future king. But her role at Court was so ill-defined that she believed her absence would readily be accepted. Finally she convinced Bernadotte that the cold winter had weakened her physically; she needed a cure at Plombières, where the waters had always proved so beneficial. On 4 June she left Stockholm for her favourite spa, with Élise de Flotte as a travelling companion. There was no formal separation of husband and wife. It was anticipated that she would return once her health was better, for she would not wish the son on whom she doted to reach manhood without her guidance.

This was a false assumption. Her influence on Oscar's upbringing was minimal once he became a Swedish Prince. Summer days with Julie at Plombières proved more congenial than anything Sweden could offer. The two sisters were still there when morning mists lingering over the wooded foothills gave the first warning of autumn. At that moment Désirée should have set off again for the Baltic. She did not: the prospect of a wearying journey through Germany followed by the dreaded sea-crossing made her feel so unwell that her doctor insisted on further rest. By the first week in September – twelve months to the day since she celebrated Bernadotte's election as Prince Royal – Désirée was back at La Grange. Soon she was in the Rue d'Anjou once more. She did not see her husband for almost three years, nor her son for eleven.

At first Napoleon was reluctant to permit the Princess Royal of Sweden to settle in France. He suspected that she would serve as her husband's spy. Soon, however, he realised that she might be a useful contact for himself or any other member of the Bonaparte family. Although she could relay salon gossip to Stockholm, it was unlikely she would pass on any information which Bernadotte's professional agents did not already know. Much of the correspondence beween Paris and Stockholm was intercepted, often by the

French, occasionally by the Swedes: Savary maintained a good counter-intelligence service within the Empire; and Bernadotte encouraged Louis Camps to build up a similar network of Swedish agents. Even their boyhood friend, Jean Gré, became a spymaster in Copenhagen, keeping Bernadotte well posted about developments south of the Baltic over the following eighteen months.

It hardly needed an extensive spy network to reveal Napoleon's next move. By December 1811 – the month in which credulous souls from Stockholm south to Lisbon watched the fearful portent of a comet in the night skies – the armies of the Empire were on the move, eastwards into Poland and along the southern shores of the Baltic. For Sweden there was one sensitive region, the small segment of Pomerania around Stralsund and the island of Rügen, a Swedish enclave in Germany since the days of the great Gustavus Adolphus. Already, in November, there had been a serious riot on the Stralsund quayside when stone-throwing Swedish youths attacked French seamen. The sympathies of the local population were with the blockade runners, making a profitable mockery of the Continental System. Napoleon dared not leave the territory under Swedish sovereignty if he advanced into Russia. What had failed abysmally at Walcheren might succeed on Rügen; for it would be a simple matter for the Swedes, supported by the British naval squadron in the Baltic, to land an expeditionary force at Stralsund and threaten the flank of the Grand Army. On 7 January 1812 Napoleon ordered the commander-in-chief of the Army of Germany to send two divisions into Stralsund and Rügen, interning the Swedish garrison and commandeering vessels bound for Sweden, together with their cargoes. News that the French had seized Swedish Pomerania reached Bernadotte on the last day of the month.

He was angry at this sudden assault, seeing it as a personal affront. The occupation was carried out by General Friant, who had led a brigade across the Alps with Bernadotte and served beside him on the Tagliamento, but the operational directive was signed by Marshal Davout, now Prince of Eckmühl and commander of the Army of Germany. Bernadotte referred to the French move as 'Davout's occupation of Pomerania' and interpreted it as yet another provocative act by his old antagonist. He also darkly noted a fact of which it is hard to believe that Davout was even aware – that the French seizure of Swedish territory took place on the Prince Royal's forty-ninth birthday. A proudly independent letter of pained reproof went off to Napoleon.

At heart Bernadotte cared little about Swedish Pomerania. Militarily the foothold in Germany was untenable; Rügen and Stralsund played no part in his plans for a Swedish-dominated Scandinavia. But he made capital out of Napoleon's move. Russophobes in the Council were won over to his argument that, in face of French hostility, it was essential to turn to the Tsar; and in the third week of February General Carl Löwenhielm was sent off to St Petersburg to negotiate with Tsar Alexander directly, and as Bernadotte's trusted friend and personal envoy. At the same time a secret emissary travelled to London. But there was still no decisive break with France. In any campaign against Russia Napoleon would prefer the Swedes to open a second front in Finland rather than remain dubiously non-belligerent. And Bernadotte was still pursuing a day-to-day policy of studied inactivity, wishing to win the backing of Russia, France and Britain for a redrawn map of Scandinavia. The Swedish consul in Paris journeyed backwards and forwards between Bernadotte and Napoleon in March and his travels continued well into the spring. But although the Prince Royal enlisted the help of Désirée, of her sister Julie and even of the Emperor's sister, Pauline Borghese, Napoleon became exasperated by his obduracy. Union with Norway remained Bernadotte's key objective, preferably without having to fight for it. He never seriously contemplated a Finnish war.

Tsar Alexander was more accommodating. In the first week of April Löwenhielm gained a remarkable diplomatic success: Russia would support a Swedish demand that Denmark should cede Norway and, if the Danes resisted, would assist Sweden by assigning an army corps of 15,000 men for action against Denmark, preferably an attack on the island of Zealand, with Copenhagen itself as the prize. In return, once Sweden and Norway formed a united kingdom, Bernadotte would send an expeditionary corps to northern Germany to aid Russia against Napoleon, should such a campaign be necessary. The British looked askance at the whole affair, particularly an attack on Denmark designed to secure what was regarded in London as the annexation of Norway. But Castlereagh, who became Foreign Secretary in the first week of March 1812, wished to tempt Bernadotte away from any dependency upon France: Sweden might count on protection by the Royal Navy, the despatch of muskets and guns and the promise of a rich sugar island in the West Indies; but no firm guarantee of British backing to take Norway.

Castlereagh did at least send an experienced diplomat to meet Bernadotte. Edward Thornton had once been British resident at Lübeck, was minister at Stockholm in 1807–8, and in 1811 had set out on an unproductive exploratory mission to Sweden. Now Bernadotte was determined to charm him into collaboration: it is easy enough to recognise a familiar figure in Thornton's description of the soldier 'who was eager to prove that he had made himself what he was by his own sword and by no favour from Napoleon', and it is understandable if the Prince Royal was interested in the latest news from Badajoz, where Wellington was about to cross from Portugal into brother-in-law Joseph's puppet kingdom; but it is a little surprising to find Thornton commenting on a 'natural, open, and unaffected manner with nothing of the fanfaronnade usual with Frenchmen of which the Prince seems to have had as little as almost any Frenchman I have ever seen'. Little came from these pleasantries; Thornton was guarded over Norway and did not have the authority to offer Bernadotte the large subsidy which he hoped he might secure from London.

Thornton and the envoys of Russia, France and Austria followed the Court as it moved from the midsummer heat of Stockholm up-country to Örebro. There the Riksdag had been summoned to approve the raising of a conscript army of men between twenty and twenty-four, the levying of special war taxes, emergency measures to curb irresponsible journalism, and supplementary grants to raise the appanage of both the Prince Royal and his son. Under pressure of great events south of the Baltic the Riksdag proved remarkably compliant. For it was at Örebro, on 27 June, that Bernadotte received the first news that the Grand Army had crossed the River Niemen; Napoleon was leading into Russia the largest concentration of troops that the world had as yet seen, over 600,000 men and more than 140,000 horses.

The Swedish response was swift. Formal treaties of peace with Britain were signed by both Russian and Swedish plenipotentiaries at Örebro on 18 July. But, while Britain and Russia once more became allies against the French Empire, the Prince Royal solemnly affirmed Sweden's neutrality in a message to Napoleon. The most he would offer his 'friend', Alexander, was good advice: a succession of letters urged the Tsar to make use of Russia's vast size and reserves, to seek to detach the Poles from Napoleon's cause, and to fall back, if necessary even as far as the Caspian Sea: 'Napoleon may possibly win the first, the second, even the third battle; the fourth may be indecisive. But if Your Majesty perseveres, it is inevitable that you will win the fifth', Bernadotte wrote.

By the time that Alexander received this encouraging message, his army was in full retreat. Vilna had fallen to Napoleon, Minsk to Davout. Less than four weeks after the start of the campaign his army commanders persuaded Alexander, with difficulty, that the right place for a Tsar of All the Russias was in his capital rather than in a military camp where only one aspect of the struggle against the enemy could absorb his attention. By 3 August Alexander was back in St Petersburg, while Napoleon had reached Vitebsk, where many of his generals wished him to establish headquarters and wait until the following spring before pursuing the enemy into the heart of Muscovy. The brief lull in the fighting enabled Alexander to think in terms of grand strategy, of his need to strike at the invader by other means. From St Petersburg he sent a letter to the Prince Royal proposing that they should meet at the end of August in Äbo – now Turku, Finland's second city, but in 1812 the Grand Duchy's capital. It was a 350-mile journey from St Petersburg but from Stockholm scarcely more than a day's sailing across the entrance to the Gulf of Bothnia.

The invitation took the Prince by surprise. He was on his way southwards to inspect the port of Karlskrona when a courier reached him. He hurried back to Stockholm but did not arrive at Äbo until the afternoon of Thursday, 27 August, three days after the Tsar. The 'summit conference' took place in Äbo Castle, a grim fourteenth-century keep looking out across a river estuary spattered with islands. Bernadotte was accompanied, not only by Chancellor Wetterstedt and General Adlercreutz, but by General Lord Cathcart, who was on his way to St Petersburg as Britain's new ambassador to the Tsar. Unlike Thornton, Cathcart was authorised to offer half a million pounds to Sweden or to Russia 'as circumstances may point out'; but this aspect of his mission Cathcart kept carefully concealed.

Most of the talking at Äbo was left to the two main participants, both of whom delighted in turning public occasions into good theatre. Alexander, always liable to lose confidence in himself, was impressed by the magnetism of Bernadotte's personality, the air of total certainty which he affected to bolster his own half-convictions. Even at Äbo, the Tsar, who liked to focus on distant vistas, may have held out to Bernadotte the prospect of succeeding Napoleon as ruler of France. He certainly considered, more than once, ways by which he might make Bernadotte commander of Russia's armies in the field, an appointment which the Prince Royal had no intention of accepting. The Tsar oversimplified Bernadotte's motives in coming to Äbo. He was not then an enemy of Napoleon, scheming for his downfall. His immediate objective was some tangible gain to please the Swedish people before they began to question the wisdom of accepting government by an ex-sergeant from Gascony.

Äbo is a set-piece in the Bernadotte legend, the first occasion upon which he was recognised as a European statesman. Yet he was less successful than his later propagandists claimed. An offer to take over the policing of Finland, so that the Tsar could concentrate all his forces for the battle against Napoleon, was rejected; understandably the Russians feared that once they allowed the Swedes back into the Grand Duchy they would have to fight another war to get them out again. In return for tolerating the eventual extension of Russia's frontiers to the Vistula, he secured a pledge from the Tsar that the size of the Russian auxiliary corps to help Sweden obtain Norway from Denmark would be raised from 15,000 to 35,000 men. A letter from Bernadotte to Charles XIII, and intended for the Royal Council, makes it clear that he believed that a Russian army from Finland would join Swedish troops in the province of Skane and subsequently seize the Danish island of Zealand, including Copenhagen; and the Tsar mentioned an operation of this kind in conversation with Cathcart (who strongly disapproved). But Bernadotte's letter gives more details of the plan; he told Charles XIII that the Russo–Swedish expeditionary force would first cross to Riga 'because it was important to confuse the enemy'. It is hard to accept that Bernadotte genuinely believed the Tsar's fleet would sail into the Gulf of Riga merely as a feint, when an under-strength garrison in the city was holding out desperately against Napoleon's reluctant Prussian ally. Who was fooling whom at Äbo?

By a formal treaty, signed on the third and last day of the Conference, Russia gave Sweden a free hand in dealing with Denmark, provided the Swedes had British approval. Yet with the vanguard of the Grand Army advancing relentlessly from Smolensk on Moscow, this last week in August 1812 was no time for the ruler of Russia to commit his troops to helping their recent enemy, Sweden, in a war against Denmark. As, of course, Bernadotte knew full well. In what Alexander regarded as a magnanimous gesture, the Prince Royal insisted that the Tsar needed every regiment he could raise in order to defend his twin capitals; only when the tide of battle had turned in Russia would the Swedes expect help against Denmark. At one moment Bernadotte even boasted that should Napoleon's army threaten St Petersburg he would himself set sail for France, land in Brittany and march on Paris, although with whom was left unspecified. The veteran Guards officer, Lord Cathcart, who had commanded the British force which attacked Copenhagen five years before, remained sceptical of all he observed at Åbo. So long as there was more talk of landing in Zealand than of ways of throwing back the French invader, he saw no reason to dip into that half a million pounds and encourage either posturing egotist.

Within a month of returning to Stockholm the Prince Royal heard of Napoleon's hard-won victory at Borodino and of his entry into Moscow. Once more urgent messages of encouragement were sent to St Petersburg; it was in Sweden's interest for Russia to stay in the war; a second Tilsit would destroy all the diplomatic preparations for the union of Sweden and Norway. During the winter months Bernadotte sought diplomatic and financial backing from London and he also mounted an effective propaganda campaign, in Scandinavia and in Europe as a whole. Local agents in southern Norway emphasised the common bonds that linked the two kingdoms of the Scandinavian peninsula. For foreign consumption, Count Engestrom produced a masterly 'report', in French, to let other governments know of the Prince Royal's patient rejection of Napoleon's blandishments; when copies reached London in early March 1813 they made a considerable impression both at Westminster and in the City. And at the end of September 1812 Germaine de Staël travelled to Stockholm from St Petersburg. She put her own literary talents – and the skilled pen of her companion, August von Schlegel – to the service of 'the true hero of our age', whose 'public life deserves the admiration of reflecting minds'. It was just fifteen years since Bernadotte's conversation first captivated her at Talleyrand's dinner table in the General's earliest days in Paris.

The Prince Royal had assured Tsar Alexander that if Russia

withstood the first hammer blows, Napoleon would be defeated. He had not, however, foreseen the disasters of the retreat from Moscow and he was deeply moved by the tragedy that engulfed so many old comrades in arms. He sent money to aid sick and destitute French prisoners held by the Russians. Politically the retreat posed for him an unexpected problem. He had assumed that the blizzards of winter would halt the campaign. In the following spring he would, he thought, have a stronger army and thus be better prepared to intervene. But by the end of the year Bernadotte and his principal colleagues in Stockholm began to have doubts. After the terrible retreat would Russia and Britain still need Swedish intervention? If Sweden remained at peace while Napoleon's empire fell apart, what chance was there of acquiring Norway? And if Bernadotte failed to bring his adoptive country either union with Norway or the recovery of Finland, why should the Swedes continue to have faith in his leadership?

The early months of 1813 were full of suspicion and intrigue. Under the influence of Mme de Staël and of Schlegel the Swedes broadened their diplomacy, seeking an understanding with Prussia and encouraging King Frederick William III to break with Napoleon. The effect of this new concern with Prussian affairs was to revive Sweden's old interest in what happened south of the Baltic and in the recovery of Swedish Pomerania to serve, as in the Thirty Years' War, as a base in Germany. On 17 March 1813 the Prince Royal ordered the first military initiative since he came to Sweden: 600 men would sail next day from Karlskrona and re-occupy Stralsund and Rügen, from which Davout had already withdrawn his forces so as to shorten his line of defence. Several thousand more Swedish troops would follow over the following weeks: and, as the Prince wrote to the Tsar, he would himself cross to Pomerania a month later, ready 'to execute all that has been agreed upon with His Majesty the Emperor Alexander'.

Britain and Russia did still need Swedish intervention but had no wish to be involved in what was to them a sideshow in Denmark. Castlereagh wanted a powerful allied force in northern Europe capable of recovering Hanover and ensuring that the city did not fall into Prussian hands again. The Russians wanted, quite simply, more men and material, for the Tsar's army, too, had suffered grievously in its pursuit of Napoleon's retreating columns. Had Alexander honoured his pledge to send an expeditionary force to help the Swedes attack Napoleon's Danish ally, there would have been no adequate army for the great 1813 Campaign, which was designed to roll back the French Empire from its eastern borders. Both the Russians and the British made independent attempts to induce the Danes to turn against Napoleon, cede Norway peacefully to Sweden and accept compensation in Germany. The chief result of these secret contacts in Copenhagen was to make Bernadotte more and more suspicious in Stockholm. So long as there was any danger of a Norwegian–Danish invasion of western Sweden, he dared not risk sailing off to Pomerania with the country's crack regiments and leaving the frontier with Norway denuded.

By late March he felt reasonably sure of British backing. A treaty concluded with Thornton in Stockholm promised Sweden a British subsidy of a million pounds and the creation of a German legion under his command provided that he transported 30,000 Swedish troops to northern Germany. If Denmark refused to cede Norway to Sweden peacefully, Bernadotte could count on support from the Royal Navy in operations against Zealand and he was also promised the eventual cession of Guadeloupe, so as to revive the interests of the Swedish West Indies Company which Gustav III had founded. Thornton let Bernadotte know that the British wished him to postpone any immediate attack on Zealand and use his troops in Pomerania to free the Hanse towns and Hamburg and advance into Holstein, so as to cut communications between France and her Danish ally. On paper, however, he was left to decide his own strategy once he landed in Pomerania.

But when would that be? Bernadotte was still reluctant to make the decisive break with Napoleon's France. An open letter, drafted as propaganda in mid-March, informed the Emperor of the sorrow with which he felt bound to 'defend the rights of the people who have invited me to the succession of their throne' against the pretensions of the French Empire; he urged Napoleon 'to embrace sincerely the idea of a general peace'; but concluded that, whatever might be the Emperor's decision over peace or war, 'I shall none the less preserve towards Your Majesty the sentiments of a former brother in arms'. The letter remained unanswered by Napoleon. He preferred to use less public ways of keeping in touch with his former Marshal.

On the evening of Sunday, 25 April, Napoleon reached Erfurt, his first field headquarters for the 1813 campaign. With difficulty he had raised an army of some 225,000 French, German and Italian troops ready to meet, somewhere beyond the upper Elbe, a far smaller force of Russians – and now Prussians, too. There was not, however, any likelihood of a clash with Swedish troops for, although several thousand Swedes had already landed in Pomerania, their commander-in-chief remained in Stockholm. It was only on the Monday morning that he bade Charles XIII farewell and set out for Karlskrona, the chief port of embarkation. He was still inspecting troops in the province of Smaland when, on 2 May, Napoleon gained the first victory of the campaign, outside Lützen, where in 1632 the greatest Swedish soldier king had perished in an even more famous battle. On this later occasion, only Napoleon's acute shortage of cavalry horses prevented him from turning a Russo–Prussian defeat into a rout. Desperately Tsar Alexander sent a personal envoy to Sweden imploring the 'friend' he had flattered at Äbo to mount a diversionary offensive in Pomerania.

Alexander's choice of emissary was unfortunate. General Pozzo di Borgo, who had served the Tsar intermittently since 1804, was a Corsican whose vendetta with Napoleon's family went back several decades. He found Bernadotte on 7 May at Karlskrona, waiting on events. Pozzo's years of exile had grafted an excessive political conservatism on a natural Corsican excitability, a combination well calculated to spark Bernadotte's explosive temper. The two men bristled with mutual antipathy at first sight. They argued fiercely hour after hour, Pozzo seeking to prove to the Prince Royal that Sweden could only secure Norway through success in the 'common cause' against Napoleon. 'We spent the whole night talking', Pozzo reported. 'Discussions with him are lively and lacking in logical formation. He speaks eloquently but without any arrangement of ideas. Vanity is shown in every word. The sun never rises except at his command.' At first Pozzo thought he had failed to prod Bernadotte into action, for he was full of recrimination at the Tsar's failure to send him the auxiliary troops he needed for the assault on Zealand. Dramatically he predicted to Pozzo, 'If I do not gain Norway and reap success, a violent death must be my destiny'; and the two men retired to bed as dawn broke, with their differences unresolved. But Bernadotte had calmed down by the afternoon; Pozzo might assure the Tsar that he was about to cross the Baltic and would send a small detachment as far as the Elbe. The allied commanders must realise, however, that he would not risk battle with Napoleon until his army was supplemented by the Russian and Prussian troops whom he expected in Stralsund.

It seemed as if Bernadotte had finally committed himself. Even so, over a week elapsed between the night-long session with Pozzo and his departure from Karlskrona. He had no intention of putting to sea until he was certain that Chancellor Wetterstedt enjoyed sufficient respect in Stockholm to uphold royal authority – *his* authority – while he was campaigning in Germany. At last, on 18 May, Bernadotte stepped ashore at Stralsund. On that same Tuesday evening, 250 miles to the south, Napoleon was manoeuvring the main body of his troops so as to envelop the Prussians and Russians on the flood plain of the River Spree. By the end of the week he had won yet another victory, at Bautzen. It was by no means certain that when, and if, Bernadotte moved south from Stralsund, he would find an allied army in the field to welcome his coming. Perhaps he might even now be spared the sorrow of having to order his troops to fire upon the French. But how, then, would he bring about the union of Sweden and Norway? The dilemma which had troubled him for the past year seemed no nearer solution.

Chapter 12
At War with Napoleon

THROUGHOUT Napoleon's Russian Campaign and the bleak months following the Emperor's return to France, Désirée remained in Paris. Everyone knew that the husband of the 'Countess of Gothland' was in alliance with France's enemies and she was cold-shouldered by former friends. Occasional letters came through safely from Stockholm; she learnt of Oscar's scholastic progress and physical growth and she received an apologetic explanation when Sweden broke off diplomatic relations with France. Far too rarely money reached her, always much less than she hoped. Both husband and wife feared Napoleon's wrath if Swedish troops clashed with the French. Bernadotte suggested she should leave Paris for Aix, cross into Switzerland and make her way northwards through Germany, an odd proposal since this route would have taken her into the main theatre of war. Désirée behaved circumspectly. Rather than flaunt her privileged status at the home she loved in the Rue d'Anjou, she rented a small villa at Auteuil. She also sold La Grange to her brother Nicholas for fear it might otherwise be confiscated, like General Moreau's estate at Grossbois. Family loyalty made her reluctant to leave her sister Julie, a sentiment not unconnected with the influence King Joseph retained at his imperial brother's Court. But, in the summer of 1813, the two sisters decided that their rheumatism would be better served by the waters of Vichy than at Plombières or any spa near the frontier, where military comings and goings might prove embarrassing. At Vichy it was easier to pass unrecognised.

Once in that spring Désirée made a determined effort to influence policy. In the third week of April a letter to Bernadotte gave, as usual, much family news; but, with the connivance of the Foreign Ministry, it also contained sound advice: 'Don't declare openly against the French', Désirée wrote, 'for fear that you will lose the popularity you still enjoy among them. If Napoleon falls, you can play a fine role in your old country, deciding who shall be Regent here (*y disposer de la régence*).' The letter was carried to Stralsund by a Swedish colonel taken prisoner there a year before by Davout and reached Bernadotte four days after he landed in Pomerania. The colonel also passed on an official message in Napoleon's name: if the Prince Royal would be content to defend the Stralsund enclave and did not march against France, 'the Emperor was willing to forgive the past'. This vague gesture of reconciliation Bernadotte ignored. On the other hand, Désirée's advice coincided so closely with his inclinations that it both intensified the caution with which he committed himself to his allies and sharpened his ambition. A few days later one of Bernadotte's aides noted in his diary that he was again taking pride in describing the warmth of his reception at Äbo: there, he boasted, the Tsar 'proposed me as Emperor of France'. For the remaining months of war the twin objectives of gaining Norway for Sweden and France for himself confused and confounded his day-to-day policies.

On 10 June Pozzo di Borgo returned to Swedish headquarters as the Tsar's emissary. Alexander formally notified the Prince Royal that Russia and Prussia had concluded an armistice with Napoleon on 4 June. At the same time he again apologised for his failure to provide the Russian troops promised as auxiliaries for Sweden's campaign against Denmark. Bernadotte thereupon lost his temper. The rulers of Russia and Prussia had betrayed him, he thundered. How dare they sign an armistice without consulting their Swedish ally? Were they about to sue for peace, accepting empty assurances written into a second Tilsit? No doubt Sweden and England would be left to continue alone the war against Napoleon. This scene of high drama, impressive to his Swedish companions, was not unfamiliar to their Corsican visitor. With rare patience Pozzo explained that the Armistice was a device intended to rally Austria behind the coalition and give Prussia time to raise and train a militia. Gradually Bernadotte was won over. Pozzo persuaded him that the allied sovereigns needed to consult him on the workings of Napoleon's military mind and that Alexander had no doubt of the mission Bernadotte was called to fulfil in the land of his birth. He should set out at once for Silesia and give advice at allied headquarters.

Accordingly, at the end of the first week in July, he left Pomerania

to meet Tsar Alexander and King Frederick William III at Trachenberg Castle. With him travelled Field Marshal Stedingk and the
brothers Carl and Gustav Löwenhielm. It was a slow journey of
more than 200 miles across Prussia. Outside Stettin an over-patriotic
French artillery officer momentarily broke the Armistice by firing
on the ex-Marshal of the Empire as the Swedish escort came into
view, and the poor Silesian roads delayed him even more. He was
expected at Trachenberg late in the afternoon of 9 July; by dusk
there was still no sign of his carriages. Yet so eager were the Tsar
and the King to flatter their temperamental guest that they waited
dinner for him. Not until midnight could they welcome him at their
table.

If Stedingk's account may be believed, Bernadotte dominated the
Trachenberg summit conference from the start. He threatened that
if the two sovereigns abandoned him he would take his army back
across the Baltic, raise Finland in revolt and march on St Petersburg
while Alexander's finest regiments were still in Poland. Fortunately
the Tsar refused to take this threat seriously. He explained that the
immediate task was to concert plans with the Austrians so as to
defeat Napoleon if he refused a general settlement before the Armistice expired in August. Bernadotte talked at great length to the chief
Austrian envoy, Count Stadion, winning from him an assurance
that Austria would not oppose the union of Sweden and Norway
and would concentrate a great army in Bohemia ready to strike at
Napoleon's southern flank. Stadion discussed with Bernadotte the
earliest plans for the campaign, already drawn up by the Austrian
chief of staff, General Radetzky. He had, however, returned to
Vienna before the allies agreed on what Lord Cathcart informed
Castlereagh was 'the Prince Royal's Plan', a grand strategy for the
allies to force Napoleon's armies back behind France's natural
frontiers.

Bernadotte's directive proposed the creation of three main armies:
the Army of Bohemia, 220,000 Austrians and Russians under a field
commander appointed by the Emperor Francis: the Army of Silesia,
95,000 Prussians under General Blücher; and the Army of the
North, 120,000 men, comprising a Swedish, a Prussian and a
Russian corps, together with small contingents from other states,
all commanded by Bernadotte himself. The three armies would
converge on the Grande Armée in a great arc, each attacking French
detached corps and falling back if threatened by Napoleon in person:

only when the allies could concentrate their united strength at one point would they engage the Emperor and his crack regiments in a setpiece battle. It was a shrewd plan, more cautious than Alexander wished, but likely to appeal to the Austrians. They had suffered too many speedy defeats by Napoleon in short campaigns to risk another disaster.

Although Bernadotte had never served as an independent commander-in-chief, he hoped to become generalissimo of the three allied armies. This was impossible. The Prussian officer corps, stung into sullen hostility by tactless reminders of who had beaten them at Lübeck, resented any show of confidence offered by their king or the Tsar to the ex-enemy Marshal. Tactfully it was suggested that Austria would be bound more securely within the coalition if the supreme command went to the Emperor Francis's nominee for the Army of Bohemia, Prince Schwarzenberg, with Radetzky as his chief-of-staff. Even the Prince Royal acknowledged the wisdom of encouraging the newest of the allies by accepting Schwarzenberg as generalissimo. At heart, however, he cared little for Austrian or Prussian top brass and was confident the Tsar's generals would follow his wishes. As commander of the Army of the North he had every intention of implementing his Trachenberg Plan in a strategy freely modified to meet Sweden's needs.

Bernadotte's Fabian strategy – his assumption that newly raised regiments in the Grande Armée could not survive a campaign of attrition so far from France – was questioned by one critic. General Moreau had arrived at Stralsund from exile in America to serve Napoleon's enemies at Bernadotte's invitation. He knew nothing of the political suspicions with which each ally regarded the others and it was as a soldier that he criticised the Trachenberg Plan. He maintained that, for any prolonged campaign in the heart of Germany, the Army of the North was in a hopeless condition: it was dependent on one inadequate base both for reinforcements from Sweden and supplies from Britain; and it was menaced by a line of fortresses along the Elbe, garrisoned by French veterans. But Bernadotte was certain his Fabian tactics would succeed. Patiently he explained his assumptions to Moreau:

> I shall not expose myself to those massive club blows which Napoleon has so often successfully employed. I shall exhaust him by manouevring
> . . . and I shall threaten his flanks by organising a kind of armed

uprising; it will withdraw when he tries to attack and then reoccupy ground once he goes away, it will feed off the resources around it while he, far from his own resources, wastes his men in hand-to-hand fighting. Our numbers are almost equal . . . He who spares his troops remains the stronger. Let us hold on! And Napoleon, despite his gifts, his power, his fame, will in the end be swept away.

Bernadotte's self-confidence was impressive, but poor Moreau had no opportunity to see the policy vindicated. He took service, not with the Army of the North but as a military adviser to Tsar Alexander, and was killed by a cannon ball at Dresden on 27 August, eleven days after the Armistice expired.

As Bernadotte assumed, Napoleon was once more counting on swift and decisive victories. His main army was concentrated in Saxony; he planned, in the first instance, to defeat Blücher in Silesia on his left flank and then advance on Prague, inflicting a second Austerlitz on the combined Russian and Austrian forces. Berthier, however, questioned the wisdom of this strategy. How would the Army of the North react, he wondered? Was it not poised for a descent on the French rear? 'Bernadotte?' Napoleon scoffed. 'He will make a show.' Yet, however much he might affect contempt for Sweden's Prince Royal, Napoleon respected Berthier's judgment too much to ignore the danger he had sensed. Even if the war were decided along the mountainous frontiers of Saxony and Bohemia, it was vital to create a strategic diversion in the German plains. Marshal Oudinot, with 66,000 men at his command, was ordered to march on Berlin, while Davout would strike eastwards from Hamburg into Mecklenburg, so as to threaten the Swedish base at Stralsund.

At first Oudinot had the ball at his feet: Bernadotte seemed prepared even to abandon Berlin rather than risk a defeat. But as Oudinot neared the city he met strong resistance from General Bülow's Corps – 38,000 Prussians attached to the Army of the North. At Grossbeeren, only eleven miles south of the Prussian capital, Bülow found the French invaders so widely dispersed that he inflicted a speedy defeat on Oudinot, won before Bernadotte and the Swedes reached the battlefield. Oudinot fell back on Wittenberg and the line of the Elbe, thus exposing Davout's right flank and forcing him, too, to order a retreat. Napoleon was furious: Ney was hurriedly sent to the Elbe with reinforcements and authority to subordinate Oudinot to his command. But this affront to Oudinot proved to be a psychological error. As Bernadotte well knew, there was as much friction between Ney and Oudinot as there had long been between Davout and himself; and he was ready to exploit the quarrels of the Marshals.

The principal battle in this theatre of war was fought on 6 September, almost halfway between Berlin and Leipzig, around the village of Dennewitz. Ney fell upon a Prussian corps, under Count von Tauenzien, forcing it back on Bülow's Grossbeeren veterans, who were encamped two miles to the north. When the battle began, Bernadotte was fifteen miles away, guarding the main route from the Elbe towards Potsdam with a combined Swedish, Hanoverian and Russian force. At once he set out for Dennewitz. Despite several days of heavy rain in the previous week, the weather was now fine, although a strong wind blew from the north-west. The countryside was open, with low hills and occasional marshy streams – easy going for any army on the march. Yet it took six and a half hours for the commander-in-chief to reach Dennewitz. By then the combatants were fighting confused actions wrapped in a blanket of ochreous dust – for thousands of men and horses charging and wheeling over the thin soil of lower Brandenburg on a gusty day had created a sandstorm. Shortly before Bernadotte's arrival Ney, unable to gain a clear impression of the terrain, mistakenly ordered Oudinot to his right flank rather than to his left. Although he doubted the wisdom of this order, Oudinot sullenly obeyed, at once opening up a gap into which Bernadotte brought his Swedish and Russian guns. Ney, sword in hand, was in the thick of the fighting against the Prussians when this sudden cannonade on his left convinced him of the need to retreat to Torgau on the River Elbe. 'I have arrived with forty battalions and the battle is won', Bernadotte informed General Bülow, ordering him to pull his tired troops back into the second line. He made no attempt to pursue Ney and Oudinot towards the Elbe.

At Dennewitz the French suffered 10,000 casualties, dead or wounded; the Prussians sustained 7000; no Swedish soldiers perished, although twenty were wounded. Next morning Bernadotte's Order of the Day paid tribute to the courage of the Prussians but it also emphasised how his own arrival, with those forty new battalions, made victory certain. Prussian bitterness over Bernadotte's leadership deepened; why had it taken six and a half hours for his troops to march fifteen miles? 'We . . . surrendered the honour of the day to those who had hitherto been mere onlookers', complained Colonel von Reiche, one of Bülow's staff officers, recalling the sandstorm battle in his memoirs.

In Stockholm Dennewitz was celebrated as a triumph for the Prince Royal's army. But, to the intense irritation of his allies, Bernadotte never consolidated the victory. He was content to remain at improvised headquarters in the town of Zerbst; four weeks passed before he crossed the Elbe, for he was afraid of being cut off by a powerful sortie by a French garrison from one of the cities along the river. Yet he was by no means inactive. Immediately after Dennewitz he made contact with his old friend Ney, writing to let him know that the Swedes were caring for a wounded aide-de-camp from the Marshal's staff and to assure him that the captive officer would have the best treatment. How wretched it was, Bernadotte reflected, that he and Ney should now be fighting for different interests. Could not Ney use his influence with the Emperor Napoleon to end the ravages of war by making a reasonable peace and thereby render great service to Europe?

There is no doubt that throughout the campaign Bernadotte, though conscious of his obligations as a Swedish prince, felt a deep repugnance at having to fight against the French. Yet he can have had little hope of securing a negotiated peace so soon after the collapse of the Armistice, especially as Napoleon won a major victory at Dresden in the last days of August. Predictably the Emperor brusquely dismissed his plea as soon as Ney broached it. But Bernadotte was content to encourage dissension among the Marshals. If they became convinced that Napoleon was fighting for himself rather than for the good of France, they might force his abdication and end the war without further bloody battles.

By now the Prince Royal was acquiring a natural instinct for what is today called 'psychological warfare'. Long ago he had admired Napoleon's skill in public relations, the demagogic appeal of his proclamations, the boost to morale given by those half-truths in the 'Bulletins of the Army'. Bernadotte had himself sought to emulate Napoleon, drafting proclamations in Hanover and, to the Emperor's anger, at Wagram and in Antwerp. Now, in 1813, his staff officers would sometimes hear him at night pacing his room, phrasing proclamations and bulletins which he would dictate in their most polished form next morning. A week after Dennewitz, while still well east of the Elbe, he called on the French soldiery to cease fighting a war designed to oppress the other peoples of Europe and rely on the goodwill of the allies to bestow a just government on their country. More effective was an appeal to the soldiers of Saxony to join him, their old commander, in a war against the oppressor: 'The French themselves wish to retire behind the limits which Nature has prescribed. Though they serve tyranny, they hate it. Have the courage to let them know your resolve to be free and these same Frenchmen will, in admiration, urge you to persevere in so noble and generous an enterprise.' To encourage the Saxons to change allegiance Bernadotte, on his own initiative, established a 'Saxon Legion', in which patriots from other regions of Germany were soon incorporated. He wished to set up a free 'Dutch Legion', too: the British, however, disliked the idea. The Scheldt estuary fell within their sphere of interest; they hoped Bernadotte would eventually help eject the French from the Netherlands, but under their political direction.

By late September all his allies were becoming uneasy at Bernadotte's hesitancy. Despite the enthusiasm with which he had outlined his master-plan at Trachenberg, it seemed clear he was reluctant to lead the Army of the North forward against the French. The three sovereigns – Tsar Alexander, Emperor Francis and King Frederick William – were together at Teplitz (Teplice) in Bohemia, preparing to march westwards into Saxony. How could they persuade their Swedish companion-in-arms, far away to the north, to put down his pen and take up the sword again? Alexander's chief adviser on foreign affairs, Count Nesselrode, had met Bernadotte at Åbo and at thirty-three was young enough to think he could read the riddles of his character. The solution was simple, Nesselrode claimed: the sovereigns must flatter the Prince Royal as victor of Dennewitz, and thus shame their battle-shy partner into action.

What followed was more appropriate to a fairy-tale ballet than to wartime diplomacy. Each sovereign despatched a personal envoy who rode a hundred miles across Silesia carrying a military distinction for presentation to the Prince Royal. From Russia came the Grand Cordon of the Order of St George, last awarded in 1812 to Marshal Kutuzov for clearing the homeland of the French invaders; from Austria, the Order of Maria Theresa; and from Prussia, the newly instituted Iron Cross. The first cavalier to reach Swedish headquarters was Alexander's emissary, Count de Rochechouart, a

French émigré much respected by the Tsar. Bernadotte was delighted with the Russian honour but, having a far more complex character than Nesselrode believed, was wryly amused by this procession of gift-bearers. He was particularly pleased that the Order of St George was presented by a compatriot who rode so swiftly that he arrived twelve hours ahead of the Austrian and Prussian cavaliers. 'My friend', Bernadotte remarked, 'as usual they have lost the race . . . That's as it should be. You are a Frenchman; they are Germans.' The jocular comment was significant. At that moment the Prince Royal's thoughts were much in France; he had recently heard of the death on 11 August of his brother, far away at Pau.

'He captivated me completely', de Rochechouart wrote later. 'He looked very martial on horseback, a little theatrical perhaps, but his bravery, his coolness in the thick of the bloodiest battles, made one forget this trivial fault. He had the most winning manners and speech imaginable.' Some habits puzzled de Rochechouart: 'At noon I found the Prince lying down with his feet raised very high, so that his knees formed a desk, while his head, which was low, rested on a bolster. "I always work best when I am lying down", he said.' But Bernadotte's political confidences could be embarrassing: 'An Emperor is not a French title', he once remarked. 'France wants a King, but a King who is a soldier. The Bourbons are played out . . . Who is there who would better suit the French than myself?' Such matters, de Rochechouart tactfully replied, were outside his competence.

A few weeks before, Napoleon had admitted in conversation with Metternich that a ruler who was the 'child of fortune' could not hope to survive military defeat: 'Your sovereigns, born to the throne, may be beaten twenty times, and still go back to their palaces; but that I cannot do', Napoleon explained. Now, when de Rochechouart conveyed to the Prince Royal at Zerbst the Tsar's plea for him to launch an offensive west of the Elbe, he found Bernadotte justifying his hesitancy in strangely similar terms: 'Ah, you must understand, my friend . . . the need for utmost prudence . . . My fortunes are staked on a single battle. Were I defeated, I might search Europe in vain to find anyone who would lend me six francs.' Gradually, however, Bernadotte recognised that the relentless pressure of France's enemies was forcing Napoleon back towards Leipzig where, as envisaged in the Trachenberg Plan, the united strength of the allies could overwhelm him in a setpiece battle. Reluctantly, on 4 October, Bernadotte ordered the Army of the North forward across the Elbe. Slowly, with Blücher and the Army of Silesia on their right, his troops thrust southwards along the Mulde and Saale rivers, threatening to cut Napoleon's links through Franconia to the Main, the Rhine and the heart of his empire. But the French, too, were manoeuvring for position, the Emperor hoping to break through the allied armies and turn on them from the rear, isolating Schwarzenberg and destroying his enemies one by one. As Schwarzenberg advanced no more than seventy miles in two and a half weeks, Napoleon remained convinced he held the strategic advantage. If Ney, Oudinot and Marmont could drive a wedge between Bernadotte and Blücher and join the French garrisons along the Elbe, once again he would be able to send his enemies 'beaten back to their palaces'.

Bernadotte, well familiar with Napoleon's military mind, feared just such a manoeuvre. De Rochechouart was astonished at the speed with which he would rattle off orders for quartering his army, without turning to a map or consulting past notes, but by the second week in October this nightly posting of troops had become essentially defensive in character, leaving clear a line of retreat. On Tuesday, 12 October, one of Ney's brigades caught a Prussian corps serving as rearguard for the Army of the North at Dessau. Ney's troops inflicted such heavy casualties that Bernadotte began once more to doubt the wisdom of pressing forward into Saxony.

The events of that Tuesday are well-documented. Before daybreak the main body of the Army of the North entered Köthen, an old fortified town halfway between Magdeburg and Leipzig. Young Philippine von Griesheim, living in the square beneath Köthen's sixteenth-century castle, described in a letter to a friend how 'from seven in the morning until the same time at night we had columns marching through – in all about 200,000 men, half of whom went by within the space of two hours. So deafening was the noise that my ears still ring with the sound of bugles, beating drums and a Turkish military band.' In reality no more than 70,000 men can have passed through the town that day, and the martial music probably came from Astrakhan Dragoons in Bernadotte's Russian Corps rather than from any Turkish band, but Philippine's letter is vivid testimony to the excitement of those autumn days in Köthen. The presence of 'Swedish regiments with their Crown Prince' delighted her; 'all our floor space was packed with military men from several nations', she wrote, describing how that night she sang duets with an Austrian, was petted by a Swedish General and introduced to the English General, Sir Charles Stewart, 'famous for his immense wealth'. But Philippine was shrewd enough to sense an air of crisis behind all this merrymaking: 'The troops are very active', she wrote to her friend. 'Couriers, orderlies and extra guard pickets gallop across the Castle Square, which seems to suggest something important is about to happen.'

She was right. On Thursday afternoon Bernadotte summoned a Council of War in Köthen Castle. He recommended that the Army of the North should fall back across the Elbe. But he was overruled, not only by the Russian, British, Prussian and Austrian envoys but by the Swedish commander, Field Marshal Stedingk, as well. They believed Napoleon to be near Leipzig and they convinced the Prince Royal that so long as the three allied armies maintained pressure on the Emperor himself, he dared not risk an attempt to turn the rear of any one army unless it allowed itself to become isolated. On Friday, 15 October, Philippine and her sister 'fetched the last fruit up from the cellar' to give to our 'unassuming, well-behaved Swedes' as they marched off. On that Friday morning, forty-five miles south of Köthen, Napoleon watched anxiously from high ground above Leipzig, as Schwarzenberg and Blücher tightened their noose around the city. So great were their numbers that the Emperor mistakenly believed Bernadotte's troops must already have joined Blücher and his Prussians.

'The Battle of the Nations' began in a damp mist at eight next morning. Throughout the Saturday there was fierce but indecisive fighting, much of it in heavy rain, the bad weather further delaying the approach of the Army of the North. Only skirmishes around opposing outposts took place on Sunday. By evening the glow of new campfires around Breitenfeld showed that the Prince Royal was at last close at hand; he established headquarters on the old battlefield where Sweden was twice victorious in the Thirty Years' War. Early on Monday morning, almost forty-eight hours after the first exchange of fire, the Army of the North went into action.

Once more Bernadotte impetuously scorned danger, riding along the line of his foremost troops in a uniform easily identifiable to any good marksman in Napoleon's army; he wore a violet velvet tunic braided with gold, carried in his hand a marshal's baton ornamented at each end by a gold crown, and his white-feathered hat was surmounted by a long plume in the yellow and light blue national colours of Sweden. 'Nothing could match the martial style of Sweden's illustrious leader', de Rochechouart wrote in his memoirs, as he recalled the Prince Royal observing the barrage of Congreve Rockets fired by a troop of the Royal Horse Artillery, the only British unit to serve under his command. Captain Richard Bogue, commander of the rocket troop, was killed by a sharpshooter in the village of Sellershausen, but Bernadotte's luck held. Next morning – Tuesday, 19 October – he was seen encouraging the Swedish Pomeranian Lifeguards who, with Russian and Prussian regiments, forced down the Grimma Gate, the entry into Leipzig from the south-east. By then Napoleon, recognising defeat, was seeking to hold an escape-route to the West.

Bernadotte's multi-national army acquitted itself well at Leipzig. The Swedes in particular won praise from the other allied commanders for their discipline and sustained good order. But the Prince Royal's chief contribution to the campaign was made long before he reached Breitenfeld. His proclamations encouraged more than three hundred Saxon soldiers to join his 'Saxon Legion' in the third week of September, and during the battle there was a steady stream of desertions. Two battalions of infantry went over on the first morning, a regiment of Hussars and a regiment of Uhlans later in the day. Some mixed German battalions – Saxons and Würtembergers – surrendered to the Army of Bohemia on Monday morning and, as the first Swedish colours were seen on the battlefield, two Saxon batteries ceased fire; their commanding officer had fought under Bernadotte at Wagram, and he now attached his ten cannon to a Swedish artillery regiment. There is no doubt Bernadotte had been popular among the Saxons in 1809; it is small wonder if, four years later, they looked to the author of these flamboyant proclamations as a protector, an enemy against whom a mere token resistance was circumspect, honourable and judicious.

Despite his late arrival at Leipzig, the Prince Royal was the first allied commander to reach the Marktplatz, the heart of the old city. There, some half an hour later, he had the satisfaction of greeting Tsar Alexander and King Frederick William, who had so often complained of his tardiness in pressing forward from the Elbe. It was their first meeting since the summit conference at Trachenberg in the second week of July; and that afternoon he also welcomed

Emperor Francis, who sixteen years before had received him at the Hofburg as emissary of a revolutionary republic. During the following two days there was a series of discussions to decide on future strategy. The Prince Royal found himself opposed by the Prussians, by the British envoys and by Metternich, the Austrian Foreign Minister, whom he had last met at Napoleon's side in Paris when he was offered the Swedish succession. He thought, however, that he could still count on the Tsar, who needed his support to counter the growing collaboration of Austria and Prussia. But from conversations Alexander held with the British ambassador it would seem that he, too, mistrusted Bernadotte; he wished to get him away from headquarters so that the three sovereigns could negotiate directly with Napoleon. The bonds holding the allies together were becoming extremely brittle.

Not surprisingly, conference table diplomacy in occupied Leipzig was often acrimonious. Once more Bernadotte threatened to withdraw the Swedish contingent, retire to Stralsund 'and await further orders from my king', unless Sweden's interests were safeguarded. Metternich treated such bluff with the scorn it deserved but, with Alexander's backing, the Prince Royal grudgingly received authority to march northwards. He was to assist the Prince Regent of Great Britain to recover Hanover and to eliminate any threat from Davout's garrison in Hamburg. His main objective, as his allies suspected, was to put pressure on King Frederick VI of Denmark, who had not yet deserted Napoleon. Uppermost in his mind was the need to force Frederick to cede Norway to Sweden as speedily as possible, so as to leave himself free to influence allied deliberations over the future of France.

From the fourth week in October 1813 until mid-February 1814 Bernadotte took no part in the main allied operations against Napoleon. He established his headquarters at Hanover on 6 November, the day on which the allied sovereigns made a ceremonial entry into Frankfurt. At Hanover Bernadotte conferred with old acquaintances in the merchant community so as to ensure that the city was well administered before the arrival, later that month, of the Duke of Cumberland as titular 'Deputy Elector'. But couriers kept him in touch with Frankfurt and on 12 November he was angered by a new directive sent to him by Alexander, allegedly an extension of the Trachenberg Plan. The Tsar proposed a four-pronged allied advance on Paris: Wellington northwards from the Pyrenees;

Schwarzenberg from Switzerland and through the Belfort Gap; Blücher from the Rhineland: and Bernadotte advancing from Hanover into the Netherlands and wheeling south. Since nothing was said of Denmark, the Prince Royal complained once more that Sweden had been betrayed by her allies. He would wait no longer. On 16 November he detached a Prussian and a Russian corps from his main army, with orders to enter the Netherlands and support a Dutch revolt. Secret agents contacted Davout in the vain hope he would evacuate Hamburg under a flag of truce. But the Prince Royal turned his main army – 60,000 men – northwards against Denmark.

He met little resistance. Denmark's political leaders counted on diplomatic support from Metternich. To Bernadotte's intense fury, an Austrian envoy sought a compromise which would have ceded only the Trondheim region of Norway to Sweden, thus leaving both the northern and southern shores of the Skaggerak in Danish hands. But King Frederick was more obstinate than his political advisers: he rejected both the Austrian initiative and a succession of proposals from the Swedes themselves, most of them made during a three-week armistice. When the war was renewed on 6 January 1814 Frederick's cause was hopeless. He had no military resources of his own with which to check the Swedish advance and no hope of help from Napoleon. This final phase of a forgotten campaign lasted a mere four days and, shortly before midnight on 14 January, the Prince Royal saw Sweden's principal war aim realised, at least on paper. By the Treaty of Kiel Denmark made peace with the allies: Norway was to be ceded 'to the King of Sweden and comprise a kingdom united with the Swedish state'; Denmark would receive monetary compensation and the cession of Swedish Pomerania, once the union of Norway and Sweden was completed.

In Stockholm news of the Treaty of Kiel prompted demands that the Prince Royal should return home. He had helped his allies free Germany: now his duty was to be at hand while the two Scandinavian kingdoms completed their merger. But Bernadotte was firmly resolved to stay south of the Baltic. He maintained that it was important for him to gain recognition of the new Scandinavia from the Great Powers. Moreover he had been warned, in a peremptory message from Castlereagh, that if Sweden withdrew from active participation in the campaign to overthrow Napoleon, he could not count on further British subsidies. Above all, his greatest personal ambition remained unfulfilled, for the Prince Royal of Sweden was still Jean Baptiste Bernadotte, from Henri IV's Pau. With questionable sincerity the Tsar continued to tempt him, as in those desperate days at Äbo: 'Soon France will have to settle her destiny', Alexander wrote. 'You will be the mediator between her and Europe – and who knows where some happy star may lead you?' The prospect was irresistible.

He left Kiel for the Rhineland on 24 January in the coldest weather anyone could remember in western Europe. Thick snow concealed a familiar countryside, but at last he began to recognise the towns; he was returning to what he regarded as the cradle of his military reputation. On 10 February he made a formal entry into Cologne. There he was moved to issue a magnificent proclamation to the people of France: he had, he explained, taken 'up arms by order of my king to defend the rights of the Swedish people'. Now he had 'avenged the insults they received', liberated Germany and crossed the Rhine. 'On seeing the banks of the river where I have so often and so successfully fought for you, I must make known to you my innermost thoughts', he continued. 'Enlightened men everywhere cherish the hope of seeing France preserved; their sole desire is to prevent her from being the scourge of the world. The sovereigns are not allied together to make war on the nations but to force your government to recognise the independence of states.' And he concluded, 'I can have no ambition save to work for the prosperity of the Scandinavian Peninsula. Would that, in fulfilling my sacred duty to my new fatherland, I may contribute to the well-being of my old compatriots.'

The proclamation was a mistake. At Leipzig he had been a star actor, able to upstage sovereigns, generals and ministers by his late entry. But for four months he had toured the northern provinces with a sideshow. Now the Tsar and General Blücher were up centre. The great river which inspired Bernadotte to reveal his 'innermost thoughts' had been crossed by Blücher near Coblenz on New Year's Day and by Alexander further south a week later; and on 10 February the Prussian vanguard was barely sixty miles from Paris. Although brilliant generalship by Napoleon checked this incursion and relieved the immediate pressure on his capital, it was clear that events had long since outstripped the Prince Royal. The Austrian and Prussian invaders cared little about preserving France and most of the allied statesmen were concerned with more material gains than with any crusading ideal of freeing the world from the French

'scourge'. Moreover, that particular phrase especially enraged Bernadotte's old compatriots. Had he not himself scourged Europe in five
of the Emperor's campaigns?

Unlike his call to the Saxons, the Cologne Proclamation brought
no response from those to whom it was addressed. When, towards
the end of the war, he proposed honourable terms to General Lazare
Carnot if he would surrender Antwerp, the one-time 'organiser of
victory' rejected the offer with proud contempt. A further proclamation, prepared by Benjamin Constant, was among Bernadotte's
papers at Cologne, ready for the moment when his advice was
sought on the transition in France from 'the usurpation called the
Empire' to a new form of government. It remained unprinted
and unpublished. By 28 February, when Bernadotte moved his
headquarters to Liège, he had come to realise that he commanded
no following in the land of his birth.

Three days after he reached Liège, the Prince Royal had an
unexpected visitor, who was passed rapidly through the French
lines and Swedish outposts. Dr Franzenberg entered Bernadotte's
service as a physician at Vienna in 1798; three years later he had set
out with the Bernadottes on their non-journey to America and more
recently he had acted as Désirée's secretary. Now he brought with
him the first letter the Prince Royal had received from his wife for eight
months. But Franzenberg came to Liège with Joseph Bonaparte's
backing and at the suggestion of Napoleon and the prime purpose of
his mission was to discover Bernadotte's immediate intentions. Was
he, as Napoleon suspected, wavering in his loyalty to the allied cause
now that his companions-in-arms had invaded France?

The Prince Royal welcomed Franzenberg warmly, but the canny
habits he had perfected during the Directory speedily reasserted
themselves and his political comments were cautiously vague. Franzenberg should recommend Joseph to advise his brother to make
peace at once, he said, firmly and positively. But when Franzenberg
told him that if he was the first of the allied leaders to reach Paris
many people of eminence who feared a Bourbon restoration would
welcome him as France's natural saviour, Bernadotte fell back on
the legalistic hesitancy he had shown at Brumaire. He could, he
explained, do nothing to divide France or precipitate civil war, but
he would respond to any call which a united nation might make to
him.

Within a few days Franzenberg reported back to Joseph and soon afterwards saw Napoleon in Rheims, passing on Bernadotte's advice that he should make peace on whatever terms he was offered as speedily as possible. For Désirée, by now once more back in the Rue d'Anjou, Franzenberg carried a letter which contained news of Oscar but was silent on political affairs, together with a diamond ring and letters of credit for 60,000 francs. To neither his wife nor her secretary did Bernadotte give any indication whether he planned to cross the old French frontier and march on the capital or remain on the Meuse, content for Destiny to catch up with him – or pass him by.

He lingered in Liège, growing increasingly resentful of Sweden's exclusion from the 'Big Four' summit conferences at Alexander's headquarters in Chaumont. What Russia, Britain, Austria and Prussia agreed there – and in intermittent peace talks with Napoleon's envoy at Châtillon – he learnt either in letters from the Tsar himself or in despatches from Carl Löwenhielm, Sweden's ambassador to Russia. Too often he was asked for advice on decisions already taken. After the exaggerated courtesies of Äbo and Trachenberg it was galling to find oneself an afterthought, and he blamed Metternich for his fall from grace. At last – on Friday, 25 March – he decided to set out from Liège incognito, with two companions, and ride through the Ardennes and Lorraine for a personal interview with Tsar Alexander at Chaumont. But he had left his departure too late. For on that same Friday Schwarzenberg, at Alexander's insistence, ordered the main allied armies (180,000 Austrians, Russians and Prussians) to press forward down the River Marne on Meaux and make a dash for Paris itself. King Frederick William accompanied the Tsar and Schwarzenberg, but the Emperor Francis, Metternich and Castlereagh were non-starters; they remained in Dijon.

Six days later, at eleven in the morning on 31 March, the first Russian cavalry reached the eastern barriers of the city. By dusk Paris was in allied hands and Désirée waited, with fading expectancy, for news that her husband had led his Swedish regiments down the Rue du Faubourg Saint-Martin, after the Russian and Prussian columns. That afternoon a Swedish officer duly arrived in the Rue d'Anjou: he was General Carl Löwenhielm, come to present his compliments to his Princess Royal. As ambassador to the Tsar he had followed Alexander into Paris that morning. He could only tell Désirée that he believed Bernadotte to be still at Liège – although he was, in fact, at Nancy and about to turn back from what he now realised was a pointless attempt to reach Russian headquarters.

That night Désirée wrote to her husband. She let him know how her sister Julie had reluctantly followed Joseph to Tours and Blois, how Talleyrand was even then dining with the Tsar and how the white cockade emblems of the Bourbons were on display in the Faubourg Saint-Germain. She also told him what she could of military movements around the capital. But at the heart of her letter came four sentences of disappointment and pained reproof: 'I am extremely sorry you did not arrive before the E.[mperor] of R.[ussia]. That would have had a fine influence on your interests and on those of people who are dear to you. It is for you to decide if you are in a position to arrive promptly with your army, which I beg you not to leave. Your presence here would be of great consequence.'

Perhaps, on that 31 March, it might have been. For, although Napoleon was still Emperor at Fontainebleau, it was clear he would soon be forced to abdicate. At that moment the de facto ruler of France was Tsar Alexander and, since he was unencumbered by Metternich or any Prussian statesman, he was also chief spokesman for the allies. Had Bernadotte been present in Paris, the Tsar could have turned to him as someone well acquainted with the recent past of France. Instead, Alexander relied on that egregious survivor from the earliest days of the Revolution, Talleyrand, at whose home on the corner of the Rue St Florentin Alexander spent his first days in Paris. He had not entirely forgotten his exchange of hopes and plans with the Prince Royal at Åbo. One evening, soon after his arrival in the Rue St Florentin, he asked his host whether, now that the Napoleonic Empire was finished, the French people might welcome the establishment of a constitutional monarchy under the House of Bernadotte rather than the return of the Bourbons. 'Bernadotte could only be one more phase of the Revolution', Talleyrand replied, and he added, with devastating logic, 'Why choose a soldier when you have just discarded the greatest of them all?'

Part IV
Sovereign Lord of the North

Chapter 13
The Dual Kingdom

BERNADOTTE made the journey to Paris, as Désirée wished. He moved the headquarters of his army from Liège to Brussels and then headed south in a fast barouche, travelling through towns where the church bells were ringing to celebrate Easter. Shortly before dusk on Tuesday, 12 April, he stepped down from his carriage in the Rue du Faubourg Saint-Honoré. Officially he took up residence in Joseph Bonaparte's old town house. Privately he spent much of the following three weeks with Désirée, in the Rue d'Anjou, close at hand.

He knew he came too late 'to play a fine role', for Talleyrand had already induced the Senate 'freely to recall Louis-Stanislas-Xavier' to the French throne. Yet, if history was in a Parisian melting-pot that week, it was as well for Bernadotte to keep his Béarnais nose within sniffing range of its aroma. Metternich, hurrying northwards from Dijon, had reached Paris two days before to give Austrian approval to the treaty dissolving the Empire of France and Kingdom of Italy. Out at Fontainebleau, during Bernadotte's first night in Paris, Napoleon tried to kill himself, swallowing a poison which had lost its potency. Eight more days passed before the 'Emperor and Sovereign of the Isle of Elba' began his slow journey into exile, historic place-names along the route seeming to mock the parody of authority he was permitted to retain. Bernadotte, too, found the past embarrassingly present for much of April. He exchanged courtesies with old colleagues like Ney, Marmont and Augereau, but he knew well enough that others still regarded him as a traitor. And there were echoes of more distant times; he received visits from Etienne Gérard, once his adjutant, from Morard d'Arces, who succeeded d'Ambert as colonel of the Royal-la-Marine, and even from General Darnaud, the commander of the 36th Infantry in

1792 when Lieutenant Bernadotte marched his battalion from St Servan to Strasbourg. At heart the Prince Royal still believed he could reconcile the opposing loyalties of his military career. He scrupulously avoided any commitment to allied policies which stripped France of the conquests made by the armies of the Revolution: a separate armistice was signed between France and Sweden; and he was content to leave the formal business of peacemaking to that experienced diplomat, Gustav Wetterstedt. Yet some public displays he could not miss, however distressing to a veteran commander of the Sambre-et-Meuse. He rode beside the Tsar of Russia and the King of Prussia on 15 April when they saluted the Austrian Emperor's entry into Paris. Next day he was seen ill-at-ease in a box at the Opéra, for the gala performance in honour of the allied sovereigns. Désirée never accompanied him to any official function; and she made it clear that her health would not allow her to return to Stockholm.

Throughout these days in Paris the Prince Royal remained acutely conscious of problems still unresolved in Scandinavia. In the Treaty of Kiel, Frederick VI of Denmark had reluctantly signed away Norway to Sweden but he made no attempt to enforce the transference of authority across the Skagerrak, where the Norwegian people proudly cherished a tradition of independence. A pro-Union party, led by Count Wedel-Jarlsberg, never had so large a following as the Prince Royal's agents claimed; and in late March reports reaching the Army of the North's Belgian headquarters indicated a mounting resistance to Sweden's takeover bid. The Viceroy of Norway was Prince Christian Frederick, a first cousin of the Danish King and also his heir. If the Viceroy refused to accept the Treaty of Kiel as binding it was clear he could count on support from communities throughout central and southern Norway. Bernadotte was worried: even his closest allies, Russia and Britain, had accepted the Treaty reluctantly; and the Austrians and Prussians were openly hostile to any united Scandinavian Kingdom. So cherished a prize could only be secure in Sweden's hands if he had the backing of at least one of the 'Big Four' allies.

'My sole aim in coming to Paris was to settle the Norwegian business', Bernadotte wrote to his royal foster-father on the Thursday after his arrival. He told Charles XIII that he had already been well received by Tsar Alexander and King Frederick William and that he hoped soon to meet the Count of Artois, who was spokesman for the Bourbons until his brother, Louis XVIII, should return to his kingdom. With Frederick William he had little success and with Artois he merely exchanged courtesies. The Tsar was more forthcoming; he was prepared to leave a Russian garrison in Holstein, threatening both King Frederick and Prince Christian Frederick if they failed to fulfil their Treaty obligations. In Paris, too, Bernadotte had his one and only meeting with Castlereagh; it was a profitable discussion, held in the Foreign Secretary's temporary home, a wing of the Ministry of Finance off the Rue Neuve des Capucines.

Castlereagh could never make up his mind about Bernadotte. In the previous summer he had spoken eloquently in the Commons on his contribution to the allied cause; and as late as October he was still prepared to praise his conduct in the Leipzig Campaign. But when he travelled out to allied field headquarters in January, Castlereagh became a close admirer and associate of Metternich: 'I get on with him as if we had spent all our lives together', he wrote three days after their first meeting. From Metternich, who disliked Bernadotte and mistrusted his policies, Castlereagh acquired a strong suspicion that the Prince Royal was intriguing with both Napoleon and the exiled Bourbons. It was Castlereagh who, at headquarters in February, insisted on transferring two Russian and a Prussian corps from the Army of the North to reinforce Blücher, brushing aside allied objections that Bernadotte would take offence with the comment that, if so, he would then loose his monthly subsidy from London. But Lord Liverpool, the British prime minister, remained well-disposed towards Bernadotte; he told Castlereagh that he thought the Norwegians should welcome the Treaty of Kiel because 'the Prince Royal offers them a free Government in the place of the arbitrary one to which they have been subjected for nearly two centuries'.

Castlereagh could not share his prime minister's Swedophile enthusiasm, but when he met Bernadotte in Paris he was prepared to be more accommodating than the Prince Royal had feared. At the end of April he told a cabinet colleague that, although 'Charles John (*sic*) has certainly forfeited all claim to personal favour' by his reluctance to keep up the pressure on Napoleon, Britain had an obligation to see that the terms of the Treaty of Kiel were fulfilled; the Royal Navy must therefore blockade Norway and discourage support for Prince Christian Frederick. At the same time Castlereagh proposed to send an allied diplomatic mission to the Viceroy. He told his emissary, Augustus Foster, that he hoped Norway would accept Swedish sovereignty without a war between the Scandinavian neighbours.

So, of course, did the Prince Royal. But, while he was in Paris, the Norwegian movement for independence made great strides forward; for a group of eminent Norwegians, backed by the Viceroy, summoned an assembly to meet at Eidsvold, a village fifty miles north of Christiania, and on 17 May issued a liberal constitution for an independent Norwegian kingdom, of which Prince Christian Frederick was elected monarch. By then Bernadotte was on his way north through Germany. It was for him a time of crisis. Of the twin ambitions he held twelve months before, one – to gain France for himself – was already a will-o'-the-wisp. Now the second objective, to gain Norway for Sweden, was becoming equally elusive.

Yet, even in the face of black news from the North, he remained a true Palois. For he delayed his departure from France long enough to pay a courtesy call on Louis XVIII at Compiègne, as that gout-stricken widower paused on his journey back to Paris. 'Rule France with an iron hand in a velvet glove', Bernadotte claimed he told Henry of Navarre's descendant that morning. He was not, however, the first ex-Imperial dignitary to offer the head of the House of Bourbon sound counsel, for Talleyrand had beaten Berna-dotte to Compiègne by three clear days, and his advice was always more immediate, practical and self-rewarding. What Bernadotte had to say was of scant interest to Louis XVIII, who thought little of his visitor, and over the following months the King tended to side with Metternich against the 'Swedish usurper'. Talleyrand, however, never questioned the validity of the Prince Royal's title.

The Compiègne meeting was Bernadotte's French curtain-call, a more subdued farewell than he had wished. On 26 May he boarded a Swedish frigate off Travemünde and never again set foot in continental Europe south of the Baltic. But he had no time to agonise over lost opportunities. Within three days he was ashore at Karlskrona, welcomed rapturously by townsfolk and by peasants hurrying in from the villages. The conquering hero who revived Sweden's prestige as a military power was back among his adopted countrymen. It was, he confessed in a letter to Désirée, a pity he could not speak their language.

Stockholm celebrated his triumphant return on 10 June – a day

when, 900 miles away, London was fêting the Tsar, the King of
Prussia and hero liberators from every allied army that had entered
Paris. England could afford to wage peace vigorously over several
months in that summer of rejoicing: Sweden could not. The Prince
Royal was angry at the apparent inability of the British Admiralty
to set aside transports to carry some 30,000 Swedish troops from
the Army of the North back across the Baltic. He needed them
urgently for, to his deep regret, a war with Norway seemed inevitable. When four allied commissioners travelled to Christiania to
talk sense to Norway's elected king, they found him unwilling to
compromise: he knew he could count on support from his cousin
in Copenhagen; he believed that it was against the commercial
interests of Britain, Russia, Prussia and Sweden to see Baltic trade
hampered by war in the Skaggerak; and he was confident that, even
if the Swedes occupied Christiania and the small coastal plains in
Ostföld and Vesföld, the Norwegians would take to the mountains
and resist as effectively as the guerrillas in Spain.

If native-born Swedes thought little of the Norwegian challenge,
their Prince Royal took it seriously; the long resistance of the Tyrol
was in his mind as well as Spain. Moreover he was aware that as
yet he had brought Sweden no territorial gains, nothing to silence
the grievances of the anti-Russian party who, at Örebro, had hoped
the coming of a Napoleonic Marshal would ensure the recovery of
Finland; and he feared that any war of attrition in Norway would
lead to such grumbling from the Swedish merchant community
that, on Charles XIII's death, another palace coup might restore
the Vasas. Reluctantly Bernadotte faced the prospect of a war along
Sweden's western border. He was, however, determined to avoid
bloodshed when possible and make peace if the Norwegians showed
a change of heart. As in the previous winter, he encouraged the
distribution of propaganda sheets, although it is doubtful if his pleas
and promises reached many communities in a terrain so different
from the town-studded plains of Germany. 'Full individual liberty'
was promised to the Norwegians under their own constitution,
provided they accepted a union similar to that which had brought
'prosperity to England'. It was an infelicitous analogy to spread
among merchants and seafarers trading with Leith and Aberdeen.

Yet no appeals to reason could prevent the Norwegians striking
heroic attitudes that summer; a people's self-esteem resented the
Kiel Treaty's assumption that they were chattels, up for barter

between one ruler and another. There was thus a certain inevitability about the Swedish–Norwegian War of 1814. Fortunately it was a brief conflict, over within three weeks, and a minor triumph for good staff-work and careful planning, which avoided needless slaughter. On 26–27 July a Swedish amphibious force occupied the Hvaler archipelago, small islands at the approach to what is now the Oslofjord. A southern army corps under General Hans von Essen and a northern army corps under the Prince Royal himself then pressed forward against the formidable citadel of Fredrikssten and the thin line of Norwegian forts along the lower Glamma, the longest river in Scandinavia. Fredrikssten Castle was invested, ready for a protracted siege. But when the small port of Fredrikstad fell on 3 August, the Prince Royal induced a wealthy merchant to act as an intermediary and set out for Christiania with generous peace proposals. When, a few days later, a Swedish general met a deputation of Norwegian parliamentarians in the busy shipbuilding town of Moss, it became clear that neither side wished lives lost and property destroyed in what threatened to become a long and senseless campaign.

For the moment, operations continued. But on 14 August, the day on which the Prince Royal's troops gained a foothold across the Glamma, armistice terms were settled, generally known as the 'Conventions of Moss': Sweden accepted the Eidsvold Constitution of 17 May, provided that the Storting (the Norwegian parliament) would transfer the Crown from Christian Frederick to the Swedish dynasty and amend other provisions so as to facilitate the union of the two kingdoms. For this purpose, it was agreed that the Storting would meet in October. Bernadotte was in a hurry. He wished the formal act of union to become legally binding before the Congress summoned to Vienna to refurbish a war-weary continent completed its task in the closing weeks of the year.

Yet while he was prepared to charm the Norwegian spokesmen into collaboration he would make no concessions either to Christian Frederick or to King Frederick VI of Denmark, whom he accused of encouraging the ambitions of his cousin in Norway: Christian Frederick must renounce his right of succession to the Danish throne and leave Norway for ever, he insisted. Moreover, since Frederick VI had failed to surrender Norway to Charles XIII, Bernadotte saw no reason why Sweden should honour other terms of the Treaty of Kiel: he refused to hand over Pomerania to Denmark or pay certain indemnities stipulated in the Treaty. This intransigent mood lost Sweden the diplomatic support of the 'Big Four', who sympathised with Denmark. They feared that Bernadotte's dynastic ambition would perpetuate resentment within Scandinavia. Four allied commissioners therefore crossed from Copenhagen to Gothenburg on a mission to persuade the Prince Royal to work for reconciliation.

They found him devious and apparently unhelpful. 'The Prince Royal is necessary to the North for his abilities and great activity', the British commissioner, Augustus Loftus, wrote in the last week of August. 'He is the proper counterpoise to Russia and it is lamentable that he should injure himself by making use of devices which tend to no possible good and only serve to throw an appearance of artifice and finesse into everything he says or does. My three colleagues are now all gone home more or less dissatisfied with him and will no doubt make their reports accordingly.' But, in his exasperation, Loftus was imperceptive. He failed to recognise that Bernadotte's fire and thunder were essentially a show of Gascon pride, a front behind which he was falling back in good order. His determination to make the Union a reality before the Vienna peacemakers looked northwards to the Baltic led him to concede points to the Norwegians and the Danes. Even so, many details of the settlement were only resolved at the Congress itself. It was, for example, not until the first week in June 1815 that treaties between Prussia, Sweden and Denmark provided for the transfer of Pomerania to the Prussians rather than the Danes, in return for monetary compensation.

Left to themselves in the autumn of 1814, the Swedish nobles would have prevaricated over Norway. 'Union', they assumed, meant 'absorption' – as it had in the ambitious policies of Charles XII and Gustav III. 'There is no reason and no need to feed the vanity of the Norwegians by according them a national existence different from that of Sweden', Carl Löwenhielm wrote to Engestrom from Paris in April. But when, in accepting the Conventions of Moss, Bernadotte recognised the Eidsvold Constitution as fundamental to the Union, he implicitly acknowledged Norway's nationhood. Thereafter it was left to the members of the Storting to safeguard their own locally democratic traditions in partnership with Sweden where, despite the constitutional changes of 1809, society remained strongly oligarchic in character. On 20 October, after a fortnight of hard bargaining, the Storting voted overwhelmingly in favour of Union: the Norwegians had substituted a royal suspensive veto on legislation for the total veto which the sovereign possessed in Sweden and they secured a guarantee that Norwegian troops would not be required to fight outside their homeland without the approval of their own parliament. Only in the conduct of foreign policy could a Swedish minister speak jointly for the dual kingdom.

The Prince Royal did not realise how tightly the shrewd legalistic minds of the Storting deputies bound the hands of their sovereign. His experience of French politics had accustomed him to short-lived constitutions, often modified under pressure from above, and he regarded the political settlement with the Norwegian parliamentarians as a practical expedient patched up in the aftermath of war. Charles XIII was solemnly elected King by the Storting on Friday, 4 November, but he was far too frail and senile to travel in person to Norway. It was therefore the Prince Royal, with his son beside him, who rode into the Norwegian capital on the following Wednesday evening. They were escorted by local militia, Bernadotte having refused a company of Swedish Guards since he wished to show confidence in the new kingdom's loyalty. Next morning, in a ceremony ratifying the constitution, he delivered a flattering speech to the Storting in elegant French, which Oscar then read out in Swedish.

Christiania – as Oslo was called between 1625 and 1925 – was still a small town in 1814, with a population of about 11,000 compared with Stockholm's 80,000 and some 20,000 in Sweden's second city, Gothenburg. In so compact a community it was possible for the leading townsfolk as well as the parliamentarians to meet their two future kings, and Bernadotte exercised the charm with which he had broken down hostility in so many German towns during the wars. On one evening in that November he needed resource to other skills. For beyond the solid walls of the Akershus Fortress, where timber-built houses clustered in narrow alleys, a small fire fanned by an inshore wind threatened to spread across the town. The Prince Royal ordered the making of firebreaks and supervised the carrying of water up from the quayside; his quick response saved Christiania from the devastation which followed similar emergencies in 1624, 1686 and 1708 and which was to sweep through the rapidly expanding city in the last year of Oscar's reign. During this first visit of the fifteen-year-old prince to Christiania the parliamentarians and burghers were impressed by his linguistic skills, for when the session of the Storting ended on 26 November, Oscar read a translation of his father's speech not in Swedish but in Norwegian. Father and son arrived back in Stockholm ten days later, at night and in a blizzard, but despite the appalling weather a crowd was in the streets of the old town ready to celebrate their homecoming. No one could doubt the popularity of the Prince Royal in his adopted country.

By going to Christiania he missed an opportunity to attend the opening sessions of the Vienna Congress. He was not sorry. The Habsburg capital held mixed memories for him. He respected Emperor Francis but loathed his chief minister, and fresh embarrassments could not be ruled out; for, just as in 1798 the city had housed French émigrés who shunned the presence of a revolutionary ambassador, so now it offered refuge to the exiled Vasas. Imperial, royal and princely families, with their retinues and hangers-on, almost doubled the population of Vienna that autumn. Bernadotte preferred to dominate a conference table, as at Trachenberg, rather than keep silent while Talleyrand and the Big Four played out their power game; far better remain in Stockholm, await the couriers with despatches from Vienna, and shape policy from a distance rather than be swayed by the passions of the moment. He knew he could rely on the diplomatic tact of Carl Löwenhielm to safeguard the interests of Sweden and the new dynasty.

Yet there were some bad moments for Bernadotte. He was uneasy over the influence of the Vasas: would the 'Big Four' wish to compensate Gustav IV Adolf's son for his lost inheritance in Sweden? The young Gustav was almost the same age as Oscar. From both Löwenhielm and the Tsar came letters suggesting that the allies might create a new duchy for Gustav in Saxony or make him Duke of Cracow. While Bernadotte would have liked the whole family to fade into the background, Louis XVIII and Metternich remained sympathetic to Vasa pretensions. But, after a few weeks, Löwenhielm was able to exploit differences between the Big Four over Poland and Saxony so as to keep the Vasas out of the limelight. Ultimately Sweden did well from the Congress: the union with Norway was recognised by all the Powers; the final transference of Stralsund and Rügen to Prussia spared the Swedes any involvement in the tortuous politics of the German Confederation; and both the Swedish state and Bernadotte himself gained considerable sums of money from Great Britain, notably as compensation for handing back Guadeloupe to France rather than ceding the island to Sweden as the British had earlier promised. Money from Prussia and from Britain helped refill Sweden's empty coffers and made the Prince Royal personally less dependent on grants from the Riksdag and Storting. At the same time, although Bernadotte's hopes of reviving the Swedish West Indies Company were dashed by the loss of Guadeloupe, he could still profit from the Caribbean sugar trade: for St Barthélemy, Gustav III's tiny island in the sun, remained a personal possession of Sweden's kings for another sixty years.

On one occasion in Vienna Count Löwenhielm was forced to take a rapid policy decision without reference back to Stockholm. When news reached the Congress that Napoleon had escaped from Elba and landed in southern France, the leading European Powers published a solemn assurance to Louis XVIII and the French people offering every assistance in restoring peace and tranquillity and Löwenheilm signed the declaration in Sweden's name. Bernadotte approved: he thought Napoleon's adventure doomed to disaster. He was not, however, prepared to mobilise the Swedish army or send an expeditionary force once more across the Baltic; he would, he told Louis XVIII's ambassador, wait and see what requests and conditions were made by his old allies in Vienna.

During these eventful weeks, no news reached him from Désirée, who was still living in the Rue d'Anjou, and Bernadotte was left to evaluate Napoleon's enterprise at third hand. He was impressed by the ease with which the Emperor regained Paris and won the backing of the French people. The restored Bourbons had irritated Bernadotte by a series of social slights and by their encouragement of the Vasa exiles; he wasted no sympathy on the wretched Louis XVIII when he fled to Ghent. On the other hand, the constitutional experiments of the Hundred Days and the support given to the Emperor by his old friend, Lucien Bonaparte (so long estranged from his brother) made Bernadotte think again and he welcomed Napoleon's assurances that his only objective in foreign affairs was the recovery by France of her 'natural frontiers' along the Rhine. Publicly the Prince Royal was guarded in his comments; privately his heart was with old friends like Gérard and Ney as they marched forward across the Sambre and the old battlefield of Fleurus. For the Bernadotte dynasty, a liberal Imperialist France was preferable to a reactionary Bourbon restoration.

'If Napoleon had won Waterloo . . .' is an old game which has long intrigued British and French writers, concerned for the most part with the fate of the Emperor himself and of the armies of Wellington and Blücher. To speculate on Bernadotte's response is equally intriguing: almost certainly, no military intervention, but an attempt to raise Sweden's international prestige by coming forward as a mediator, particularly between Paris and St Petersburg. Such a role was denied him by the decisive nature of an allied victory over which the Swedes kept their silence. When, after news of Waterloo had reached Stockholm, the French ambassador arranged for a *Te Deum* to be celebrated in honour of Louis XVIII's second restoration, it was attended by no representative of the Swedish court or high ranking dignitary.

For Bernadotte the day-to-day business of government was concentrated on narrowly Scandinavian affairs. Many matters came easily to him: the encouragement of intensive farming in southern Sweden and the establishment of a peacetime dual army for Sweden and Norway, for example. Over some problems, such as the appointment of a good Lutheran pastor to the bishopric of Bergen, he was out of his depth – and reluctant to admit it. Occasionally, liberal proposals sparked off angry outbursts of Gascon temperament: thus when the Riksdag met in 1815, an attempt by the clerical deputy and former soldier, Frederick Bogislas Schwerin, to borrow the concept of a loyal Opposition from British parliamentary practice alarmed Bernadotte. A recollection of distant feuds with Sieyès made him unsympathetic to churchmen constitutionalists: '*Opposition? C'était conspiration*', he snapped.

This was an ominous reaction. Like Napoleon during the Consulate, Bernadotte was beginning to see imaginary conspiracies in gatherings of politicians. They were, he believed, subsidised from abroad, by agents working on behalf of the Vasa exiles. An ignorance of the Swedish language and a limited comprehension of constitutional liberties increased his paranoia. Yet these fears were not entirely groundless. In March 1817, on the ninth anniversary of Gustav IV Adolf's deposition, the police in Stockholm picked up reports of a plot to assassinate Bernadotte – and, possibly, Oscar – either by poisoning his food or by a swift sword thrust. Extra precautions were taken throughout that spring. Two months later a young cavalry officer, Lieutenant Anders Lindsfelt, was arrested, interrogated and found hanged in his cell. The episode increased the Prince Royal's reliance upon secret agents, organised in the first instance by his compatriot Camps. Even the Fouché family helped him; the old regicide himself died in 1820, having enjoyed a comfortably wealthy exile in Trieste, but his son settled in Sweden and was soon appointed a Court Chamberlain.

The Prince Royal sought to stand impartially above Swedish society, gaining from this isolated eminence a fuller authority in government. He could count on the goodwill of Charles XIII and his consort and he was still closely attached to the Mörners, his earliest contacts among the Swedish nobility; one of the family, Count Carl Mörner ap Tuna, became the first Lieutenant-Governor of Norway. With the Löwenhielm brothers, too, he remained on good terms, but their skill in diplomacy ensured that they were almost always absent from Sweden. His warmest Swedish friendship was with a slightly less distinguished family. When Bernadotte arrived in Stockholm, Count Magnus-Frederick Brahe had already been a member of Charles XIII's household for several years. The newcomer was pleased, not only by the Count's tact, but by the assiduity with which his son, Magnus Brahe, fulfilled the duties of an aide-de-camp and by the charm and beauty of Aurora Brahe, the old Count's second wife. Aurora's cousin, Mariana Koskull, a lady-in-waiting to Queen Hedvig, was widely believed to have consoled the Prince Royal for Désirée's absence. Their relationship may have been platonic but, if so, Mariana showed fortitude as a listener and persistence in willingly playing cards evening after evening. Yet since the Brahes and Mariana spoke French fluently, Bernadotte could relax in their company, slipping easily into a mood of 'I told the Emperor . . .' reminiscence and occasional 'When I was a Sergeant . . .' anecdotage.

Most easily he would cast aside the cares of government at Rosendal, the villa he built in an old deer park three miles down the Saltsjo from central Stockholm. As if to link past and present in his life, the villa looked out across Djurgardsbrunnsviken bay to a cavalry barracks on the mainland. The Brahes were, of course, frequent guests at Rosendal but it never became simply the Prince Royal's private country house. He entertained the Queen there; and, at least once, he was even host to that scurrilous gossip, the French ambassador.

As King Charles XIII's health grew feebler month by month so the Prince Royal felt a need to hold in check the affable *'mon vieux'* familiarity of his small talk. He assumed the mantle of royalty more self-consciously than had he been born close to the throne. A letter to Carl Mörner ap Tuna in September 1816 speculated, rather pompously, on 'the great difference between the man and the Prince'. More precisely, it sought to justify a change of heart by explaining why, despite earlier indignation, he was now prepared to treat a minor rebuff to his Norwegian policies with magnanimity: 'I was a man before I was a Prince', he admitted, but, 'as a Prince I must stand above that feeling of mortification which is born of human ingratitude, a sentiment which if you look closely at it is, perhaps, only a consequence of wounded vanity.' Increasingly, in those first years of the dual kingdom, he was reminding himself of the role 'destiny has called me to fulfil', and an unspoken 'As a Prince I must . . . ' became his watchword.

At the end of January 1818 Charles XIII gave a banquet for several hundred guests to mark Bernadotte's fifty-fifth birthday. But hardly had the King entered the hall of the palace than he collapsed with an apoplectic fit. For another week he lingered on, while the Prince Royal once again exercised full powers of Regency. At ten o'clock at night on 5 February, Charles XIII died. Jean Baptiste Bernadotte ascended the throne as King Charles XIV John, 'King of Sweden, of Norway, of the Goths and of the Vandals'.

It was a smooth and speedy succession. Before midnight a long line of parliamentary deputies, members of the nobility and Stockholm burghers had begun to file into the Queen's throne room to pledge loyalty to their new king. By the end of the month he had received messages of condolence and congratulation from his brother sovereigns throughout Europe. The strangest gesture of all, however, was a letter addressed to King Charles John and entrusted to a courier from Basle; for, at this opening of a new reign, it contained a message of goodwill to the Swedish people from the pathetic refugee of 1809, their deposed king, Gustav IV Adolf.

Désirée's status caused problems of social etiquette abroad. King Louis XVIII sent the Duke of Aumont to the Rue d'Anjou to convey his greetings to the 'Countess of Gothland' and ask if she wished to be acknowledged as Queen of Norway and Sweden; but on Charles John's instructions, Désirée declined as yet to accept the new title. Bernadotte hoped that she would sooner or later return to Sweden. In the previous year he received confirmation from Désirée's doctors in Paris that her health would hardly stand a protracted sojourn in a cold climate. He made certain that she received, not only regular letters from himself and their son, but a pension of 50,000 francs a quarter, conveyed to her by one of Louis Camps's couriers. And in what now became Scandinavia's 'Coronation Year', he kept her well informed of all the festivities in Sweden and in Norway.

Momentarily he thought of postponing the ceremonies until Désirée could rejoin him. But he was a shrewd judge of public opinion. He wished to secure the backing of the Church for his dynasty while the novelty of accession was still prompting demonstrations of loyalty in the towns and villages of the two kingdoms. Although he let Désirée know his regret at not having her beside him, he did not press her to return. He saw no reason why weeks of state mourning should continue into the spring and summer. Coronation Day in Stockholm was fixed for Monday, 11 May 1818. It was the thirtieth anniversary of Sergeant Bernadotte's promotion to Sergeant-Major.

'No expense has been spared to make the establishment of the new dynasty a matter of popular interest and amusement', the British minister to Sweden reported back to London with haughty disdain as the coronation festivities in Stockholm came to an end. The sneer was unjust. The King's greatest concern was, not simply to win cheers from the people, but to emphasise a continuity with the Vasa past, although his Gascon sense of theatre prompted him to improvise traditions where they were lacking. Notable among these were the heralds who rode through the capital in the days preceding the coronation so as to make certain that everyone was aware of the great ceremony which would give them a holiday in the following week.

Charles John was interested in every detail of the plans for his coronation, both in Sweden and in Norway. The sixteenth-century crown of Eric XIV – most ambitious of the early Vasas, five times the failed suitor of Elizabeth of England and once of Mary of Scots – was polished up and redesigned, with diamonds provided by Charles John himself, who also presented a blue-enamelled orb. For the short procession down the Slottsbacke from the palace to the Storkyrka ('Great Church') he wore silver woven robes beneath the simple crown of a prince, moving forward with slow dignity under a canopy plumed with feathers. He was crowned and anointed by Archbishop Jakob Lindblom, with the sacred ceremonies permitted

by the Canon Law of 1686, which recognised that the National
Lutheran Church was subject to the King's authority. Hardly had
he returned to the palace, through cheering crowds and with the
church bells ringing throughout the city, than he began to sound
out his Norwegian advisers on the coronation ritual of his second
kingdom. He knew that Trondheim, not Christiania, was the spirit-
ual heart of Norway; the long days of high summer would, he
thought, offer a fine occasion for a crowning in the fjords.

On 21 June, however, he had to write in genuine sorrow to his
Governor of Norway, telling him of a grievous loss. Queen Hedvig
Charlotte was not four years older than her royal foster-son; she
had, however, long suffered from occasional agonising pains in the
stomach. Yet in these early months of widowhood she seemed
remarkably well and on 19 June she dined with Charles John out at
his Rosendal villa. In the small hours of the morning she was seized
with appalling stomach cramp and, to the new king's consternation,
within a few hours she was dead. There was now no matriarchal
figure at the Swedish Court. The Countess of Gothland remained
in Paris, about to set out for the spa waters of Aachen. Even though
the Norwegian coronation was postponed until September in order
to observe the decencies of mourning for Hedvig Charlotte, there
was never any possibility of Désirée joining her husband in time for
the ceremonies at Trondheim.

Nidaros Cathedral, built on the site of the shrine of St Olav,
Norway's warrior patron saint, was in a poor condition in the early
years of the nineteenth century; and Trondheim itself was so small
a city that all the dignitaries who hurried north for the coronation
on 7 September were forced to remain aboard ships moored off the
harbour, in the bay of the fjord. But, once again, Charles John was
crowned with great solemnity, surrounded by all the principal
military and civil leaders of the kingdom. The ritual was simpler
than in Stockholm, the senior prelate of the Norwegian Lutheran
Church officiating. As in May, Charles John was fortunate with the
weather, bright sunshine and a cloudless sky. On the following
evening a coronation ball was held in the largest timbered house of
the old city. Elaborate fire precautions were observed throughout
the week but, surprisingly, there was no emergency on this occasion.

'Their shouts of joy warmed the cockles of my heart', Charles
John told his Viceroy, after riding back from Nidaros Cathedral
into Trondheim. No one now could rightly dispute the crowned

sergeant's royal titles. Two thrones were his with parliamentary consent and sanctified by a solemn crowning in each realm. He was well-satisfied with 'the fulfilment of our destinies'. Three and a half million subjects owed him their allegiance – and the dual kingdoms over which he ruled were twice the size of Bourbon France.

Chapter 14
Dynasty Building

T HE Stockholm and Trondheim coronations may have added
divine sanction to Charles John's personal titles, but had the
royal House of Bernadotte come to stay? For in 1818 the new
dynasty comprised a man of fifty-five and a son not yet twenty.
Although Charles John might look robust he had suffered from
chronic bouts 'of spitting blood' since before Oscar's birth and was
probably tubercular. A recurrence of the illness during weeks of
tension and stress could prove as dramatically disastrous as an
assassin's knife. Moreover for both father and son there was always
the possibility of a bad fall from a startled horse. The dynasty
needed a good marriage for Oscar and, as soon thereafter as possible,
grandsons for Charles John.

Désirée had long favoured a marriage between her only son and
a first cousin. After 1815 she spent much of her time in Paris
safeguarding the interests of Julie's family and she hoped Oscar
would choose either Zenaïde or Charlotte Bonaparte, the daughters
of ex-king Joseph and Julie. But such a marriage was always a
non-starter. Charles John was looking for a daughter-in-law who
possessed more valuable political connections. He was, moreover,
less sympathetic towards Désirée than a few years before. At the
Congress of Aix-la-Chapelle (Aachen) she pursued Louis XVIII's
chief minister, the Duke of Richelieu, with such tenacity that gossip
insisted they were lovers. Richelieu's tastes and prejudices made
such a liaison unlikely but Désirée's general conduct aroused considerable disquiet and Charles John wrote sternly to her soon after
returning from Trondheim. In curiously oblique phrases he warned
his wife that so long as she continued to behave foolishly she was
in danger of undermining the social authority which he anticipated

she would enjoy as queen, 'when next spring you are reunited to those you love'.

The gossips did not entirely spare Charles John or his son either. The King's attachment to Mariana Koskull no longer aroused comment, but he was said to be attracted to the outrageously flirtatious wife of the Dutch envoy and to have been fired with dishonourable intentions by the blonde consort of a provincial governor who, though not quite a lady, aspired to be a queen of fashion. In so censorious a society it was enough for Oscar to enjoy sharing a spontaneous and innocent zest for living with one of the younger Löwenhielm wives to start tongues wagging. Not surprisingly, the Prince acquired a reputation for diffidence at Court functions. His father and closest intimates looked for suitable brides for Oscar among princely families across Germany, in the Netherlands and even in Russia, despite the strong resentment which the loss of Finland to the Tsar still aroused in Sweden. But Oscar refused to be hurried into matrimony. He was prepared to wait and to travel; better to search for a bride than rely on reports from his father's agents.

In the last week of July 1821 Charles John was genuinely saddened by the news from St Helena that Napoleon had died at Longwood two and a half months before. 'He was the greatest captain that has appeared upon the earth since Julius Caesar', the King wrote to Oscar – characteristically qualifying this high commendation with the comment that, if Napoleon 'was the greatest man of his age in military planning, I surpassed him in method and calculation'. A rush of sentiment made the former Marshal well-disposed towards his old comrades-in-arms, as once before, during the Hundred Days. It was therefore not surprising that when Baron von Bonen, an expatriate Swede from the Bavarian Court, sought an audience with Charles John soon afterwards, he found the King readily receptive to the suggestion of a link between the families of Bernadotte and Beauharnais. Napoleon's stepson, Prince Eugène, was also the son-in-law of King Maximilian Joseph of Bavaria, who had created him Duke of Leuchtenberg and Prince of Eichstatt; and Bonen claimed to have come straight to Sweden from Munich to discuss a possible marriage between Prince Oscar and Eugène's eldest daughter, who was named Josephine in honour of her grandmother, the Empress.

Technically Bonen told the truth. Eugène, however, knew nothing of the Baron's business. Not until early October did Bonen visit the Beauharnais' favourite home, the *Residenz* in Eichstatt. Bonen gave no indication on that occasion of having already met Charles John and Eugène decided he was a well-meaning crank with whom there was no harm in agreeing on the merits of a marriage link with the Bernadottes. Since Josephine was only fourteen and since Bonen disappeared from Eichstatt as suddenly as he came, neither Eugène nor his wife, Augusta, attached much importance to his suggestion; they were preparing to move into their new Munich palace, the Leuchtenberg, within a fortnight. There Bonen reappeared early in January, bringing with him a cordial, one-soldier-to-another letter from Charles John to Eugène, together with the blue ribbon of the Order of the Seraphim, and written authority to discuss the marriage of Oscar and Josephine. A miniature, also entrusted to Bonen, showed a tall and slim young man with black curly hair and dark eyes, as handsome as any prince Josephine had ever seen. His character, Bonen confidently assured Eugène and Augusta, was above reproach.

Two problems troubled Josephine's parents: her youthfulness and her religion. She was born in March 1807 and Eugène insisted that there could be no wedding until she was sixteen. The religious issue was not such a stumbling block as he had feared. When Napoleon had suggested, twelve years before, that Eugène should be a candidate for the Swedish succession, his stepson had explained that he could not accept Lutheranism. But now Bonen could reassure Eugène and Augusta: although a future king must be a Lutheran there was no need for their daughter to abandon her catholicism, any more than had Désirée. Once these two points were settled, Baron von Bonen went back to Stockholm with a portrait of Josephine and an invitation for Oscar to visit Eichstatt during the grand European tour his father was planning for him in the coming summer.

Charles John welcomed the Beauharnais marriage project. It would, he explained to Désirée, give the Bernadottes a link with the old order – the Wittelsbachs of Bavaria were as ancient as any dynasty in Europe – and also with the new Bonapartist order, which might yet return to favour. Oscar was unenthusiastic; as he explained apologetically to his future father-in-law a few months later, he had become tired of 'third persons' who 'meddle with my future'. Although both Charles John and Eugène regarded the matter as settled before their children even met, Oscar believed he retained some freedom of decision. He was determined to set out on his Grand Tour; he would see Germany, the Netherlands, Switzerland and Italy before allowing his betrothal to be announced.

Not that Charles John wished to stop him. A short list of eligible reserves, would-be brides from Copenhagen southwards to Wilhelmshöhe, was drawn up for Oscar's earnest perusal. But the King had other motives in sending Oscar abroad in that summer of 1822; he knew Oscar would meet his mother early on his travels and he hoped their son's charm and tact might coax Désirée back to Sweden. Moreover, Tsar Alexander and Metternich had already agreed that a Congress of the European Powers should gather in Florence that autumn. Although Charles John did not wish Oscar to play at round-table diplomacy with the top professionals, a Congress was a good social occasion at which to make an international debut.

All went as Charles John wished, despite a press leak by Baron von Bonen which intensely angered the aready highly embarrassed young prince. Désirée met her son for the first time in eleven years at Aachen on 23 June and was delighted with him. They agreed that Oscar would seek his father's permission to cut short the tour of bridal inspection and head for Eichstatt, once he had paid a courtesy call to Het Loo, where the optimistic Oranges were putting twelve-year-old Princess Marianne on view. Désirée's interests were now centred on her son's immediate future, a preoccupation made all the easier by the death of the Duke of Richelieu in May. She arranged for Oscar to visit his aunt Julie in Brussels (where cousin Zenaïde had recently married Lucien Bonaparte's eldest son) and undertook to join him in Switzerland after he had been to Eichstatt so that he could meet Josephine's aunt and Désirée's old friend, Hortense Beauharnais. Désirée never doubted for a moment that Josephine would gladly become Oscar's wife.

She was right. Oscar reached Eichstatt early in the evening of 23 August, with a suite of seven Swedish noblemen, all of whom had so large a following that the Princess Augusta, who kept a detailed record of Oscar's visit, feared the palace was too small to accommodate them. She noticed that throughout that first evening Oscar kept glancing at Josephine, but he appears to have said little to her. Two days later he told Eugène frankly that he had wanted to marry the daughter of a reigning monarch since he believed that would be politically advantageous for Sweden; his father, however, had insisted he could never do better than marry the daughter of the Prince 'whose spotless reputation was of greater worth than the crown of which he had been deprived'. Eugène wished to know if Oscar was convinced that Josephine would make him happy. Oscar did not doubt it: 'I have decided', he replied. 'She is still very young; but in a year she will be able to marry, will she not?' Nothing was said to Josephine until after Oscar had visited her aunt Hortense. Then there were a few days of amateur theatricals, a visit to the opera, and finally what everyone in Eichstatt had long since expected – a solemn proposal of marriage. The young Princess agreed that she would be very happy to become Oscar's wife; no announcement would be made until his return from Italy and his initiation into Great Power politics.

The whole Swedish cavalcade duly travelled south of the Alps to Milan, Rome and eventually Verona, where the Congress was to be held rather than in Florence. Oscar and his retinue made a fine impression on the Duke of Wellington, on Emperor Francis and Tsar Alexander and even on Metternich. Then back to Munich at the end of the first week in November for the formal ceremonies of betrothal. It was agreed that there would be a proxy ceremony in Munich soon after Josephine's sixteenth birthday and that she should go to Stockholm for a midsummer wedding.

Within a few months of the betrothal the bride's father became seriously ill. Eugène suffered a cerebral haemorrhage on Easter Day; he willed himself to recover sufficiently to welcome guests for the ceremony in Munich's Herzogsspitalkirche eight weeks later. Hortense came, together with her fifteen-year-old son, the future Emperor Napoleon III, but etiquette ruled out the presence of Désirée or any of the Clary family. Poor Eugène was too weak to attend the banquet afterwards and it was thought that the sorrow of parting from his favourite daughter would cause a relapse. He lingered on, however, for ten more months, occasionally summoning the strength to travel out into the Bavarian countryside and always eager, above all, for news from Stockholm.

Josephine's progress northwards through Germany and across to Sweden in that spring of 1823 was a triumph. And at Lübeck her presence achieved what had long seemed an impossibility, the boarding of a Swedish vessel by Sweden's Queen. For Désirée had decided that she wished to return to Stockholm and enjoy life at a Court whose solemnities would be lightened by the presence of the young couple. Contrary winds delayed the departure of the ship for several days and when eventually it sailed Désirée was, as she feared, ill so long as the vessel was on the open sea. But, unlike her own first arrival in Sweden, the weather was royally kind to Josephine once the ship reached the islets of the Saltsjö and sailed up between the rocky, wooded banks towards Stockholm. On the afternoon of 3 June, they landed at Manilla, three miles short of the city. Josephine was escorted into a gold and purple state coach, pulled by eight greys, which carried her to Gustav III's summer villa at Haga. There a cheering crowd greeted her. She thanked her wellwishers in a short speech in Swedish, carefully conned for the occasion. Almost unobserved by the crowd, Désirée slipped back to the royal palace in Stockholm. From there she joined her husband and son at Drottningholm. Only when the wedding festivities began a fortnight later did the Swedes realise a Queen was among them once more.

Charles John was delighted by Oscar's sixteen-year-old bride. He had first admired her grandmother during those heady days in Lombardy over a quarter of a century ago. The Princess possessed some of the Empress Josephine's grace and charm, but she was fair, tall and sylphine, like her mother. At her wedding, on 19 June, she moved with astonishing natural majesty. Not only Désirée was impressed but also Princess Sophie Albertine, Gustav III's septuagenarian sister, once Abbess of a convent in the Harz mountains. A few weeks later Désirée, writing to her younger niece Charlotte, praised Josephine's good looks and kindness; she commented, in particular, on 'the care she shows towards me over small matters'. Poor Désirée, by now considerably overweight, missed some of the protracted wedding celebrations, having slipped when stepping down from a carriage and badly dislocated her shoulder. Yet so much pleased her in Sweden that she wondered why she had hurried back to France so precipitately thirteen years before. To have arrived in midwinter was a disastrous mistake, she reflected; today, so she told Charlotte, 'the nation, my husband, my son – everything is perfect for me'. She did not add that, while on her earlier visit she was constrained by the social etiquette prescribed by Queen Hedvig Charlotte and the widowed Sophie Magdalene, she was now First Lady of Sweden and Norway in her own right.

Court life had fallen into disarray since Charles John's accession. He insisted that ceremonial occasions should be observed with dignity and parade ground orderliness but for much of the year he was content to conduct the business of government with an efficient informality. State councillors seeking an audience knew that he was as likely to receive them in his bedroom as in one of the smaller rooms of the palace. For, while Napoleon always liked to get up early, Charles John saw no point in leaving the comfort of his bed until the day was well advanced, especially in winter: his knees served as an improvised desk for letter-writing, as so often during his campaigns; and he was as well able to dictate from a recumbent position in bed as pacing across a study floor.

Désirée's return made little difference to his methods of work. Her presence at Court ensured that there was a regular pattern of meals: a light lunch; dinner at five o'clock; supper at ten. Charles John, like Napoleon, always ate little and preferred simple food rather than gourmet dishes. Désirée found her husband's personal foibles too well established for change. To most of them she was well accustomed: why question old habits? Some she readily shared, notably his determination to keep palace stoves so well stoked up in the winter that room temperatures never fell below 16°C (60°F). Like his ministers and councillors she was fully aware he had a keenly developed sense of smell and particularly loathed tobacco; he would keep a bottle of eau-de-cologne handy and sprinkle a noxious offender with it liberally if he believed he had recently been smoking. Yet in one respect Charles John changed over the years, for as he grew older he became almost a teetotaller. He was alarmed at the high incidence of alcoholism throughout the kingdom once restrictions on distilling *brannvin* ('potato brandy') were lifted early in the century: '*Brannvin* will be the ruin of the Swedish people', he once declared. But King and Queen still appreciated good French wine at their banquets, which became more frequent with the widening of Court life after Oscar's wedding.

Despite the casual way in which he conducted so much royal business Charles John was not indolent. His printed correspondence with the lieutenant-governors in Norway shows a careful attention to detail and he undertook frequent journeys away from Stockholm so as to see for himself the problems of his subjects. On the average 1000 official documents were presented to him for signature every month. Each had to be translated from Swedish into French and so too did the agenda and minutes of the Council of State. Often particular points had to be explained to the King by a minister or civil servant who could speak French well. Non-linguist politicians resented exclusion from inner government. Moreover as early as 1823 the British minister, William Fitzgerald, reported that members of the Riksdag were complaining of government by 'mutilated translations', a grievance on which fifteen years later another British envoy, Sir Thomas Cartwright, also commented. Charles John himself suspected from time to time that he was being misrepresented. At first he welcomed Oscar's ability to act as a go-between who spoke Swedish, but there were occasions when the fluency of his son and daughter-in-law irritated him and threw him into a black mood of Gascon temperamentality. Eventually he succeeded in memorising a few Swedish phrases of conventional greeting which he would use at military reviews or state receptions.

Some ventures in both kingdoms won his support as soon as they were broached. As early as 1809 the Riksdag had approved the construction of a canal linking Gothenburg and the Baltic by way of Lakes Vanern and Valtern, and this undertaking was warmly backed by Charles John, both before and after his accession. Canal building was a familiar concept to him: Napoleon had planned to provide France with 2000 miles of new canals, and civil engineering enterprises of this type were under discussion during the period Bernadotte served on the Council of State in Paris. But Charles John encouraged the Swedes to look to Britain rather than to France for financial backing and expert advice. The artificial waterway linking the lakes was less than sixty miles long; even so, it needed the building of fifty-eight locks and it was only in the autumn of 1832, fifteen years after his accession, that Charles John was at last able to open the Gota Canal. Like Napoleon, too, he promoted the building of roads to unite his kingdoms. If the fallen Emperor, reminiscing on St Helena, listed the 'carriage ways' over the Alpine passes as among his greatest achievements, then Charles John in old age could also be proud of having opened a route from Trondheim across the mountain divide of Swedish Jamtland and southwards to Gavle, Uppsala and Stockholm.

Yet while the King would support commercial projects familiar to him, he was as suspicious of new ventures as he had been of military observation balloons in the Rhineland. Steamships he accepted: there was a steamer on Lake Malar in the year of his accession and paddle wheels were churning up the southern fjords by the summer of 1825, when he accompanied Désirée on her first visit to Norway. Railway talk he ignored: John Ericson, an engineer who had worked on the Gota Canal, constructed a steam locomotive which he sent to England for the famous railway competition of 1829, but Charles John showed no interest in Ericson's invention; Sweden's first railway was not opened until twelve years after the King's death. Industrial growth was slow, partly because Charles John assumed that homecraft textile production and sawmills dependent on the flotation of logs better suited the economic geography of Sweden and Norway than mechanised looms and steam sawmills. During the King's later years there were complaints that he was too set in his ways to understand modern needs, a point of view with which Oscar had some sympathy.

Politically Charles John liked to think of himself as a crowned republican, gradually advancing popular government in his two kingdoms. In Sweden, however, the hereditary aristocracy continued to dominate the Council of State throughout his reign; he had been on the throne for nine years before the first commoner, Hans Schwan, was admitted to the Council. Whenever there was a conflict between liberals urging the modernisation of the Riksdag or relaxation of the press laws, Charles John and most of his advisers were firmly on the side of the conservative traditionalists.

Towards Norway Charles John was, as he thought, generous. He supported reforms to improve the country's economy and modernise the towns and harbours. When Frederikshald was destroyed by fire in June 1826 the King piously observed that the Almighty may have inflicted this disaster upon the townsfolk so as to test their faith; they must glorify God by working hard so as to make good their losses – but he also ordered his Lieutenant-Governor to provide what aid he could in rebuilding the devastated town. Charles John remained popular throughout Norway: Karl Johans Gate, a fine road completed in 1852 and now the chief shopping street of modern Oslo, perpetuates his name almost a century and a half after his death. Yet he treated Norway's parliamentarians oddly. For, although in 1821 he strictly observed the constitution by letting the Storting abolish the nobility despite his earlier veto, he later allowed a trivial dispute to become, at least in his eyes, a major crisis.

The issue, which came to a head in 1827, was simple: the Storting wished to celebrate Norway's national day on 17 May, the anniversary of the Eidsvold Constitution: Charles John preferred to commemorate 4 November, the day the Storting accepted Charles

XIII as Norway's King. So deep was the feeling aroused by this dispute that in January 1828 Charles John dismissed Johan Sandels, his wise and conciliatory Lieutenant-Governor. For several months that spring he went into residence in Norway himself, ready to quash rebellion. There were small demonstrations in Bergen and Christiansand, but it was in the capital that Charles John anticipated most trouble on 17 May and he prepared to meet the challenge resolutely. Throughout that Saturday he waited booted and spurred in Christiania's makeshift palace, a single-storeyed building that had belonged to a timber merchant; news came to him of stone-throwing students jeering at troops between the market place and the quays. Ought he to ride out and take command?

On another Saturday market day, almost exactly forty years before, the incensed townsfolk of Grenoble pelted Colonel d'Ambert's marines with tiles from the rooftops rather than accept a loss of privileges. Perhaps Charles John recalled the incident. For, following his natural inclination, he took no action at all. The demonstrators dispersed without shots being fired. In this 'Battle of the Market Place', as patriotic Norwegian writers call the episode, there were no serious casualties and, it would seem, no losers. For the King returned to Stockholm at the end of July convinced that, since 17 May had not been commemorated by the Storting this spring, he had made his point; and the Norwegians, ignoring their sovereign's spluttering indignation, went on celebrating 17 May as Constitution Day each year throughout Charles John's reign and beyond. They still do.

Désirée had wished to leave Sweden in that summer of 1828 and visit Julie in Italy. The King forbade her to go: once across the Baltic would he ever tempt her back again? In a letter from Norway he explained that it was essential for the Bernadottes to be seen as a happy and united royal family, an example and inspiration for the kingdoms as a whole. By now the Bernadotte dynasty was an established institution. Princess Josephine gave birth to her first child in May 1826, Charles Ludwig Eugène (King Charles XV, 1859–72); a second son, Gustav, followed in June 1827; and she was pregnant for the third time, with the boy who would reign from 1872 to 1907 as King Oscar II. Rather than have Sweden's grandmother matriarch a voluntary exile once again, Charles John proposed to recognise Désirée's status as queen-consort in a coronation ceremony of her own. It was accordingly agreed that the

Marseilles merchant's daughter, an occasionally devout Catholic, would next summer be crowned Queen Desideria of the Swedes, Goths and Vandals in Stockholm's Lutheran Storkyrka. The Latinised form was considered more dignified than the name by which her husband, brothers and sisters called her.

Charles John chose 21 August 1829 for Désirée's coronation, the nineteenth anniversary of his election as Prince Royal. He was annoyed when, a few days before the event, a Riksdag deputy sought to secure the backing of the Diet for a deputation to the Queen begging her to accept the Lutheran faith. But the Diet would have nothing to do with such a suggestion and the coronation ceremonies went well. The Archbishop of Uppsala anointed the Queen and, assisted each time by a different representative of the nobility, placed the crown on her head and invested her with orb and with sceptre. In one respect Désirée was less fortunate than Charles John, for as her procession moved slowly back to the palace a heavy shower of rain broke over the city, but for most of the ten days of celebration the weather was good. There were balls, firework displays and a naval review which, with proper concern for Her Majesty, took place in waters tactfully distant from the open sea. On the last Sunday in August the parklands of Drottningholm were opened to the people of Stockholm. They were pleased to find the King and his heir so confident of their personal safety that they could risk what a later generation would call a 'walkabout'.

Yet for how long could the Bernadottes continue to count on such respectful adulation? In the following winter there was momentary concern over the King's health for the first time since his accession. By the spring of 1830 he seemed strong again, ready to join his subjects in welcoming the birth of a princess, Josephine's only daughter, Charlotte Eugénie. But within four months Charles John was surprised by news from Paris: a 'revolution stopped halfway' had replaced Charles X as King of France by the head of the Orléanist branch of the Bourbons, Louis Philippe, who became King of the French. Fifteen years ago, after Waterloo, Charles John would have welcomed the Orléanist succession. Now, with a nicely ironic twist to history, the July Revolution embarrassed him. For Paris changed, not only kings, but flags too; out went the Bourbon white lilies and back came the familiar colours of the Republic. Not surprisingly, when Marshal Ney's son arrived in Stockholm on a special mission from Louis Philippe, he unfurled a red, white and blue tricolour above the French Legation, as Bernadotte had once done in Vienna. In royal Stockholm, however, the gesture was unacceptable; and Charles John made certain the young man received a kingly reproof. The offending flag was lowered. No one rioted in the streets.

In such proceedings there was a cumbersome pomposity which deserved to be deflated. But how? The Swedish press, subject since 1812 to laws protecting the institutions of the monarchy from attack, began to resent the continuance of regulations originally introduced as a wartime expedient. Within a few months of the flag episode a radical member of the lesser nobility, Lars Johann Hierta, found ways of pouring good humoured scorn on the absurdities of government and, in particular, the Gascon rhetoric of His Majesty's speeches from the throne. In December 1830 Hierta brought out the first number of an evening paper, the *Aftonbladet*, which by allusion and thinly disguised parallels pricked the inflated pretensions of the King and his narrowing circle of French-speaking advisers. *Aftonbladet* had such good sales that the King and Council were worried. They found grounds on which, under the Press regulations, the paper could be closed down. But they could not prevent Hierta from publishing a new evening paper with a slight variation of title and a different nominal editor. When that too was banned Hierta repeated the procedure. New titles followed each other every few months, waging endless campaigns for civil liberty, free trade, cabinet government and modernisation of the Riksdag. By 1840 Hierta had the largest newspaper circulation in Sweden and was publishing what he called 'The 21st Evening Paper' (*Det tjugonde-forsta Aftonbladet*). The satire that amused Stockholm in the evening would be spread among the smaller towns next morning, for half the sales of the *Aftonbladet* were outside the capital.

Since Charles John could not read Hierta's articles himself, he had to employ press secretaries to translate and summarise them for him, and – a difficult task – to convey the right sense of allusive sarcasm. He found lampoons on 'The Reign of King Long Nose' singularly unfunny. Ever since 1796, when the *Gazette Générale de l'Europe* misrepresented his conduct in Nuremberg, he had deplored the ease with which press liberties became personally licentious. At times the sustained satire of Hierta's attacks made him choleric with anger. His health deteriorated, with pains in the duodenum as well as the coughing of blood. Within five months of the first appearance of Hierta's *Aftonbladet* the King became so ill that for most of the year he had to entrust Oscar with the business of government.

For Charles John there followed almost a decade of chronic political tension, interspersed with recurrent bouts of ill health. The Swedish press, in Gothenburg as well as Stockholm, became more and more outspoken. The King particularly resented criticism of his approach to foreign affairs, arguing that he understood the balance of power in Europe better than did his subjects, who did not readily recognise his skill in maintaining good relations with Russia while not antagonising Britain. The newspaper attacks encouraged Charles John's inclination to isolate himself socially; he gradually lost contact with the Swedish bourgeoisie who had welcomed his arrival during the war years. By 1834 he rarely emerged from his palaces, except to take part in formal ceremonies and inspect the army. Yet when, in the last days of July 1835, fire swept through inner Stockholm he hurried in from Rosendal at half-past three in the morning to take command of the fire-fighters and troops with all his old energy.

Occasionally foreign envoys would comment, somewhat mischievously, on a royal outburst of frustrated envy when, for example, Oscar's knowledge of Swedish enabled him to score a personal success with politicians whom the King could not hope to charm. 'The King is so jealous upon his power and popularity that he cannot bear public demonstrations of affection even towards the Crown Prince', the British Minister in Stockholm informed Palmerston in April 1833. But outsiders did not appreciate that throughout this bleak decade Charles John drew satisfaction and strength from enjoying a close-knit family life; it was a new experience for him. Soon, however, husband and wife acknowledged that it was easier to relax in Norway than at Drottningholm or Rosendal, which were too close to Stockholm. The royal family was treated with greater respect in Christiania and Trondheim; and, though members of the Storting were frequently in conflict with the King, they found him sympathetic to their problems, especially when they complained of Swedish exploitation. He was prepared to include Norwegians among his close advisers and allow ships to fly the white-bordered blue cross on a red background rather than Sweden's yellow cross on a blue background. Everywhere, in this post-Napoleonic era, national feeling wished the right flags to fly where they might most proudly be observed. That sentiment Charles John well understood by now.

In earlier years Charles John had himself employed the Press to boost his cause and in 1833 he tried again, feeding information to Wallmark, the editor who had been his tutor in Swedish more than twenty years before. But the columns of Wallmark's *Journalen* lacked the verve of Hierta's paper and the royal propaganda, some of it dictated by Charles John himself, proved ineffective. A second journalistic initiative, support for Anders Lindeberg who edited and owned the *Stockholm Posten*, badly misfired. For Lindeberg, disappointed not to receive permission to open a playhouse, went over to the Opposition and accused the King of managing a theatre monopoly for his own financial gains. Lindeberg was arrested, charged with inciting contempt for the crown, and sentenced to death. Charles John wished to frighten other journalists, but he had no intention that Lindeberg should die, as the judges well knew. When, however, the King commuted the sentence to three years' imprisonment, Lindeberg exercised his constitutional right and refused to accept a reprieve, at once becoming a hero martyr-to-be for the liberal Press. Throughout the summer of 1834 Charles John was assailed as an enemy of free speech, as tyrannical in his treatment of Lindeberg as Napoleon in 1806, when the Emperor ordered the execution of Johann Palm in Bavaria for 'spreading defamatory writings'. But Charles John showed his old subtlety in extricating himself from this embarrassment. To mark the twenty-fourth anniversary of his arrival in Sweden the King issued an amnesty for those held in detention for the crime of lese-majesty. Only Lindeberg fell into that category.

By now the King was ageing: 'I fear the King is declining certainly and rapidly', the American minister reported home in April 1835. He remained an impressive figure, taking the salute from the saddle at a summer review, but he was wretchedly querulous at the council table during the long, dark hours of a Scandinavian winter. Death had begun to rob him of many close associates from his earliest years in Sweden. The grim winter of 1837–38, when ice closed the harbour of Stockholm and the sea froze in the southern fjords, claimed in quick succession the lives of Marshal Stedingk, Chancellor Wetterstedt and that sorely tried ambassador in Paris, Gustav Lagerbielke. Charles John, however, survived. The coming of spring in 1838 found him, at seventy-five, tiring easily but still painstakingly seeking to keep himself informed of problems which troubled his subjects, insisting that, after so terrible a winter, his ministers should attend to poor relief and the needs of the hospitals. He continued, too, to study despatches from his envoys in other capitals. While keeping Sweden's defences on what was virtually a war footing, he was always anxious to assert his kingdoms' neutrality. The chronic feud between Russia and Britain especially troubled him; and, in the spring of 1838, he welcomed the news that Grand Duke Alexander, the eldest son of Tsar Nicholas I, would come to Stockholm that summer and discuss Russo–Swedish relations.

The Grand Duke's warship sailed up the Saltsjo on Sunday, 10 June. While Oscar went to the quay to welcome Sweden's guest, Charles John remained in his rooms. The King was reclining casually on a sofa when suddenly the chamberlain informed him that Tsar Nicholas himself had arrived unheralded at the palace, having travelled incognito with his son and slipped ashore unobserved. The Tsar's three-day visit caused consternation to his host and hostess and suspicion among their critics. For while Charles John and Désirée improvised entertainments fit for the Tsar of All the Russias in a city which still resented the loss of Finland, the politicians assumed that Nicholas had made the journey from St Petersburg in order to enlist Charles John's support for an imperial and royal crusade against liberal constitutionalism. Nicholas was present at a military review and a ball at Drottningholm, both originally planned in honour of the Grand Duke. The two rulers held private talks in which Charles John confirmed his intention of staying out of any war in Europe unless an attack was launched on his own realm. But rumour continued to link the Tsar's visit with Sweden's internal affairs. Hardly had Nicholas left the country than there were demonstrations in Stockholm over the arrest of Magnus Crusenstolpe, a pamphleteer who complained of favouritism and political discrimination by the King in the promotion of junior officers. Accusations of this character particularly angered Charles John, for he always weighed carefully every problem concerned with the army and its establishment.

While the Crusenstolpe affair was still exciting Stockholm's young radicals, the King suffered his worst accident since coming to Sweden. On 6 July he was returning from Rosendal when the young horse he was riding bolted. Fearing that some onlookers would be trampled down, Charles John succeeded in forcing his mount against a barrier – but only at the cost of a heavy fall, which fractured his collar-bone. He was still in pain when, in the small hours of 20 July, he was awoken with news of such serious riots on behalf of Crusenstolpe that, for the first time in his reign, the soldiery had been forced to open fire, killing two demonstrators. That night Désirée, disturbed by the commotion in the palace, found her husband, arm in sling, pacing down the long gallery threatening that these two deaths were only a beginning: 'I shall decimate all of them! Torrents of blood shall flow!' he shouted. 'Take no notice of him', the Queen countered, 'he wouldn't hurt a chicken; he wouldn't drown a kitten!' She knew when her husband was acting the role of a tyrant. The crisis passed without further bloodshed. But it left Charles John more cautious than usual; for when, in the early autumn, his plan to remove Jewish disabilities provoked anti-Semitic demonstrations, the King agreed on a compromise which fell short of full emancipation rather than risk more deaths on the street. At his accession he had chosen as a motto, 'The people's love shall be my reward'. It was becoming hard to live up to so noble an ideal.

The burden of 1838 – the winter hardships, the sudden visit from the Tsar, the Crusenstolpe affair and the anti-Semitic demonstrations – made recovery from his riding accident slow. In the first week of December his doctors and family induced Charles John to travel to Norway and formally allow Oscar the powers of regency which he had himself so often exercised in Charles XIII's reign. Many people assumed that Charles John would never again preside over the day-to-day business of royal government. Perhaps it would have been wiser for him to have left Oscar as Regent. Pride and obstinacy forbade it. He wished to make certain his subjects acknowledged his achievements as a ruler. At midsummer in 1839, after six months of rest, Charles John took back the reins of government from his son.

Long before Christmas it was clear that January's meeting of the Riksdag would be stormy. In the past the deputies had concentrated their attacks on individual grievances. Now they sought the King's abdication. The dynasty itself was not in danger, only the rule of His Majesty and his French-speaking inner councillors. Unusual attention was given to the King's opening speech: even *The Times* of London reported it in full. Charles John was present but, as usual, his fine-sounding French phrases were read to the deputies by Oscar in a Swedish translation.

The King contrasted the prosperous kingdom of 1840 – urban population growing rapidly, commerce and industry and agriculture all flourishing – with the sad, impoverished Sweden to which he was summoned thirty years before. He spoke of the great canals linking Baltic and ocean, of codes of civil and penal law which could soon be approved by the Riksdag, of the friendship which had replaced old enmities between the Swedish and Norwegian peoples, and, above all, of the long period of peace in northern Europe. Soon, he assured the deputies in his peroration, 'I must be summoned to another life. There I shall implore the blessed mercy of the Creator on the two people who, when left to themselves, are adorned by so many virtues, and who have given me so many touching proofs of their affection and their gratitude.'

As an appeal to sentiment the address from the throne was magnificent. But perhaps his eloquence lost some of its appeal in translation. For the speech did not win Charles John the speedy vote of confidence on which he had counted. As amendments to the address, remonstrances at the activity of favourites around the throne, lists of proposed reforms and threats of impeachment followed, week after week, the Riksdag seemed in danger of becoming Sweden's long parliament. The deputies – still divided into the archaic system of four estates – remained in session for eighteen months. Friction between the estates and the need to get a two-thirds majority for any major constitutional amendment prevented the hostility of the more radical deputies from enforcing any drastic change in the sovereignty of the nation. But Charles John would not abdicate, even when all four estates attacked his use of secret service funds. To hand over the crown to Oscar would be to admit defeat. He preferred a rearguard action, sustained longer than any in his campaigning days. At the end of the year, as his battle with the Riksdag was at its height, French newspapers reached him with accounts of the return of Napoleon's body from St Helena. As he read of Soult, who was given his baton on the same day as Bernadotte, ceremonially receiving the Emperor's coffin and of General Gourgaud placing the sword of Austerlitz on the bier, he exclaimed bitterly, 'You could say of me that once I was a Marshal of France, and now I am only King of Sweden.'

The long Riksdag dispersed at last in June 1841. As so often in

Charles John's reign all the storm and stress ended in compromise. One, and only one, member of the Council of State was induced to resign due to old age (although he was younger than his sovereign) and, in a step towards the British concept of cabinet government, Charles John recognised that councillors of state should have ministerial responsibilities rather than be advisers chosen by the King. The promise of further reforms silenced the critics who, realising that Charles John's health was failing, were ready to await Oscar's accession before renewing an assault on the royal prerogative. They were prepared for the reign to end in sunset glow.

In February 1843 there was one last round of festivities, the silver jubilee of Charles John's accession. There followed an unusually hot summer. In late June the King felt so fit that, for the first time since his serious accident five years before, he took the salute mounted on horseback, remaining in the saddle for more than three hours. In August the temperature climbed above 30°C (86°F) in the shade, so Désirée told Julie. She insisted on escaping to the countryside. Her husband, delighted by the magnificent summer, was content to remain at Rosendal, reminiscing more and more about those early days, when he was a sergeant serving King Louis XVI under a Mediterranean sun. But within four months, husband and wife were back to the realities of a Baltic winter.

On 26 January 1844 all Sweden and Norway celebrated their king's eighty-first birthday. Yet Charles John himself knew nothing of the festivities. A valet had found him unconscious at six in the morning, felled by a stroke as he sought to get out of bed. Later that day he regained consciousness but never complete clarity of thought. By 1 February Oscar was once more Regent. His father lingered on throughout the month, his pulse rate varying for three weeks until it seemed so much better that Désirée wrote optimistically to her sister. Her confidence was misplaced. Early on 8 March the King had a relapse: 'Oscar, Oscar, we must defend ourselves', someone heard him say. In the middle of the afternoon, he died.

Seven weeks went by before the state funeral. For King Oscar wished for a dignified ceremony, emphasising dynastic continuity. At last, on 26 April 1844, the remains of Jean Baptiste Bernadotte, once a citizen of Pau in Béarn, were laid within Stockholm's Riddarholms Kyrka, beside the tombs of Gustavus Adolphus, Charles XII, Gustav III and Charles XIII. On a red porphyry sarcophagus was inscribed 'Carl XIV Johan', which said nothing and everything.

Chapter 15
Legends and Legacy

THE king's funeral obsequies honoured a ruler of Sweden and Norway, a warrior who treasured peace deeply. South of the Baltic, however, news of Charles John's death evoked a different response. In France, Britain and the German lands he remained the Marshal who had fought beside the Emperor at Austerlitz and Wagram and against him at Leipzig. For Charles John outlived the post-Waterloo revulsion against the French Empire and its achievements, the mood in which writers like Southey called for vengeance on Napoleon's 'accursed head'. By 1844 the generation of Frenchmen conceived between battles could find in the faint memory of past glories a greater inspiration than the material successes the dull Orléanist dynasty could offer. Already, during his lifetime, Bernadotte's name was inscribed among the heroes of the Empire on the vaulting of the Arc de Triomphe and his portrait hung in the Gallery of Marshals at Versailles. But around his reputation there lingered a shadow of doubt. Did pride and ambition make him disloyal to the Emperor? As a Frenchman by birth and a Swedish prince by adoption was he justified in joining the enemies of his homeland in the last grand coalition?

Charles John cared about such matters. 'Don't talk of 1813! My heart aches when I think of it. Had I a thousand kingdoms to give to France, I could not pay the debt of gratitude I owe her', he remarked to a French visitor towards the end of his reign. At first he hoped to stifle his critics. When, in 1822–23, O'Meara and Las Cases put on sale their respective memoirs from St Helena the King tried to hamper their circulation in Sweden. Both men quoted bitter reproaches. O'Meara reported Napoleon as saying that Bernadotte, although not treacherous, behaved 'ungratefully to me, since I was the author of his greatness'. Las Cases was more forthright:

'Bernadotte was the snake we nurtured in our bosom', Napoleon once remarked to him. 'It was he who gave the enemy the key to our policies and the tactics of our armies.' Small wonder if a few years later Charles John bought up a whole stock of imported memoirs rather than risk the spread of tales to discredit him.

Suppression was a panic expedient. As a good publicist, the King knew the value of positive propaganda, of creating a Bernadotte Legend to counter the distorted myths from the South Atlantic. Briefly he hoped to win support from the author whom Goethe praised as 'the easiest, the most celebrated narrator of the century'. In 1826 reports that Sir Walter Scott was writing a multi-volume biography of Napoleon caused excited speculation in literary salons on both sides of the Channel and even among the expatriates of Stockholm. Charles John became so eager for Scott to accept his version of the more contentious moments in a recent past that he encouraged the despatch to Britain of material copied from the archives. To Scott's astonishment 'a great cargo of papers' reached Abbotsford from Sweden in April 1827. But, like their donor on so many occasions, they arrived too late: the relevant sections of the biography had been finished two months before and Scott could make no use of them. His printed journal makes it clear that he felt a certain relief in being able to ignore them; a few years earlier, he had encountered Gustav Vasa in Edinburgh and was touched by the resignation with which that pathetically inadequate exile met the buffetings of fate. Personal sentiment left Scott, and other Tory romantics, hostile to 'the child of Revolution' who still reigned in Scandinavia.

Charles John was no more successful in finding a fluent pen in his native France. Mme de Staël, his old admirer, had died before he came to the throne, and a Bernadotte Legend held little appeal for other French writers during his lifetime. Fifteen months after Louis Philippe's accession the Orléanist politician and historian Adolphe Thiers spoke generously about Bernadotte in the Chamber of Deputies; but the first volume of Thiers's massive chronicle of the Consulate and Empire did not appear until a year after Charles John's death. Meanwhile, to his intense annoyance, he was ridiculed on the Parisian stage: the comedy, *Le Camarade de Lit*, opened at the theatre beside the Palais Royal in May 1833 and was presented four weeks later at a special fête in the Champs Elysées, given under Louis Philippe's patronage. Six months later a second play, *Le Prix de Folie*, covered Bernadotte's brief term as Minister of War; it gave the impression that he was a vain and empty-headed muddler whose errors were so grave that Napoleon hurried back from Egypt to save France from the Minister's follies. Libels of this type strained relations between Sweden and France. The Bernadotte whom Parisians mocked in their theatres was far removed from the image of an intrepid and chivalrous soldier which he wished preserved and presented to an admiring posterity.

Nearer to that ideal came a character of popular fiction, created by Alexandre Dumas a few months after Charles John's death. D'Artagnan, like the young General from the Sambre-et-Meuse, was a shrewd and hot-headed Gascon, boastful and brave. His adventures, set in the days of Cardinal Richelieu and Anne of Austria, were taken by Alexandre Dumas from the fabricated memoirs of a soldier of fortune, but there may well have been in the author's mind some links with a more recent campaign. For in 1797 the novelist's father, General Thomas-Alexandre Davy de la Palletière Dumas, had fought beside Bernadotte's newcomers from the Rhine Front at the crossings of the Tagliamento and the Isonzo. General Dumas knew General Bernadotte at the time when his Béarnais theatricality made him the most talked about divisional commander to have joined the battle-hardened veterans of the Army of Italy. It is not improbable that General Dumas's tales of Gascon pride and foolhardiness left an impression on the young Alexandre which newspaper reports of Charles John's death brought back to mind more than a generation later.

But if Dumas grafted some traits of Bernadotte's character on to his fictional d'Artagnan, neither he nor any contemporary did justice to the extraordinary range of the Marshal's military gifts. His personal courage, generosity to the enemy, concern for the welfare of his troops and inspiring leadership are apparent in his surviving letters and in every memoir of the campaigns. Added to these talents were a shrewd economy in manpower, concern for the minutiae of planning, and a sense of grand strategy as broad-ranging as Napoleon's but less inclined to lose itself in a distant perspective of remote horizons. Against these qualities must be set three defects which deny Bernadotte a place among the greatest commanders: hesitancy in executing plans of which he had himself approved; a reluctance to fulfil unquestioningly the strategies of his superiors; and an excessive partiality for empty rhetoric which, by extrava-

gantly praising troops under his direct command, aroused resentment in other regiments which had borne a heavy strain of battle.
At times he was accused of tight-fisted parsimony, of ingratitude
towards those who had helped him by undertaking particular
missions, and of fantasising over the past while boasting emptily of
the future. Yet while he expected public compensation for the loss
of private funds in the Empire, he gave generously to Uppsala
University and himself paid for the diamonds which enriched the
Norwegian crown at his Trondheim coronation; and, if he was
ruthless towards the disgraced General Sarrazin, he loyally tried to
save the Marquis d'Ambert. However bellicose his small talk might
be, once he came to the throne he never doubted that war was a
scourge which would threaten his dual kingdom with disaster.
Occasionally he envied his son's linguistic skills and easy manner
with his future subjects, but Court life was never strained by long
family quarrels or rivalry between factions backing the sovereign
and his successor. Towards his wife Bernadotte showed loyalty,
affection and a generous tolerance.

Désirée, for her part, became the most convincing of his apolo-
gists. She survived him by sixteen years, living on in Sweden, never
returning to the house and garden in Paris she had so loved. When
she was approaching her eightieth year she summoned up the
courage to embark for France, only to turn back again at the first
pitching and tossing as the ship reached the open sea. Yet, so long
as she could remain firmly on land, she retained into old age traces
of that exuberant vitality which was a distinguishing characteristic
of the Clary sisters in their girlhood. Often in her husband's lifetime
Désirée would puncture his Gasconades with down-to-earth realism,
but as a widow she became devoted to his memory, eagerly setting
right fabrications built upon mere rumour. She encouraged
Touchard Lafosse to complete a biography of Bernadotte and
before she died had the satisfaction of reading his sound factual
narrative. Others might question his judgments on Bernadotte's
character; Désirée welcomed his presentation of her husband as a
romantic hero who cherished traditions of chivalry through an age
of revolution and impossible loyalties.

To her chamberlain, Baron Hochschild, Désirée told what she
thought worth knowing about her personal life and he incorporated
her reminiscences in a small book. But the most interesting word
portrait of her in old age comes from the memoirs of General

François Canrobert, who came to Stockholm after commanding Napoleon III's troops in the Crimea for eight months in the hope of encouraging Sweden to join Britain and France in military and naval operations against St Petersburg. Canrobert found Désirée at 78 still fascinated by a French general newly back from the wars. Her small talk, in these short days of 1855, was partly about Paris and its couturiers, but she also enjoyed losing herself in memories of the past. A portrait on her table of a general in the uniform of the Republic did not, as he first supposed, show a slim and young Bernadotte, but General Kléber: 'We liked him very much', Désirée explained. 'He it was who pushed Bernadotte and had him promoted to General.' Canrobert could see that there were older loyalties, too, in Désirée's heart. Before the General left her room, she took from a drawer a small packet of love letters: they had come, she explained, not from Bernadotte but from Napoleon in her girlhood. Désirée's life spanned the Deep of Time. Less than two years after Canrobert caught these echoes from her past, she was holding in her arms the future ruler of neutral Sweden in World War I and World War II. King Gustav V Adolf did not die until October 1950; and it was therefore Désirée's last grandson who sent royal congratulations from Stockholm to London on the birth of the present Prince of Wales.

King Charles John's most enduring achievement was the founding of a modern dynasty. No ruler in Europe can claim the Emperor Napoleon I or any of his brothers as an ancestor. But descendants of Bernadotte – and therefore, through his daughter-in-law, of the Empress Josephine, too – reign today in Sweden, Norway, Denmark and Belgium and are heirs-apparent to the Grand-Duchy of Luxembourg and the crown of Greece. Yet Sweden has remained a monarchy through six generations only because Charles John's successors were prepared gradually to shed the royal prerogative as the old oligarchic kingdom met the challenge of democracy. Oscar I, whose chief interests were in foreign affairs, proposed parliamentary reforms soon after his accession, but became increasingly illiberal in his later years, especially towards the Press. It was his eldest son Charles XV (reigned 1859–1872) who allowed major reforms to be carried through in 1865–66 and permitted government initiative to pass from the sovereign to his council, thereby facilitating the growth of cabinet government. But it was not until 1975 that the seventh of the Bernadotte kings, Charles XVI Gustav, became in effect a figure-head president for life, 'the symbolic representative of the whole realm'.

The union of Norway with Sweden, which Charles John counted as his greatest contribution to the well-being of Scandinavia, continued for more than sixty years after the King's death. In reality the two peoples had few common interests and, although geographical neighbours, were kept apart by the mountain range running north to south between them. It is to the credit of Oscar II (reigned 1872–1907) that, however much he was saddened by the destruction of his grandfather's work, the secession of Norway in 1905 was accomplished without bloodshed. Moreover the first Norwegian King – a Danish Prince who took the title of Haakon VII – was himself, on his mother's side, a great-great grandson of Charles John. At Haakon's coronation in Trondheim in July 1906, he used the regalia which had been redesigned for Charles John eighty years before and carried his ancestor's Leipzig sword. The royal families of Scandinavia, closely linked by marriage bonds, remained on good terms. Gustav V Adolf (reigned 1907–1950) was a natural reconciler whose wedding at Karlsruhe in 1881 brought together Sweden's two royal Houses, Vasa and Bernadotte; the bride, Princess Victoria of Baden, was a great-great-granddaughter of Gustav IV.

Charles John's conviction that Sweden had much to lose and little to gain by participating in the major quarrels of Europe encouraged the pursuit of neutrality and peace. Gustav V Adolf trod warily in both World Wars, sympathetic to the Kaiser's Germany but loathing the evils of the Third Reich. Over 8000 Danish Jews found sanctuary in his kingdom and he appealed directly to the Hungarian authorities in the summer of 1944 to stop the deportation of Jews to Hitler's concentration camps. Briefly in the 1940s the name Bernadotte appeared in newspaper headlines in Europe and America. Count Folke Bernadotte, who as the second son of Oscar II's second son was the King's cousin, had won widespread respect for the humanitarian relief work which he undertook for the Red Cross in the First World War and its aftermath. In October 1943 and again eleven months later Count Bernadotte arranged an exchange of sick and disabled prisoners of war at Gothenburg and he acted as an intermediary for abortive peace talks between Nazi leaders and the western allies in February 1945. He presided over the Swedish Red Cross and the Swedish Boy Scout movement. His work for refugees and for survivors from the concentration camps made it seem natural for him to serve as a peacemaker for the United Nations. In May 1948 he agreed to travel to Jerusalem as a pioneer United Nations Mediator in Palestine. He sought a truce between Jews and Arabs in the first month of Israel's existence as an independent state. But in September 1948, only seventeen weeks after the start of his peace mission, he was assassinated by a hit squad of Zionist extremists. This rebuff to a creed of human brotherhood aroused deep resentment throughout Scandinavia, where the memory of Folke Bernadotte is cherished today while so much accomplished by the founder of the dynasty seems as remote as the earliest wars for mastery of the Baltic.

Much stone and mortar in Charles John's life has vanished from the landscape. Of Bernadotte's homes in Paris there is no trace: Désirée's town house in the Rue d'Anjou disappeared beneath the Boulevard Malesherbes soon after her death; civil marriages may still be celebrated at a Préfecture of Sceaux, but the neighbouring hilltop, where after their marriage Désirée shared her husband's bachelor villa, is crowned by an estate of middle-class luxury flats, the names of Bernadotte and his bride commemorated by private roads between the apartment blocks; and, though their house in the Rue de Monceau (sometime Rue Cisalpine) survived the Second World War, the headquarters of an electricity board cover the site today. In Stockholm there are still royal palaces associated with his reign and Oscar I dutifully erected a statue to his father south of the old town. Charles John is better remembered in a city where he might well have been forgotten. More than eighty years after Norway's separation from Sweden a magnificent equestrian statue, inscribed 'The people's love is my reward,' stands in front of the royal palace of Oslo, looking out across parkland and down the street that is named in the King's honour to a parliament house built twenty years after his death.

But Bernadotte comes more readily to life in Béarn, far away from the prancing statuary of his two kingdoms. At Pau the house in which he was born has become a small museum, enriched since 1975 by valuable archives and many photocopies of documents from Stockholm. Outside the museum fly the flags of both France and Sweden; a Société des Amis du Musée publishes an occasional Bulletin and fosters links with the kingdom of the North. Across the town and beyond the casino a plaque beside a fine copse of trees records that they were planted in 1899 by Oscar II when he visited his grandfather's birthplace. A narrowing world has brought Béarn and Stockholm closer together. In June 1963 it was possible for Gustav VI Adolf and Queen Louise to fly down to Pau for a dinner and concert to honour the King's great-great-grandfather in his bicentenary year.

The people of Pau do not seem to take any special pride in the royal attorney's son who became a Marshal of the Empire and a twice crowned King. There is no statue of him in the town and, though he is commemorated by a street-name, so are two later Palois Marshals, Pierre Bosquet and Charles Bourbaki (who both fought at Inkerman) and Marshal Foch, from neighbouring Tarbes. The great hero of Pau still remains the King born in the castle, Henri IV, first sovereign of the House of Bourbon; and in the summer of 1989, while all France kept the bicentenary of the Revolution, the people of Pau celebrated the quatercentenary of Henry of Navarre's coronation. Yet to those who are intrigued by the crossed lines of royal genealogy, it is a pleasing thought that one contemporary sovereign unites in his person the two dynasties from Pau: for King Baudouin I of the Belgians can trace descent on his father's side from Henri IV and on his mother's from Jean Baptiste Bernadotte.

Notes and Sources

Unless otherwise stated works in English are published in London, French in Paris and Swedish in Stockholm. B. throughout Notes and Sources is for Bernadotte; Nap. for Napoleon.

Abbreviations of titles:

AHRF: *Annales historiques de la Révolution française.*
Barton 1: Sir D. Plunket Barton: *Bernadotte, The First Phase 1763–1799* (1914).
Barton 2: same, *Bernadotte and Napoleon 1799–1810* (1921).
Barton 3: same, *Bernadotte, Prince and King, 1810–1844* (1925).
BL: British Library, London, formerly the British Museum Library.
BMB: *Bulletin du Musée Bernadotte*, published from 1956 onwards by La Société des Amis du Musée Bernadotte, Pau.
Chandler: David Chandler, *The Campaigns of Napoleon* (1966).
Corr. Nap.: *Correspondance de Napoléon I* (1857–1870).
FO: Foreign Office papers in the Public Record Office, Kew.
Girod B: Gabriel Girod de l'Ain, *Bernadotte, Chef de Guerre et Chef d'Etat* (1968).
Girod D: same author, *Désirée Clary* (1959).
Höjer 1: T. Tson Höjer, *Carl XIV Johan, Den Franska Tiden* (1939).
Höjer 2: same author, *Carl XIV Johan, Kronprinstiden* (1943).
Höjer 3: same author, *Carl XIV Johan, Konungstiden* (1960).
HT: *Historisk Tidskrift*, published by Svensk Historisk Forening.
Monr: *Le Moniteur* (more fully, *La Gazette nationale ou Le Moniteur universel*); first published November 1789.

An abridged edition of Barton's three-volume study appeared as *The Amazing Career of Bernadotte* (1930). Höjer's three volumes have been translated from Swedish into French: Höjer 1 in 1943, the whole in two volumes in 1971, but it is rare in British libraries.

Notes and Sources

Chapter 1: Royal Marine

B.'s early life and background: Barton 1, pp. 3–50; Höjer 1, pp. 5–22; Girod B, pp. 22–50. For additional material on the family see articles by Françoise Debaissieux, BMB no. 5 (Nov. 1960) and no. 6 (Dec. 1961): Mlle Debaissieux also wrote about his birthplace, BMB, nos 7–8 (Dec. 1963). On pre-revolutionary Pau, A. Young, *Travels in France*, ed. C. Maxwell (Cambridge, 1950) pp. 53–4. On Béarn see the paper by Christian Desplat, *Béarn, A Geographical and Historical Unit*, circulated in English by the Société des Amis du Musée Bernadotte, Pau (1988). For the Régiment Royal-la-Marine: S. F. Scott, *The Response of the Royal Army to the French Revolution* (Oxford, 1978), especially chapters 1 and 4; and also the article on the regiment by Yves Barjaud, BMB, nos 23–4 for 1978–79. On Marshal Gassion see Uno Lindgren, 'La Compagnie de Jean de Gassion au service du Roi Gustav II Adolphus de Suède', BMB no. 20 (Dec. 1975). For B.'s companion Jean Gré, the article by Françoise Debaissieux, BMB no. 6 (Dec. 1961). For Corsica at this time see X. Villat, *Le Corse de 1786 à 1789* (1925). Some of B.'s early letters home are in Barton 1, pp. 22–3, 47–8. On B.'s masonic initiation Harald Qvistgaard, BMB No. 22 (Dec. 1977), with facsimiles of his signature reproduced on p. 44.

On Grenoble's 'Day of Tiles', G. Lefebvre, *The French Revolution* (London and New York, 1962), p. 101. Arthur Young in Marseilles, his *Travels in France*, p. 229. For the Clarys at Marseilles, Girod D pp. 21–5 and the same author's article, 'Le Souvenir de Désirée Clary à Marseille', BMB no. 1 (June 1956). Désirée's account of the billeting incident is in Baron Hochschild, *Désirée, Reine de Suède et de Norvège* (1888) p. 2. For the revolution in Marseilles, S. Vialla, *Marseille révolutionnaire, L'armée-nation* (1910); and especially on the Marquis d'Ambert affair, Monr for 28–9 March 1790, and Scott's *Response of the Royal Army* pp. 35–6 and 139–41. See also René Cuzacq, 'Bernadotte et l'émeute de Marseille', BMB no. 20 (Dec. 1975) and Olivier Baulny, 'Documents', BMB nos. 23–4 (1978–9). For Lambesc, Monr 12–14 June and 11 July 1790.

Chapter 2: The Revolution at War

The route of the 36th Infantry Regiment's march to the frontier in Barton 1, p. 51 needs correction from the material summarised in Höjer 1, pp. 18 and 454; but for B.'s letters, see Barton 1, pp. 55, 57. On Eugène de Beauharnais at Strasbourg, Carola Oman, *Napoleon's Viceroy* (1966), p. 35. The classical military account of operations remains A. Chuquet, *Les Guerres de la Révolution*, I–II (1886), but cf. J-P. Bertraud, *Valmy, la démocratie en armes* (1970) and see A. Soboul, *L'armée nationale sous la Révolution 1789–1794* (1945) and its successor, *Les Soldats de l'An II* (1959). The Rulzheim letter is in Barton 1, pp. 59–60 and Höjer 1, p. 30; further letters, Girod B pp. 52–5. For the effect of the Amalgam on the army, Scott, *Response of the Royal Army*, pp. 179–82. For B.'s activities on the northern frontier see Barton 1, pp. 85–7, G. Sarrazin, *The Philosopher* (London, 1812), I, p. 11. On Carnot see M. Reinhardt, *Le Grand Carnot* – vol. 1, *De l'ingénieur au conventionnel 1753–92* (1950) and vol. 2, *L'organisateur de la victoire, 1793–1823* (1952). For Saint-Just's activities on the northern frontier and at Fleurus see E. N. Curtis, *Saint-Just* (New York, 1935), pp. 247–73 and, in general, the later study by J-P. Gross, *Saint-Just, sa politique, ses missions* (1976). G. Lefebvre has a constructive review of Curtis's book reprinted in his *Etudes sur la Révolution Française* (1963), pp. 138–43. V. Dupuis, *Les Opérations militaires sur la Sambre en 1794* (1907) is almost entirely concerned with Fleurus, but reveals much about the nature of the campaign.

On B., Jourdan and Kléber see A. Chuquet, *Quatre Généreaux de la Révolution*, III (1914), also R. Valentin, *Le Maréchal Jourdan* (1956). Kléber's letter to Jourdan of 1794 praising B. and Ney is quoted (in French) from the archives in Höjer 1, p. 456; for B's balloon reconnaissance, Höjer 1, pp. 48–9 and 457. The fullest biography of Marceau remains N. Parfait, *Le Général Marceau* (1892), but for his close relationship with B. see also Barton 1, pp. 78–81, 120–7 and Höjer 1, p. 457. For B. at Kreuznach, Barton 1, p. 117. Kléber's letter of Easter 1796 about the canoness of Cologne is in Höjer 1, p. 458; and on the Pottgeiser family see Girod B pp. 71–2 and G. Sarrazin, *Philosopher,* Vol. II, pp. 15–16. Battle of Deining: Höjer 1, p. 77 and Barton 1, p. 149–51, with B.'s letter to his brother after his lance wound; ibidem for the Würzburg affair (pp. 159–60) and death of Marceau (p. 166–7).

For the *Gazette Générale*'s attack on B. and his response, Sarrazin, *Philosopher* II, pp. 88–92 and Monr 10 November 1796. Nap.'s Italian campaign and requests for reinforcements, Chandler, pp. 103–15 and Corr. Nap. II nos 1182 and 1235. For the introductory letter from Directory to Nap. about B. Girod B p. 73, cf. Corr. Nap II no. 1402.

Chapter 3: Beyond the Alps and in Paris

B.'s letter to Kléber from Metz, 19 January 1797, BL Add. Mss. 26053; his previous day's letter to Nap., with itinerary, Girod B pp. 74–6. B.'s crossing of the Alps is covered briefly by Höjer 1, pp. 93–5 and more fully by Barton 1, pp. 183–6; see also Sarrazin, *Philosopher* II, pp. 95–7, L. J. Lahure, *Souvenirs de la Vie Militaire*, 1787–1815 (1895) and C. F. François, *Journal du Capitaine François* (1903), I, pp. 149–50; Nap.'s reply received by B. at Chambéry, Corr. Nap. II, no. 1469. The report on the 'fine young men' by the royalist agent, Abbé de Pons, is fully printed in Girod B p. 79.

B.'s arrival in Italy: Corr. Nap. II, no. 1503; Barton 1, pp. 186–9; Sarrazin, *Philosopher* II, pp. 97–8 (including B.'s dispute with Dupuy and Berthier), Lavallete, *Memoirs* (London ed., 1831), p. 115. For Nap.'s warning on his 'different' method of warfare, Corr. Nap. II., no. 1402; B. reviews troops on reaching Italy, *Journal* of C. F. François I, p. 153. For critical analysis of reports of first meeting between B. and Nap. see Höjer 1, pp. 96–7. Nap. on B.'s 'fine troops', Barton 1, p. 196, citing Montholon.

For the campaign from the Tagliamento to Leoben, see Chandler, pp. 121–4; Lahure, *Souvenirs* I, pp. 118–19; C. F. François, *Journal*, I, pp. 152–8; Corr. Nap. II, nos. 1600–3. Report from the priest at Postojna, R. Chélard, *Les Armées françaises jugés par les habitants de l'Autriche* (1893) I, pp. 13–14. For B.'s monetary rewards from the campaign, see Girod B 85–6; Sarrazin, *Philosopher* II, pp. 105–6. For the rioting at Laibach (Ljubljana), J. Godechot's article, *Les Insurrections Militaires*, AHRF Vol. 5 (1933), pp. 211–12. Nap.'s refusal of leave for B., Corr. Nap. II nos. 1808 and 1818; fuller letters in Girod B pp. 87–8. On B. and d'Antraigues, Corr. Nap. III, nos. 1861 and 1885 and Barton 1, Chapter 39, need supplementing by: A. Ollivier, *Le Dix-huit Brumaire* (1959), pp. 42–62 and 76–91; R. de Grandsaignes's article, 'L'Affaire du portefeuille d'Antraigues', AHRF, Vol. 34 (1962) and H. Mitchell, *The Underground War against Revolutionary France, the Missions of William Wickham* (Oxford, 1965), Chapter 5. On B. in Milan at 14 July Review, François, *Journal*, I pp. 162–3. For Desaix on B., see L.C.A. Desaix de Veygoux, *Journal de voyage de Général Desaix en Suisse et en Italie 1797* (1907 edition), p. 291. Nap.'s letter to the Directory of 15 July 1797, Corr. Nap. III, no. 2014. B.'s republican letter and its consequences: Barton 1, p. 240; Girod B p. 92; *Morning Chronicle*, 6 September 1797.

On the Directory: M. Lyons, *France under the Directory* (Oxford, 1975); G. Lefebvre, *The French Revolution from 1793–1799* (1964); J-P. Garnier, *Barras, Roi du Directoire* (1937); P. J. F. N. Barras, *Memoirs*, edited by G. Dury (London, 1896).

B.'s first visit to Paris: Nap. on 'this excellent general', Corr. Nap. III, no. 2083; Sarrazin, *Philosopher*, II, pp. 115–18; Höjer 1, pp. 114–17; Barton 1, pp. 249–60. Talleyrand's political inaction in September 1797: Laure, Duchesse d'Abrantès, *Histoire des salons de Paris (1838)*, VI, pp. 80–4; G. Lacour-Gayet, *Talleyrand* (1928) I, p. 245; J. Orieux, *Talleyrand, The Art of Survival* (1978), p. 194. See also A. Dry, *Soldats ambassadeurs sous le directoire* (1906), pp. 338–40.

On Pichegru see J. Godechot, *The Counter Revolution, 1780–1804* (1972, original French edition 1961), pp. 273–4. For the Fructidor Coup and B.: Lyons, *Directory*, pp. 210–16; Barton 1, pp. 258–64. The Memoirs of Barras (1895–6) were 'ghosted' by Roussélin de Saint-Albin who was briefly one of B.'s secretaries; they are more reliable as an account of B.'s activities than for other matters; for the Fructidor events, Barras, *Memoirs*, III, pp. 5–37. See also J. Sarrazin, *The Memorial* (1811) pp. 22–4. For B.'s refusal of the Midi command, Barton 1, pp. 265–6. Sarrazin has two passages dealing with the Passeriano meeting with Nap.: Sarrazin, *Philosopher* II, pp. 119–31 and 153–75; see, too, Barton 1, pp. 272–77.

Chapter 4: Undiplomatic Interlude

B.'s activities in the winter of 1797–8 are treated in some detail in Girod B pp. 10–22. For B. and the Ionian Islands: Barton 1, p. 286. On his brief command of the Army of Italy: Barton 1, p. 287. For B. as an ambassador see part 2 of F. Masson, *Les diplomates de la Révolution* (1882) and Vol. 2 of Dry's *Soldats ambassadeurs*. Modern studies include Rodolphe Entz, 'Bernadotte, ambassade de France, jugé par la police autrichienne', BMB no. 21 (Dec. 1976) and Alabert Thabault, 'L'ambassade à Vienne du Général Bernadotte', BMB no. 27 for 1987 (published 1988), a long article using Austrian and French diplomatic archives. BL 931527 is a translation of a contemporary pamphlet, anonymously ascribed to 'Eyewitness', *A Factual Account of the Riot in Vienna* (1798). The reports to the British Foreign Secretary, Lord Grenville, from Sir Morton Eden, the ambassador in Vienna, are filed at the Public Record Office in FO 7/51 and contain much detailed matter concerning B.'s brief embassy, notably: FO 7/51/18 of 17 March, on 'the disposition of the public mind' towards B: FO 7/51/25 of 11 April, reporting the events of Easter: FO 7/51/26 of 14 April, reporting the riot itself; FO 7/51/27 of 16 April, blaming B: FO 7/51/28 of 16 April reporting Thugut's belief that the incident will lead to Austrian re-entry into the war. The file FO 7/51 also contains letters from Grenville on British cabinet reaction to the incident, notably (in a letter dated 28 April) the naval orders sent to Admiral Lord St Vincent in the Mediterranean. For the reaction of the Metternich family and the Congress of Rastatt, see A. Palmer, *Metternich* (1972), pp. 30–2. For a pejorative use of the word 'Bernadottes', see *The Times*, 9 October 1798, cited Barton 1, p. 320.

Chapter 5: Sceaux and the Rue Cisalpine

B.'s 'simple and quiet life' letter is dated 16 May, Höjer 1, pp. 164 and 469. On B at Sceaux and his Dourdan property, Girod B pp. 123–5 and the author's interesting article 'Les "Campagnes" de Bernadotte', BMB nos. 3 and 4 (June 1958 and June 1959). Although the romantic novel by Annemarie Selinko, *Désirée* (1953), is often factually inaccurate, the description of the small house in Sceaux at the beginning of Part II rings true. For B.'s contacts with Joseph Bonaparte, M. Ross, *The Reluctant King* (1976), pp. 69–71. Comtesse de Chastenay, *Mémoires* (1896) I, pp. 350–2 places B. in his social setting. On d'Ambert's fate, Barton 1, pp. 334–5 and Höjer 1, p. 166. On the Clary family and B.'s marriage see Girod D pp. 111–14 and Appendix IV. For Laure Junot's comments on married life at Sceaux, Duchesse d'Abrantès, *Memoirs* (1831) I, p. 287.

Alleged contact of British agents with B.: Talbot to Grenville, 3 November 1798, FO 74/22/30; rising imminent, 25 November 1798, FO 74/22/31. Reply from Grenville, 25 January 1799, FO 74/23. See also H. Mitchell, *Underground War against Revolutionary France*, pp. 225–6 and Godechot, *Counter Revolution*, p. 341. B.'s letter to Joseph Bonaparte, Barton 1, pp. 350–2; his illness, Barton 1, pp. 365–6 and Höjer 1, p. 184 (making use of the doctor's report). For the coup of Priarial 1799 and the re-emergence of Sieyès, Lyons, *Directory*, pp. 225–6; B. as Minister of War, Barton 1, pp. 377–427; Höjer 1, pp. 186–212 and, more critically, A. Ollivier, *Le dix-huit Brumaire*, pp. 130–7; J. Gohier, *Mémoires* (1824) I, pp. 88–9; Barras *Mémoires* III, pp. 360–96, with Roussélin's description of his working habits. For the birth of Oscar, Girod D pp. 125–6 and the same author's article 'L'Acte de Naissance d'Oscar Bernadotte', BMB no. 12 (Dec. 1967). On the revival of Jacobinism in 1798–9, see: I. Woloch, *Jacobin Legacy* (Princeton, 1970); Lyons, *Directory*, pp. 215–29 passim; cf. Monr 9 July 1799. For B.'s resignation, Barton 1, pp. 419–27; Monr 14 and 16 September 1799; Gohier, *Mémoires*, I, pp. 136–7 and, for the journey of the two Directors out to B.'s home, p. 144.

Chapter 6: Brumaire and After

Nap.'s return from Egypt: C. Herold, *Bonaparte in Egypt* (1963), pp. 327–32; A. Marmont, *Mémoires du Maréchal duc de Raguse* (1857), II, pp. 43–5; C-F. de Ménèval, *Memoirs to Serve for the History of Napoleon I* (1895) I, pp. 8–10; Gohier, *Mémoires* I, pp. 198–201 (dinner for Nap. and Sieyès, p. 202). For Kléber's indignation, Herold, p. 341. Relations with B. on eve of conspiracy: Barton 1, pp. 440–3; Girod B pp. 146–9 Girod D pp. 133–6; Joseph Bonaparte, *Mémoires et correspondance du roi Joseph* (1855) I, pp. 70–80. On the banquet to Nap. and its consequences, see Lucien Bonaparte, *Memoirs* (1835), pp. 78–9 and Gohier's *Mémoires* I, pp. 223–6. For the lunch on 16 Brumaire, Sarrazin, *Memorial*, p. 130.

The basic histories of Brumaire are A. Vandal, *L'avènement de Bonaparte*, Vol. 1 (1903), J. Thiry, *Le Coup d'Etat du 18 brumaire* (1947) and Ollivier's *Dix-huit Brumaire*, already cited; see also, D. J. Goodspeed, *Bayonets at St Cloud* (1965), especially pp. 107–64, and Lyons, *Directory*, pp. 230–4. Nap. and B. conversation about being 'in uniform', L. Bourrienne, *Mémoires*, (1831) I, p. 282 (but cf. Joseph's *Mémoires* I, p. 78 and Höjer 1, pp. 228–9). The most vivid eye-witness account of what happened at St Cloud is in A. C. Thibaudet, *Mémoires* (1913) pp. 6–7. For Sarrazin's version of events on 18 Brumaire and on B. in hiding, Sarrazin, *Philosopher* II, pp. 200–6; and for Gohier's account see his *Mémoires* I, pp. 229–32 (for 17 Brumaire) and pp. 266–95 for the following day. See also Carola Oman, *Napoleon's Viceroy* (1966), pp. 101–9.

The Murat wedding, Ross, *The Reluctant King*, p. 86–7. B. as Councillor of State and as commander in the West in 1800, Barton 2, pp. 9–20; Girod B pp. 161–75. Nap.'s letter to B. on setting out for Italy, J. Sarrans, *Histoire de Bernadotte, Charles XIV Jean* (1845) I, p. 42. On Cadoudal: H. Lachouque et J. Arnna, *Cadoudal et les chouans* (1950) and J. Godechot, *The Counter Revolution*, pp. 375–8. On Nap.'s Marengo campaign, see Chandler, pp. 286–302. Désirée's letters from Brittany, Girod D pp. 146–7. See also G-M. Thomas's article 'Bernadotte en Bretagne', BMB no. 9 (Dec. 1964).

Chapter 7: 'That Hot-Headed Southerner'

Thomas's article cited above is relevant for this section, too; and see Françoise Debaisieux's article 'Ceracchi et son buste du Général Bernadotte', BMB, no. 2 (June 1957). G. Hué, *Un complot de police sous le Consulat* (1909); J. Lordean, *La machine infernale de la rue Saint-Niçaise* (1924); L. de Villefosse and J. Bouissounouse, *L'Opposition à Napoleon* (1969); Gabriel Girod de l'Ain, 'Notes inédites de Rousselin de St-Albin', BMB no. 15 (Dec. 1970); Barton 2, pp. 22–3; L. Madelin, *Fouché* (1901) pp. 317–30. On the purchase of La Grange, Girod D pp. 147–9. Nap.'s complaint against the 'hot-headed southerner', T. Jung, *Lucien Bonaparte et ses Mémoires* (1882) II, pp. 107–8. On Ange Chiappe: B. Nabonne, *Bernadotte* (1946) pp. 112 and 145–8; Gabriel Girod de l'Ain's article, 'L'Ami Chiappe, 1760–1826', BMB no. 21 (Dec. 1976). For the Idéologues see L. Bergeron, *France under Napoleon* (Princeton, NJ, 1981), pp. 90–7; G. de Staël, *Dix années d'exil* (1904 edition) pp. 70–5; G. Savary, *Mémoires du duc de Rovigo* (1828) I, chapter 29. For the reopening of the churches and the Notre Dame Easter Mass in 1802, J. M. Thompson, *Napoleon Bonaparte, His Rise and Fall* (Oxford, 1958) pp. 181–2; Girod B p. 184. For the conspiracies against Nap.: Barton 2, pp. 47–58; Höjer 1, pp. 261–3; A. Merry to Lord Hawkesbury, 12 May 1802, FO 27/62. On B. and the Récamier social circle at Clichy see the article (in two parts) by Torvald T'son Höjer, 'Carl Johann et Madame Récamier', BMB no. 3 (June 1958) and no. 4 (June 1959) which appears to be based on an earlier study in a Swedish periodical and Nabonne's *Bernadotte*, pp. 115–18. For the Louisiana proposals, Girod D pp. 157–8; Joseph, *Mémoires*, I, pp. 215–16; Barton 2, pp. 66–72; A. Merry to Lord Hawkesbury, 28 April

1802, FO 27/62. Proposed diplomatic mission to USA, Barton 2, pp. 66–70; Nap.'s letter to Talleyrand about B.'s failure to set out for America, 1 April 1803, Corr. Nap. VI, no. 6663; Lord Whitworth to Lord Hawkesbury, 11 April 1803, FO 27/68; letters of Désirée and B. from La Rochelle, Girod B pp. 190–1. For Nap. on the cliffs above Ambleteuse see letter to Second Consul Cambacères of 16 November 1803, Corr. Nap. IX no. 7279. For the conspiracies of 1804 see H. Gaubert, *Conspirateurs sous Napoléon* I (1962). On B and Moreau, Barton 2, 56–7 and 71–2; on B. and Lucien, Jung, *Lucien Bonaparte et Ses Mémoires*, p. 445; Barton 2 pp. 79–82; Girod B p. 193. For B.'s reconciliation with Nap.: Barton 2, pp. 72–5; Monr 14 May 1804. Creation of the Marshalate: Chandler, pp. 311–12, Ceremony of making Marshals at St Cloud: Girod B pp. 184–7.

Chapter 8: The Marshals Go to War

For B. at Hanover: Barton 2, pp. 84–91; Girod B pp. 197–200 and pp. 202–5. Although G. Servières, *L'Allémagne français sous Napoléon I* (1904) is mainly concerned with the Hanseatic ports, his third chapter has material on the links between Hamburg and Hanover; for Rumbold, see Servières, pp. 66–70, H. A. L. Fisher, *Studies in Napoleonic Statesmanship, Germany* (1903), pp. 89–92; see also Corr. Nap. X, no. 8100. The papers seized when Rumbold was abducted remain in the Archives Nationales in Paris. For the fullest treatment of Nap.'s coronation, F. Masson, *Napoleon and his Coronation* (1911) and, with a more modern approach, H. Gaubert, *Le Sacre de Napoleon I* (1964). For B.'s monetary rewards, Girod B pp. 200–3; for Désirée's visit to Hanover, Girod D, pp. 165–6.

On the 1805 campaign plans: Höjer 1, pp. 301–2; Chandler, pp. 389–92; Barton 2, pp. 103–10 (violation of Ansbach territory, p. 108). For Ulm and the battle of Austerlitz: Chandler, pp. 392–432; C. Manceron, *Austerlitz* (Paris 1962; London 1966); A. Palmer, *Alexander I, Tsar of War and Peace* (1972) pp. 103–12; Corr. Nap. XI, nos. 9274, 9482, 9491, 9492, 9493; Girod B pp. 211–20. B.'s term as Governor of Ansbach and his creation as Prince of Ponte Corvo are covered in Barton 2, pp. 121–8; Höjer 1, pp. 314–23; cf. Corr. Nap. XI nos. 9937, 9940, 9942, 9994–5. Nap.'s letter to Joseph about the Ponte Corvo title, 5 June 1806, Corr. Nap. XII no. 10314.

For the Prussian Campaign of 1806 see Chandler, pp. 452–506, although pp. 495–6 seem unduly critical of B. Barton 2, pp. 134–46, considers the campaign and in pp. 152–9, defends B.'s reputation. Nap.'s most hostile letter to B, 23 October 1806, Corr. Nap. XIII, no. 11060. For contrasting military assessments of B.'s conduct at Jena compare the article by Lt.-Col. Titeux, 'Le maréchal Bernadotte et la manoeuvre d'Iéna' in *Révue Napoleonienne* no. 4 for April and September 1903 and General H. Bonnal, *Le manoeuvre d'Iéna* (1904). The fullest account of Jena-Auerstadt is in the closing section of D. Reichel, *Davout et L'Art de la Guerre* (Neuchâtel, 1975). See also: Girod B pp. 228–40; the collected letters of Davout edited by his daughter, A. L. de Blocqueville, *Le Maréchal Davout, Prince d'Eckmuhl* (1879–80) II, 220–44; and the biographical essay on Davout by Chandler himself in D. Chandler (ed.), *Napoleon's Marshals* (1987) pp. 94–115. Nap.'s comments on the storming of Halle, Barton 2, p. 149, citing Houssaye. The pursuit of Blücher: Höjer 1, pp. 341–3; R. Parkinson, *The Hussar General* (1975) pp. 69–71. Barton 2, p. 169 cites FO material (FO 73/76) on reports of treatment of Swedes at Lübeck; see also M. de Marbot, *Mémoires* (1891) I, pp. 238–9.

Chapter 9: Changing Fortunes

For the winter campaign in Poland see Chandler, pp. 509–51; Nap.'s directive from Willemburg, 28 January 1807, Corr. Nap. XIV no. 11709. For B.'s letter to Joseph on 'vilest place in the world' and for Berthier's courier captured by Cossacks, Girod B p. 243; cf. Barton 2, pp. 180–2. Ney's comment on Eylau, Chandler, p. 555, citing Fezensac. Nap.'s conciliatory letters to B. on 22 and 27 February 1807, Corr. Nap. XIV nos. 11855 and 11896. For Désirée's visit to East Prussia, Girod D pp. 170–1; B.'s wound at Spanden, article by Michel Ferron, 'La Blessure de Bernadotte à Spanden', BMB no. 2 (June 1957); and Corr. Nap. XV no. 12743. A section of B.'s letter to Désirée of 12 July 1807 describing his reception by Nap. at Königsberg is printed in Girod D pp. 171–2. For B. as Governor of the Hanseatic towns: Barton 2, pp. 190–200 (with problem of Spanish troops, pp. 191–4); Höjer 1, pp. 358–90. For Désirée at Hamburg and Odense and for family attempts to induce Nap. to give B. a command in the field, Girod D. pp. 173–80. B.'s illness in February 1809: Girod B p. 259.

  B. and the Saxon army, Barton 2, pp. 213–21; Girod B, pp. 259–60 for B.'s unexpected arrival at Dresden; Höjer 1, p. 394 and p. 493 for B.'s complaints of persecution by Imperial Headquarters. Nap.'s military rebuff at Aspern, Chandler, pp. 700–7. For Nap.'s gestures of goodwill towards B. and invitation to Schönbrunn, Corr. Nap. IX nos. 15408, 15423, 15426. Chandler pp. 713–30 gives a fine account of the battle of Wagram but, in following Marbot's memoirs (op. cit. II, pp. 272–3), Chandler repeats on p. 724 the frequent assertion that B. was dismissed from his command during the battle, cf. Barton 2, pp. 222–5, Girod B pp. 272–3. On the campaign in general see S. Bowden and C. Tarbox, *Armies on the Danube* (Arlington, Texas, 1980) and J. Thiry's account of the battle, written in lively French, *Wagram* (1966). Both Barton (pp. 226–8) and Girod (p. 273) print B.'s provocative Order of the Day praising the Saxon army.

  The Walcheren Expedition is treated in some detail in A. Bryant, *Years of Victory* (1944), pp. 326–44. For B.'s swift response to the landing, Barton 2, pp. 234–40, with his second controversial Order of the Day printed on p. 241. Touchard-Lafosse, *Histoire de Charles XIV, Jean Bernadotte* (1838), II, pp. 118–20 gives what is virtually B.'s own account of his reception by Nap. in Vienna: see Barton 2, pp. 247–9. For B.'s return to La Grange, Girod B p. 296.

Chapter 10: The Making of a Prince Royal

Nap.'s Austrian marriage and the birth of the King of Rome: V. Cronin, *Napoleon* (1973 paperback ed.) pp. 382–3; Palmer, *Metternich*, pp. 72–9. For Swedish officers in the French royal army see the article by Yves Barjaud, 'La Tradition du Régiment Royal Suèdois dans l'armée française', BMB no. 19 (Dec. 1974). On Gustav III, F. D. Scott, *Sweden, The Nation's History* (Minneapolis, 1977), Chapter X; for Gustav's visit to Versailles, V. Cronin, *Louis and Antoinette* (1974), pp. 195–7. The two important works on Fersen are A. Soderhjelm, *Fersen et Marie Antoinette* (1930) and H. Arnold Barton, *Count Hans Axel von Fersen, Aristocrat in an Age of Revolution* (Boston, 1975). For the Finnish War and the Swedish Revolution of 1809, Scott, *Sweden*, pp. 292–300. For B.'s candidature as interpreted by the French, Girod B pp. 297–319, a very full examination of the available material. All the main diplomatic correspondence which passed between Paris and Stockholm from June to September 1810 is printed, in French, in *Historiska Handlikar*, Volume 17 for 1899 (hereafter abbreviated as HH), published by the Kunglija Samfundet fur Utgifvande af Handskrifter Rurande Skandinaviens Historia in Stockholm. For the events of 20 June in Paris, Höjer 2, pp. 6–7. B.'s first meeting with Mörner, HH p. 55; and with Wrede, HH pp. 56–7. On Fournier: Höjer 2, pp. 24–7; Barton 2, pp. 277–80; Girod B p. 304; and the biographical entry by Nils F. Holm in *Svenst Biografiskt Lexikon*, Vol. 16 (1964–6), pp. 402–3. For B. and Désirée at Plombières, Girod D p. 188 and Girod B pp. 305–6. Contemporary evidence on Nap.'s backing for Eugène, Méneval, *Memoirs*, II, p. 331; the question is discussed in Carola Oman, *Napoleon's Viceroy* pp. 307–8. Return of Mörner to Stockholm, HH p. 110. Wrede's praise of B., Girod D p. 189, citing Hildebrand's *History of Sweden*. B. well informed over events in Sweden, HH p. 262. For Fournier's speedy journey, Höjer, pp. 15–16. Engestrom's letter of 15 August, HH p. 197–201, describes events at Örebro and includes the 'two days more' phrase. Popularity of Oscar's portrait, C. J. B. de Suremain, *En Suède sous la république et le prémier empire* (1902), pp. 233–7; Barton 2, p. 289. For the final decision of the Diet, see Engestrom's letter to Lagerbielke of 18 August, HH p. 251. On Mörner's journey to Paris with the news of the election, Barton 2, p. 257. Reaction in Paris: Girod B pp. 320–1, with Nap.'s reference to an 'honourable monument', HH

p. 281. For the million francs made available by Nap. for B., Corr. Nap. Vol XX, no. 16906. On B.'s final 'stormy interview' with Nap., Barton 2, p. 302; F. D. Scott, *Bernadotte and the Fall of Napoleon* (Cambridge, Mass. 1935), p. 12. Account sent to Sweden of B.'s formal leave-taking of Nap. and the Marshals, HH p. 304; cf. Girod D p. 197; for letters from B. to Désirée on his journey, ibid. pp. 198–9. Arrival in Sweden and reaction of the King, Barton 3, pp. 3–5. Désirée and Oscar's journey to Sweden, Girod D p. 202 and Höjer 2, pp. 52–3 (with adverse comments of Queen Hedvig Charlotte); Girod B pp. 372–3.

Chapter 11: Whose Ally?

Aleksander Chernyshev to Russian Foreign Ministry, Dec. 1810 (in French), *Sbornik Imperatorskogo russkago istoricheskago obschchestva* (St Petersburg, 1880), Vol. 121, p. 87. 'Orders in Gascon', L. A. A. Langeron, *Mémoires* (1902), p. 326. On his freemasonry in Sweden, Harald Qvistgard's article already cited, BMB no. 22, Dec. 1977, p. 41. On Wallmark, Höjer 2, pp. 51 and 65. For Gré, see the article by Françoise Debaissieux in BMB, no. 6 (Dec. 1961); for Camps, Höjer 2, pp. 51–2 and several other references, notably pp. 366–70. For General Sarrazin's misfortunes see the appendix to Barton 1 and the article by Höjer, 'Bernadotte och Bonaparte', HT, Vol. 61, iii (1941) pp. 237–38. Alquier on the absurdity of Sweden's declaration of war on Britain, Barton 1 p. 12. B.'s relations with Nap. and birth of King of Rome: Corr. Nap. XXII nos 17196, 17936, 18233; Barton 3 p. 16; Girod D p. 205. Early Tsar Alexander and B. exchanges, Höjer 2, p. 74, Barton 3 pp. 21–22. Gentil's long report of his conversation with Nap. on 10 February 1811 is printed in full (from a copy in the Archives Nationales) by Girod de l'Ain, see Girod B pp. 375–6: see also the extract quoted from Swedish sources by Höjer in the article cited above, HT, Vol. 61, iii (1941) p. 340. For Désirée's return to France: Suremain, *Mémoires*, pp. 249–50, 257–8; Hochschild, *Désirée, Reine de Suède et de Norvège*, pp. 55–6; Girod D pp. 208–10; Höjer 2 p. 53. Friant's occupation of Swedish Pomerania: Corr. Nap. XXIII, nos 18378, 18391, 18444, 18447; Höjer 2, p. 107; Girod B pp. 395–8; Scott, *Sweden*, p. 308.

Two distinguished works – both highly prejudiced against B.'s policy in 1812 – are A. Vandal, *Napoléon et Alexandre I* (1897) volume 3, and, more selective in its evidence, L. Pingaud's *Bernadotte, Napoléon et les Bourbons* (1901). For Löwenhielm in St Petersburg in the spring of 1812: Grand Duke Nicholas Mikhailovich, *L'Empéreur Alexandre I* (St Petersburg 1912) I, pp. 498–506. Castlereagh's attitude towards B. in 1812 was analysed by Sir Charles Webster, *The Foreign Policy of Castlereagh, 1812–1815* (1931) pp. 92–101. Thornton's correspondence, which was used by Webster, is now filed under FO 933/41–43; for Thornton's comments on B.'s personality see his despatches of 9 and 16 April. The Örebro Diet and Nap.'s invasion of Russia: Höjer 2, pp. 132–6. For the exchange of letters between B. and Tsar Alexander at the start of the war, see their *Correspondance inédite de l'Empéreur Alexandre I et de Bernadotte pendant l'année 1812* (compiled and introduced by an anonymous editor for the 'Librairie Militaire' in Paris, 1909); inevitability of winning 'the fifth battle', B.'s letter of 11 August, p. 27. For the Äbo meeting: Höjer 2, pp. 138–45; Girod B pp. 412–14; Barton 3, pp. 38–41; Webster, pp. 98–9; see also the article by Sten Carlsson, 'Abofördraget och krigsrustningarna 1812', *Scandia* Vol. 18, pt 2 (1947) pp. 192–201, including (pp. 194–5) the letter to Charles XIII mentioning the feint attack on Riga. For the report by Engeström which so impressed the English in March 1813, see Franklin D. Scott, 'The Propaganda Activities of Bernadotte, 1813–1814' in D. C. McKay (ed.) *Essays in the History of Modern Europe* (1936), pp 17–18.; and for Mme de Staël and Schlegel see Scott, *Fall*, p. 81. On the reoccupation of Stralsund and Rügen, ibid pp. 51–2. On Thornton's treaty with Sweden, see Webster's *Castlereagh 1812–1815*, pp. 120–1. B.'s open letter to Nap. of 23 March 1813 is printed in *Receuil de Lettres, Proclamations et Discours de Charles Jean* (2nd edition, Stockholm, 1839, hereafter cited as *Receuil*), pp. 88–96; for its effect, see Scott in McKay's *Essays*, pp. 19–20. For Nap. and Lutzen, Chandler pp. 882–7. For Pozzo's account of his meeting with B. at Karlskrona, Barton 3 pp. 65–6 and for Pozzo's general attitude, see the best biography of him, P. Ordioni, *Pozzo di Borgo, diplomate de l'Europe française* (1935). B lands at Stralsund, Girod B p. 434.

Chapter 12: At War with Napoleon

Désirée's activities in Paris: Girod D pp. 225–30, with her letter of April 1813 on p. 228; for its reception by B., see Suremain, *Mémoires*, pp. 262–88, with diary entries on all B.'s actions and conversations in Stralsund including (28 May) B.'s claim that the Tsar wished to become 'Emperor of the French'. For Trachenberg Conference: Höjer 2, pp. 174–7; Barton 3 pp. 74–5; Girod B pp. 441–3; B. von Schinke, *Mémoires posthumes du feld-maréchal de Stedingk* (1843) Vol. 3 pp. 218–24; F. D. Scott, *Fall of Napoleon*, pp. 81–90; the despatches of Thornton and Cathcart for July 1813 in, respectively, FO 933/43 and FO 65/86. For Moreau see Barton 3, pp. 83–8 and the article by Gabriel Girod de l'Ain, 'Charles-Jean, Moreau et Armfeldt (1811–1813)', BMB no. 11 (Dec, 1966); for 'massive club blows' see B.'s letter of 6 August 1813 in F. Schulze, *1813–1815* (Leipzig, 1912), pp. 121–2; a slightly longer translation in A. Brett-James, *Europe against Napoleon* (1970, hereafter cited as Brett-James) p. 36. For Nap. on B. making 'a show', H. von Boyen, *Denkwürdigkeiten und Erinnerungen 1771–1813* (Stuttgart, 1899), p. 319.

B., Oudinot and Grossbeeren, Chandler, p. 905; Parkinson, *Hussar General*, pp. 135–6; with maps of both Grossbeeren and Dennewitz in Höjer 2, endpapers. See the detailed treatment of Dennewitz by T. Heathcote in Chapter 2 of D. Chandler (ed.) *Napoleon's Marshals*, pp. 35–7 together with the extract from Reiche's *Memoirs* in Brett-James, p. 35. B.'s letter to Ney of 9 September 1813, *Receuil*, pp. 102–3. His appeal to the Saxons (ibid. pp. 104–5) is considered as a propaganda move by F. D. Scott in McKay's *Essays*, pp. 21–2; cf. Scott's *Fall*, pp. 101–2. Flattery of B. by allied sovereigns: Barton 3, pp. 96–100; Comte de Rochechouart, *Sovenirs 1788–1822* (1899) pp. 244–57. B.'s advance across the Elbe and the skirmish at Dessau, Chandler p. 918. For the events of 12–13 October 1813 at Kothen: Boyen II, pp. 377–79; Philippine von Griesheim's letters are here cited from Edith von Cramm's collection of her *Briefe einer Braut, 1804–1813* (Berlin, 1905) pp. 183–6, but there are several editions of them and longer extracts in Brett-James, pp. 73–4 and 75–6. Brett-James (pp. 117–234) prints some 70 extracts from eye-witness accounts of the battle of Leipzig, including Rochechouart's description of B. (pp. 184–5) and material relating to the British rocket battery (pp. 185–8). Fullest account: Chandler, pp. 924–36. Inter-allied diplomacy after Leipzig: Webster, pp. 166–8; Palmer, *Alexander I*, pp. 273–5; Palmer, *Metternich*, pp. 108–11. For B.'s Danish campaign: Höjer 2 pp. 201–34; Barton 3 pp. 111–17; Girod B pp. 471–82; and on the Treaty of Kiel, F. D., Scott, pp. 144–8. The text of B.'s appeal to the French from Cologne of 12 February 1814, *Recueil* p. 106–7; anger it caused in France, Barton 3 p. 120. On the Franzenberg mission to B.'s hreadquarters: ibid pp. 121–2; Ross, *The Reluctant King*, p. 225 and see also pp. 231–2; Corr. Nap. XXVII nos. 21367 and 21503; Höjer 2 pp. 257–61. For Löwenhielm's championship of B at Châtillon see T. Th. Höjer, *Sverig och kocgressen i Chatillon* (Uppsala, 1940, with the book summarised in French); and for B.'s general policy, see the article by F. D. Scott, 'Bernadotte and the Throne of France, 1814' in *Journal of Modern History* (Chicago, 1933) V, pp. 465–78. Entry of Tsar Alexander into Paris and limited support of B: Palmer, *Alexander I*, pp. 280–4; Barton 3, p. 132. Désirée's letter of reproof to B.: Girod D pp. 234–5 (full corrected version).

Chapter 13: The Dual Kingdom

B.'s last visit to Paris: Barton 3, pp. 131–4; Girod B, pp. 506–11; Höjer 2 pp. 271–4. For events in Norway see: T. K. Derry, *A History of Modern Norway, 1814–1972* (Oxford, 1973) pp. 5–16; Scott, *Sweden* pp. 312–13; Webster, pp. 306–9. For B.'s meeting with Louis XVIII at Compiègne: Höjer 2, p. 274; and B.'s letter to Désirée of 4 May, printed in Girod D, pp. 238–9. Further letters to Désirée on the journey home to Sweden, ibid pp. 239–41, including (p. 241) B.'s regret at not speaking Swedish.

Military operations in Norway: Höjer 2, pp 305–7; B.'s proclamation to the Norwegian people, 17 July 1814, *Receuil* pp. 113–17. Loftus on B. in August 1814, F.O. 188/3/12, also quoted (in English) in Höjer 2, p. 497. Löwenhielm to Engestrom on Norwegians, 14 April 1814, letter (in French) Höjer 2, p. 495. Sweden and the Congress of Vienna: Girod B, pp. 528–35; Höjer 2, pp. 335–85; and see also the article by Olivier Baulny, 'Bernadotte et L'Ile de Saint-Barthélemy', BMB nos 23–24 (1978, published 1980). B and the Hundred Days: Barton 3, pp. 144–5; Höjer 2, pp. 361, 380–4; Girod D, p. 248. 'Opposition' and conspiracy remark (18 May 1815), Höjer 2, p. 393. Administrative problems in Norway, including the Bergen bishopric: letters of B. (in French) to Carl Mörner af Tuna in S.A. Lindbaek, *Karl Johans brev till rikstathallaren Mörner 1816–1818* (HH 30, pt 1, 1935). Plot threatens life of B. and Oscar in March 1817: Höjer 2, p. 429; Girod B p. 554; Lindsfelt's death, Höjer, 2, p. 430. On Magnus Brahe see in particular Höjer 2, pp. 444 and 460 and Höjer 3, pp. 443–5; for Maria Koskull, Höjer 2, pp. 439 and 444 and Girod B, p. 580. B.'s letter of 23 September 1816 to Carl Mörner on having been 'a man before a Prince', Lindbaek in HH 30 pt 1, pp. 8–9.

Death of Charles XIII and B.'s accession: Girod B, pp. 559–60; Barton. 3 p. 156. Désirée's reactions: Girod D, pp. 256–7. British Minister in Stockholm's report on Swedish Coronation festivities: Lord Strangford to Castlereagh, 21 May 1818, FO 933/104/34. Stockholm ceremonies: Höjer 3, pp. 16–18. Death of Queen Hedvig Charlotte, Girod B, pp. 565–6. Trondheim coronation, ibid and Höjer 3, p. 19: 'shouts of joy' letter, HH 30, pt 1 pp. 183–4.

Chapter 14: Dynasty Building

Désirée and Richelieu: Girod D. Chapter 13. B. and death of Nap.: Barton 3, p. 171; Höjer 3, pp. 48–9. The fullest account of Oscar's courting of Princess Josephine Beauharnais in English is in Carola Oman's *Napoleon's Viceroy*, pp. 455–65; see also the article by Gabriel Girod de l'Ain, 'Le Mariage du Prince Oscar', BMB no. 20 (Dec 1975). For Désirée's movements and homecoming: Girod D, pp. 290–6; Höjer, 3, pp. 63–75; see also B's letters of June to September 1823 in E. Andeslkold, *Karl Johans Brev till Rikstathallaren J. A. Sandels*, 1818–1827 (HH 35, ii 1955); p. 221 for the Queen's injury. For Sophie Albertine, Höjer 3, p. 62 and for Désirée's letter of 16 August 1823 to Charlotte Bonaparte, Girod D, p. 297. On court life, Barton 3, pp. 220–3; B.'s comment on Brannvin, Scott, *Sweden*, p. 306; language problem, Barton 3, p. 220. On the Gota Canal, Höjer 2, pp. 408–9 and for industry generally see Scott, *Sweden*, pp. 444–7. B.'s letter of 27 June 1826 on the reconstruction of Frederikshald after the fire, Sandels in HH 35 ii, p. 274. On the Norwegian crisis: Höjer 3, pp. 212–28, with pp. 222–5 on B.'s presence during the 'Battle of the Market Place'; Barton 3, pp. 184–6. For B.'s letter of 19 July 1828 opposing Désirée's wish to visit Italy, Girod D, p. 316; the same book (pp. 321–2) reprints the account of Désirée's coronation given in the *Moniteur*, 8 September 1829. On the revolutions of 1830 and the tricolour flag incident, Höjer 3, pp 234–8; Hierta and *Aftonbladet*, ibid pp. 349–51; Lindeberg and the later Press war, ibid pp. 505–10. American Comments on B. in 1835, Höjer 3, pp. 556–7; letters of Sir John Bligh to Palmerston 1835–37, are in BL Add. Mss. 41273, folios 177 –93. See also for the Stockholm fire of 1835: Sir Edward Desbrowe to Palmerston, FO 933/61/38 of 31 July 1835; Barton 3, p. 225. For the Russian imperial visit, FO 933/173/44 and 49 of 13 and 27 June 1838. B.'s Rosendal accident, Girod B, p. 620; Höjer 3, p. 561. The Crusenstople affair in 1838 and Désirée's comment, Barton 3, p. 193–4; Girod B p. 621; and ibid pp. 622–3 for the anti-semitic demonstrations and Oscar's regency. King's address to Riksdag 1840: Barton 3, p. 229; Girod B, pp. 625–6. Return of Nap.'s body to Paris, Barton 3, p. 172. The letters printed in Girod D, pp. 347–50 give a vivid impression of B.'s last year of life; cf. Höjer 3, pp. 561–3. Funeral: see the article by Pierre Schommer, 'Les Funerailes de Bernadotte', BMB no. 5 (Nov. 1960).

Chapter 15: Legends and Legacy

'Don't talk of 1813', Barton 3, p 209, citing Pingaud. Barton's Chapter 27 (ibid pp. 166–72) is a useful survey of R.'s reactions to Napoleonic propaganda. For Sir Walter Scott on B. see Alan Palmer, 'Napoleon's Earliest English Biographer' in A. N. Wilson (ed.) *Essays by Divers Hands*, Vol. XLIV (1986) p. 95. On B. and Parisian theatres: Höjer 3, p. 265; Barton 3, pp. 205–7. For General Thomas-Alexandre Dumas as B.'s companion in arms in Italy, Höjer 1, p. 112. For B. and Norwegian crown jewels: Prince Michael of Greece, *Crown Jewels of Britain and Europe* (1983) p. 89. On D.'s proposed visit to Paris, Girod D p. 364. For General Canrobert's meeting with Désirée see C. G. Bapst, *Le Maréchal Canrobert*, Vol. 3 (1909) pp. 26–8. On the humanitarian service of Folke Bernadotte, see R. Hewins, *Count Folke Bernadotte, His Life and Work* (Minneapolis, 1950). For the visit of King Gustav VI Adolf to Pau in 1963 see the commemorative articles in BMB nos 7–8 (Dec. 1963), including the King's speech on that occasion. Genealogical links may be traced most conveniently in *Burke's Royal Families of the World*, Vol. 1 (1977). Books of interest not cited above include two English short lives: Simon Dewes, *Sergeant Belle-Jambe* (1943) which ends on B.'s accession; and Lord Russell of Liverpool, *Bernadotte, Marshal of France and King of Sweden* (1981).

Index

Abbreviations: B. for Bernadotte, N. for Napoleon I

Index

Index

Index